CRUEL AND UNUSUAL

The Supreme Court
and Capital Punishment

CRUEL AND UNUSUAL

The Supreme Court and Capital Punishment

Michael Meltsner

RANDOM HOUSE NEW YORK

TO HELI

*But faced collectively and in action,
death changes its countenance; now
nothing seems more likely to intensify
our vitality than its proximity.*

—*Hannah Arendt,* On Violence

Contents

Preface

Most writing about the law tends to ignore the critical role of lawyers and instead focuses attention on the judges who grant or deny legal claims, the rules of law themselves, or the clients who are hurt or helped. When the literature deals with the practice of law, the advocate is often so romanticized—the earnest professional, always at the ready—or abused—hostile, egomaniacal, greedy—as to make him unrecognizable. Although lawyers can do little without grieving clients and willing judges, their role as workers deserves more attention.

In 1961 I began a long association with the NAACP Legal Defense and Educational Fund, Inc., an organization whose staff has developed public interest advocacy to a fine art. During my nine-year tenure as a staff attorney, and after 1970 when I served as a consultant, Fund attorneys held the executioner at bay until the Supreme Court was ready and willing to abolish the death penalty. This book tells much about the operation of the Court and the law of capital punishment, but its primary purpose is to convey the craft and cunning of the lawyers who orchestrated a stunning legal victory; of the means they employed to right a deeply felt, historic wrong.

The reader is forewarned that I saw the events that are

the subject of this book as both lawyer and reporter. Although I have attempted to identify and state fairly points of view at odds with my own, distortion is inevitable. Secondly, where the reader encounters speculation about the motives of judges or the inner workings of courts, he should be aware that the truth will yield, if at all, only upon the eventual publication of data that are at present confidential—memoranda, draft opinions, and correspondence. Fortunately, the death penalty draws swarms of writers and researchers. I have no doubt that historians will straighten the record where I have left it crooked.

A third difficulty complements these two. A lawyer is not at liberty to reveal certain aspects of cases in which he served as counsel. Here matters of taste mingle with the professional obligation emanating from the lawyer-client privilege of confidentiality. In this respect, I have sought to balance the reader's interest in grit with the professional's need for privacy. If I have erred in such calculations, my repentence will be long and painful.

Because this book is not aimed exclusively at lawyers, excerpts from Supreme Court arguments have been summarized and rephrased to permit a more ready grasp of the colloquy; quotation marks designate language used by the Justices and the lawyers appearing before them. Chapter notes are provided to assist independent inquiry, but in order to avoid crowding the text with distracting notation marks, I have not attempted to document every reference or to acknowledge each of my numerous debts to the scholarship of others.

CRUEL
AND
UNUSUAL

The Supreme Court
and Capital Punishment

1

The Fund

Typically, Americans have dealt with their complex feelings about capital punishment by one of those intricate compromises with which our culture manages conflict too powerful to resolve. Though the morality and effectiveness of execution was the subject of long and often bitter controversy, before the early 1960's no one questioned the legality of the premeditated killing of human beings by government. Capital punishment was justified as a deterrent to crime, yet the killing was done infrequently and in privacy; its victims were reportedly the most depraved of criminals, but they were rarely considered so beastly as to be insane. Jurors, judges, and governors ensured that the death penalty could be imposed in only a small proportion of the cases where it was an available punishment but opinion polls, referenda, and legislative votes evidenced substantial support for retention of capital punishment as a potential sanction. Despite repeated claims of racial and economic discrimination in the selection of the men who were killed, reform of the legal procedures used in death penalty cases was of the lowest priority. Politicians avoided the issue, for abolition of capital punishment attracted no natural constituency. As any serious interest in the subject required confrontation with unpleasant details of death and dying, the public ignored it. Those few who condemned the horrors of gassing and electrocution were treated with the indifference which a secular and pragmatic society reserved for its zealots and true believers.

No one could have predicted that within a few years gas chambers and electric chairs would be dismantled; that the Supreme Court would rule the death penalty had been administered in so random, illogical, and discriminatory a fashion that it was unconstitutional; or that the issue before the public would not be whether to heed the abolitionists but what to do about pleas that the machinery of death be restored. We still have not sorted out the reasons why these events occurred, but there can be no doubt that they grew out of a rare conjunction of vigorous men and ripe ideas. While energy and scholarship were necessary, they were not sufficient. The actors in this drama needed a structure to give their efforts shape.

Only recently have lawyers associated in numbers to bring court cases in a systematic attempt to change the character of American institutions. The ranks of defense funds, public interest law firms, community law offices, and legal centers which now readily challenge corporate and governmental conduct—from air pollution to prison conditions, selective service to exclusionary zoning—were almost empty ten years ago. Two institutions of any size made law reform the organized and planned objective of a full-time staff of attorneys.

One was the American Civil Liberties Union (ACLU), founded in 1920 by a nonpartisan group, including Clarence Darrow, Eugene V. Debs, Felix Frankfurter, and Roger Baldwin, to defend the Bill of Rights. Today the Union has 170,000 members, 48 state affiliates, and 350 local chapters, but for most of its existence it subsisted on a shoestring with only several thousand dues payers. The Union legal program was primarily defensive, aimed at beating back incursions on personal liberty rather than systematically enlarging the scope of constitutional rights.

ACLU's few staff lawyers had their hands full litigating free speech and assembly cases, dealing with the havoc produced by McCarthyism, and coordinating the activities of scattered affiliates, contentious members, and volunteer attorneys; they had little time and money to spend on test cases brought to change the law.

The other organization was the Legal Defense Fund (LDF), a group of lawyers who originally banded together in order to prod Americans to repay an old debt to the black man but who ultimately found that justice was a chain inescapably linking black and white. Structured differently from the ACLU, LDF had a board of directors and a legal staff but no affiliates or members. Unlike the Civil Liberties Union, whose first mission was to protect the citizenry from an intrusive state, the Legal Defense Fund had no great fear of big government—so long as it acted in the interests of black people. By now, the civil rights story is familiar to everyone, but I must begin by retelling a chapter. There is simply no other way to appreciate why and how the death penalty came to collide with the Constitution.

In 1939 influential members of the National Association for the Advancement of Colored People had formed a corporation known formally as the NAACP Legal Defense and Educational Fund, Inc., but soon dubbed "the Legal Defense Fund," "the Inc. Fund," or simply "the Fund," in an attempt to distinguish it from the parent NAACP. The Fund quickly obtained approval from New York State courts to provide legal assistance to the poor despite a state law prohibiting the practice of law by a corporation, but its goals were not local but national: to pursue equality for blacks by bringing test cases in the courts challenging the laws and customs on which racial segregation rested. This was a course the NAACP itself had embarked upon some years earlier, under the leadership of a brilliant Washington black lawyer and Howard Law School vice-dean, Charles Houston, and soon to be appointed Howard Law School

Dean (later federal judge) William H. Hastie. The proposed legal program was not severed from NAACP for reasons of policy, but rather to attract the tax-deductible donations which the Internal Revenue Code denies to organizations that devote a substantial part of their time, as did the Association, to lobbying and propaganda.

Today, the Fund is a well-known instrument of American liberalism—a professional resource available to the loosely connected efforts of those who seek to forge a powerful tool of institutional reform from the politics of race and poverty. LDF has a yearly income raised entirely from private sources of almost four million dollars; a staff of some twenty civil rights lawyers stationed in New York City; field offices in California and in four Southern states; and a network of about two hundred, mostly black, cooperating lawyers. Attached to the Fund by ties of various lengths and strengths are social scientists, educators, commercial lawyers, law professors, foundation executives, liberal politicians, corporation and government administrators, community workers, a Mexican-American legal defense fund, a law reform unit that specializes in cases involving discrimination against the poor, and a scholarship program.[1]

The Fund, however, like the ACLU, grew to national prominence from humble origins. In 1940, its full-time legal staff consisted of a young Maryland lawyer named Thurgood Marshall. LDF's income of $10,000 paid Marshall's salary as well as expenses; he worked out of the NAACP's modest New York offices. Some twenty years later, the budget had climbed to $500,000; the full-time legal staff to five. After Southern Senators obtained an Internal Revenue Service ruling that the two organizations could not have common directors, the Fund became totally independent of the policies and leadership of the NAACP.

In 1954 it was Fund staff lawyers and their academic consultants who—capping a twenty-year effort—finally broke the iron grip of segregation on the Constitution by persuading the Supreme Court of the United States to reject the "separate but equal" doctrine of an 1896 decision, *Plessy v. Ferguson*.[2] The Court held that the system of dual public schools, then operated by seventeen states and the District of Columbia, violated the Due Process Clause of the Fifth Amendment and Equal Protection Clause of the Fourteenth Amendment.

Following decision of The School Desegregation Cases, known as *Brown v. Board of Education*,[3] LDF's small New York legal staff devoted its energies to challenging in the federal courts every form of state-required, supported, or sanctioned racial discrimination: in schools, courtrooms, public facilities, employment, hospitals, housing, voting. Staff lawyers fought a war of attrition against recalcitrant Southern school officials, and defended those who were charged with crime in the early 1960's when they took the civil rights movement to the streets: freedom riders, sit-inners, and protest marchers. Top priority went to protecting workers in Dr. Martin Luther King, Jr.'s campaigns in St. Augustine, Florida; back-country Mississippi; Montgomery, Selma and Birmingham, Alabama.

The Fund paid the legal bill for local protest movements across the South, in places like Danville, Virginia; Americus and Albany, Georgia; Jackson and Belzoni, Mississippi. LDF lawyers represented King, James Meredith, Medgar and Charles Evers, Ralph Abernathy, Stokely Carmichael, Floyd McKissick, James Foreman, Father James Edmund Groppi, James Farmer, Bob Moses, Dick Gregory, as well as hundreds of their followers. They counseled NAACP branches, the Southern Christian Leadership Conference (SCLC), the Student Non-Violent Coordinating Committee (SNCC), and the Congress of Racial Equality (CORE). Those sued by the Fund were as impressive a list—Orvil Faubus, George Wallace, Ross Barnett, "Bull" Conner, Lester Maddox, Jim Clark, and countless rural sheriffs, school boards, and state public officials.

During these years, few Southern lawyers would represent the civil rights movement. They were spread out like frontier outposts, whose presence was the movement's only protection against constant harassment. Although the Department of Justice dispatched more lawyers and FBI agents to the South after its jurisdiction to do so was clarified by the Civil Rights Acts of 1964, 1965, and 1968, Department intervention cannot even now be realistically expected in any but the more serious or violent racial confrontations. In the early 1960's, the Department's civil rights program was a sick joke told by haggard, circuit-riding attorneys and scarred civil rights workers. But even if Justice Department lawyers and FBI agents, almost all of whom were white, had been stationed in every town in the South, there still would have been an enormous gap of trust and communication between them (ultimately responsible to the Administration in power and its concept of political necessity) and the men and women whose civil rights it was their duty to protect.

Other legal organizations—the National Lawyers' Guild, the Lawyers' Constitutional Defense Committee, the Lawyers' Committee for Civil Rights under Law, and the ACLU—were too poor or understaffed on the front lines to account for more than a fraction of the steadily increasing legal needs of the civil rights movement. By choice as well as necessity, all factions in the black community came to the black attorney in times of stress, but there were few available and fewer still who were able to manage significant civil rights litigation by themselves. They were in the right place at the right time, but were helpless without outside money and manpower and new ideas.

The success of the Fund's legal program was in large measure related to its ability to connect these isolated attorneys to the lawyers and institutions which serviced the New York and Washington liberal leadership. Because the Fund linked the two, it looked in both directions: its legal staff and board of directors were interracial and national; its contributors mostly white and Northern; its clients at first Southerners, although eventually blacks from every region. Due to its relationship with Southern black lawyers, LDF maintained a virtual monopoly over civil rights litigation.

At the high-water mark of civil rights activity, lawyering for the Fund was like being a member of one of those highly trained, specially assembled raider groups which are occasionally deployed in wartime but regularly portrayed in films. These were years when each day brought news of another confrontation between peaceful blacks and outraged segregationists in places that most Americans had never heard of—like Gadsden, Alabama, Orangeburg, South Carolina, and Clinton, Louisiana; when many readers greedily opened *The New York Times* to the "race page"—a concentration of civil rights stories usually located somewhere near the middle of the paper's first section—to learn the results of the previous day's protests much as a baseball fan turns to the sports page to check box scores and batting averages.

Practicing attorneys rarely have worked so close to the front lines. A staff lawyer might be awakened late at night, called upon to travel to a small Southern city, pass through the hostile white section, and establish himself in the often decrepit offices of a local black attorney or, when there were no such offices, in the back room of a local mortuary or the vestry of a church. He would grind out the legal papers, affidavits, complaints for injunction, and briefs of law which often, but certainly not always, sufficiently restrained Southern white communities until cooler heads—usually those that thought of "new industry" and "image"—realized that, unless their cities were to be torn apart, they must reach an accommodation with angry blacks.

Mapping legal strategy under battlefield conditions, the movement lawyer might be arrested, threatened with injury, or forced to watch his clients suffer intolerable perversions of law—phony charges, high bail, perjured testimony, excessive sentences. But following the fateful 1955 arrest of black seamstress Rosa Parks, for failure to give up her seat on a Montgomery, Alabama, bus to a white man, the lawycrs stood between the "race-mixers," as they were then called, and the barely suppressed fury of the Southern legal system. If today many lawyers find themselves as closely identified with their clients' causes as their cases, it is only because this Southern experience radicalized a portion of the profession. William Kunstler, for example, had a humdrum commercial practice before he went South.

Whatever glory may attach to those civil rights lawyers must be kept in perspective. Change was largely the work of courageous Southern blacks, SNCC and SCLC community workers, and their student helpers. The lawyers' work was auxiliary. Material deprivations are unworthy of mention when one considers the existence scratched out by civil rights movement organizers. The physical dangers were small compared to those experienced by any black, especially those who challenged the status quo. Although the hours were long and the work hard, LDF lawyers did not often offer their bodies to night raiders, church burners, dynamite-mad klansmen, or hefty rural sheriffs who preyed viciously on those who had no one watching from New York.

Thurgood Marshall presided over the affairs of the Fund with a steady hand until his appointment in 1961 to the United States Court of Appeals for the Second Circuit by John F. Kennedy. A tireless traveler in the days of long-distance trains and erratic air travel, Marshall was not only a sharp reader of the judicial mind, a successful fund raiser for the cause, and a seasoned advocate who had been to the well in many a hostile Southern town, but a folk hero with a reputation that inspired many to hopes for a courtroom revolution. Marshall's personal record of success was enviable. He argued scores of cases before the Supreme Court of the United States and won all but a handful. His appointments in 1965 as Solicitor General of the United States— the man who argues before the Supreme Court on behalf of the federal government—and later as the first black Associate Justice of the Court were surely fitting. Marshall was as familiar with the mechanics of constitutional litigation as most lawyers were with drawing up a deed or a will.

The Fund's success in turning around the constitutional law of race relations spoke of more than Marshall's legendary courtroom accomplishments: influential friends, skillful money raising, and a talented staff made possible his personal recognition. When he selected as his successor Jack Greenberg, a white man who had received his law degree from Columbia Law School, Greenberg inherited not only a litigation program regularly blessed by the Supreme Court, but surprising power, good will, and friendships.

On the surface, the two men were very different. The older man was long-limbed, the younger compact. Marshall usually was relaxed, though his temper could sting like fire; Greenberg was a bundle of energy. Marshall spun yarns in a folksy drawl that suggested the amiable country boy, though he was raised in Baltimore. Greenberg was more the abrupt, businesslike, city boy. But both shared a twenty-four-hour-a-day passion for the Fund's work. They were single-minded, tough leaders who knew how to take command and to strike hard, fast, and, where necessary, without traces.

The modest victories of American liberals are easy enough to identify—projects funded, legislation enacted, a case won, a judicial candidate rejected—but the winning combination is often difficult to find. A successful test case, for example, reflects an invisible politics: tedious skull sessions that hammer out strategy, money-raising lunches at the Ford Foundation, calls to mandarin partners at Wall Street law firms, the intervention of bar associations, an ex-Attorney General, a law school dean, a labor union general counsel. Fund lawyers did not always wait for clients to appear at their door; often they planned a case and then sought out those wishing to sue. These were the keys on which first Marshall and then Greenberg played with confidence, enabling the Fund to earn a reputation as an organization consistently able to put together the coalition of lawyers, clients, staff, consultants, and expert advisors required for success in each project.

Greenberg shared direction of the Fund's civil rights program with Constance Baker Motley until her selection in 1965 as borough president of Manhattan and thereafter as the first black woman appointed to the federal bench. Mrs. Motley was a strong woman, built as solid as an oak tree; she knew exactly what she wanted and suffered little nonsense from white Southerners who stood in her way. This daughter of a Yale University chef took upon herself the most demanding of litigation assignments when she began to commute to Mississippi, laying the groundwork for the state's first experience with integration. The other member of the Fund's Mississippi team was Derrick Bell, Jr., a spirited young black lawyer who had quit the Justice Department during the Eisenhower years shortly after a superior suggested that NAACP membership was inconsistent with his duties. As there were only three black lawyers in the entire state, Motley and Bell carried federal law to Mississippi twice a month, via jet.

Another senior lawyer at the Fund was Yale Law School graduate James Madison Nabrit, III, who was appointed the Fund's associate director after Mrs. Motley became borough president. Jim Nabrit had been weaned on the plans that brought The School Desegregation Cases to the Supreme Court. His father had argued one of the cases; later Nabrit Senior became dean of the Howard University Law School and president of the university. Greenberg tended to be unpredictable; Nabrit on the other hand, while a young man, was a cautious lawyer of the old school. He combined an imposing technical skill with great prudence. At freewheeling strategy sessions, Nabrit defined the limits of the possible to often frustrated, angry colleagues who were anxious to thrust the broadest grounds for decision on a reluctant judiciary, and occasionally preferred to lose in order to "expose the system" rather than to win what they thought to be a paper victory. His was the hard head that reminded all that nothing could be accomplished without craft. Scores of young lawyers passed through his hands with the assurance that they might take upon themselves the difficult task of employing the legal system as a political instrument without the added burden of professional ignorance.

The lawyers that Greenberg, Motley, Nabrit, and Bell attracted to the Fund in the 1960's were not always those who had received the highest grades at law school, but as clever manipulators of the judicial system they had few equals. As a group, they showed a special capacity to seize upon new ideas and tenaciously bend them to their uses. Other attorneys may have logged as many hours, but none more imaginatively served their clients' interests or more readily responded to calls for help which came through a switchboard which seemed to be plugged into the sources of American racism.

When in 1961, after spending my first year after Yale Law School brooding in Europe and the Middle East, I returned home to take up the lawyer's trade, at first it was with reluctance. There were few places that suited my taste where my legal training could be used. The New York Civil Liberties Union employed only one attorney at that time, there were no "public interest" law firms, neighborhood legal service offices were years away, and consumer advocate Ralph Nader was an adjunct professor of history at the University of Hartford. Interviews at the then-lethargic Civil Rights Division of the United States Department of Justice dissolved what little optimism about the American legal system I had managed to nurture in a year abroad. Even after nine months of Robert F. Kennedy, an Attorney

General who at least seemed open to the movement's message, a veteran Civil Rights Division lawyer told me: "The Department won't act until blacks take to the streets."

The few places available for someone who wanted to practice public law for a private organization were not always highly regarded by leaders of the profession. When Thurgood Marshall offered me a job as a Fund staff attorney, both a former teacher and a prominent federal judge warned that this was frenetic work ("a finger in the dike job," one said) in which a young lawyer never would have the time to do his job well. He might squander his talents on the insatiable demands of clients whose every claim required maximum exertion. This led inevitably, they argued, to shortcuts, hurried arguments, reflexive responses—all well perhaps for a few years of "service" but ultimately devastating to intellectual growth, to the evaluative process which is a precondition to professional development. While in many respects they accurately predicted the hazards, their conclusion that a new member of the bar might better apprentice at large Wall Street or Washington law firms, where knowledge accumulated gradually and responsibility came late, failed to take account of the rewards of helping the people who needed help the most and of identification with more than a client's bankroll. Though the training and working conditions of many of my law school classmates were lavish and their pay astonishing, it seemed to me, and to several other young lawyers who eagerly joined the Fund's staff when jobs were available, that they had abandoned too much in return. A job at the Fund offered me a chance to deploy my naturally combative urges on behalf of the underdog and to make my mark in the world.

If my colleagues at the Fund were the first wave of young lawyers who rejected the rewards of commercial law for a new professional ideal, we were not as a group particularly radical in politics or life-style, fitting more than most would admit De Tocqueville's description of lawyers as men with "certain habits of order, a taste for formalities, and a kind of instinctive regard for the regular connection of ideas, which naturally renders them very hostile to the revolutionary spirit . . ."[4] As bourgeoisie, rather than topple the norms of our profession, we sought to change them piecemeal, by example, and without jeopardy to the good life.

During the early 1960's, while protests and litigation combined to eliminate the legal basis for all state-supported and much privately sponsored racial discrimination, challenging capital punishment was not on the Fund's agenda. The death row population was several hundred. Roughly two men a week were sentenced to death; an execution was held an average of once a week, about half of them in the South. The blatant racism displayed in many Southern death cases —frequent death sentences when the defendant was black and the victim was white, beatings, coerced confessions or, most common practice of all, indictment and trial by all-white juries—provoked LDF intervention, but a campaign against the death penalty, even in its more discriminatory manifestations, would have been thought a flight of fantasy. There was simply too much else to do. The Department of Justice denied that it had the power to bring school desegregation suits; *Brown v. Board of Education* would have remained words in a book if the Fund had not attempted to enforce it. One school case could tie up a staff lawyer for months. It took a thick slice of lawyer time and an outrageous amount of money to desegregate a hospital, a lunch counter, or a public park.

The Fund took on many death cases involving Southern blacks. Staff lawyers told themselves that the cases presented an opportunity to advance LDF's general interest in eliminating racial discrimination from the operation of the criminal law by establishing more just rules of criminal procedure. In several, Marshall and Greenberg had persuaded the Supreme Court to make new law by striking down several coercive police interrogation practices. Mrs.

Motley had won an important extension of the indigent's right to counsel—applying it to arraignment proceedings—in a 1967 death case that she and Nabrit had carried to the Supreme Court.[5] It is doubtful that the hard-pressed handful of lawyers would have accepted many of these cases if they had not been capital, but no serious thought had been given to the possible unconstitutionality of the death penalty itself or even to challenging the legal procedures by which courts decided who died and who went to prison.

A case headed for the Supreme Court that came to my attention in 1963 illustrates the prevailing approach to death cases. Johnny "Big Time" Coleman, an Alabama black man, had been sentenced to death in a rural court for murdering "Screwdriver" Johnson—a white, whose nickname derived from the implement he always carried in a leather holder on his belt. Because there had been no witnesses to the homicide, the state had been forced to establish Coleman's guilt by an extended series of inferences—shells found near the body had been stolen from a general store; Coleman had been seen in the vicinity of the store before the robbery; a shirt of similar make to those sold at the store was found in the cabin where Johnny "Big Time" lived.

Whatever the relevance of this Sherlock Holmes-like evidence to Coleman's guilt—especially when presented to the jury by a government toxicologist who made his living testifying as a prosecution witness in such cases—the facts hardly seemed a concrete basis for capital punishment. One might at most surmise that "Big Time" and "Screwdriver" had become involved in a fight which had led to Johnson's death. But an all-white jury in Greene County, Alabama—a county where 80 percent of the adult population was black—decided not only that Coleman was guilty but that he should be electrocuted.

Greene County is many miles from the office of a Negro attorney, but Coleman's mother finally found one in the person of plucky Birmingham lawyer Orzell Billingsley, Jr.

At the mother's request, Billingsley entered the case after the jury verdict, but before time for seeking a new trial had expired. His first act as Coleman's lawyer was to challenge the racial composition of the trial jury, as well as the grand jury which had found enough evidence to indict. These were motions that his white, court-appointed, predecessor had neglected to make and they were brushed aside by the Alabama courts.

Unfortunately for men condemned on slender evidence like Coleman, the Supreme Court of the United States usually does not have the authority to decide whether or not the evidence in a state criminal case supports the defendant's guilt; the Court more rarely may decide that a particular sentence is unjustified. Even when the Court's jurisdiction is clear, the Justices have the power to select the cases they will review; they choose only those that involve legal issues of utmost importance. In order to fashion an appeal which might interest the Court, it was necessary to press Coleman's contention that he had been denied the opportunity to prove that blacks had been systematically excluded from Greene County juries by the failure of his white lawyer to raise the question.

Beginning in the 1880's, the Supreme Court had long labored to eliminate racial discrimination from Southern state jury selection. But exclusion of blacks persisted, in part because of difficulties encountered in proving it, and the Court often set aside criminal convictions because racially selected juries had sat in judgment on black defendants. As the Court favored deciding the jury discrimination issue in capital cases, it was not particularly surprising that, in 1964, a brief order of the Court announced agreement to review Coleman's case. Several months later, the Justices unanimously set aside the conviction on the ground that Coleman had not been given a satisfactory opportunity to offer proof of racial discrimination;[6] the case was sent back to Greene County for a new hearing.

Billingsley subsequently offered evidence that no black

had ever served on a Greene County jury, but the local court was unimpressed and reinstated the death sentence. Incredibly, the Supreme Court of Alabama also ruled that Coleman had not, after being given the opportunity, proven exclusion of Negroes from the juries. In 1967, however, the Supreme Court of the United States again disagreed with the Alabama courts and ordered a new trial for Johnny "Big Time."[7]

Twice reversed by the Supreme Court, elected in an area of the state where blacks had begun to vote, the local district attorney whimsically permitted the new trial to take place before a jury of twelve black citizens of Greene County—apparently the first time such a jury had been empaneled in the South since Reconstruction. Coleman was acquitted of Johnson's murder, and he became one of the few death-row inmates to leave prison a free man. But six months after his release, he died—of natural causes—at the age of thirty-eight.

Until the mid-1960's only techniques of the sort used in Coleman's case were available to the condemned. Their lawyers searched the records of trial court proceedings for procedural errors, most of which related to the issue of guilt rather than to the death penalty, but many men on death row were without legal representation. The law frowned on claims that the evidence offered at trial was insufficient to justify capital punishment. A challenge to the constitutionality of the death penalty or the procedures by which it was imposed held little promise. A few lawyers fought to have appellate courts declare the death penalty cruel and unusual punishment, or attacked the peculiar characteristics of the capital trial, but such efforts were haphazard, last-ditch attempts to save a life and all had flopped.

The Supreme Court scrutinized appeals in death cases with great care, but it still agreed to decide far less than half of those presented to it. If the condemned man's case offered an interesting, exploitable, or challenging legal issue, he had a chance to win a new trial and eventually escape a sentence of death. If the defendant's lawyer failed to see such issues, or if his case simply contained none, he was like a moneyless patient with a commonplace disease—out of luck.

2

The Court

But times were "a-changing." The mass slaughters of the Second World War and the legacy of a century bloodied by revolutionary and counterrevolutionary violence had led to a modest reaction against state-imposed killing. In 1930, 155 Americans had been executed; by 1960 the total was down to 56. The territories of Alaska and Hawaii and the state of Delaware abolished capital punishment during the late 1950's.[1] In Delaware, the first state to abolish since 1917, the legislative struggle was particularly well-publicized and stirred abolitionist activity elsewhere. In 1960 a small group of New Jersey citizens, outraged by attempts to execute several unrepresented blacks and by the legislature's indifference to abolition bills, held a week-long, Easter-time vigil before the Trenton State House. The controversy surrounding Caryl Chessman's interminable courtroom battles to upset his death sentence for kidnaping with bodily injury (stayed eight times by three California governors) commanded national and international attention, especially among the young.

In England, where a death sentence was mandatory after a murder conviction, abolitionists grew bolder. The imposing 1953 Report of the Royal Commission on Capital Punishment, chaired by Sir Ernest Gowers, armed them with an impressive array of documented arguments against the death penalty. The Report did not recommend abolition, for the Commission held to its Royal Warrant, framed to restrict inquiry to "whether liability under the Criminal Law in Great Britain to suffer capital punishment for murder should be limited or modified."[2] But repudiation of the death penalty was implicit in much of what the Commission had to say. Parliament must face the future of capital punishment squarely, the Commission concluded, for it was an "inescapable" truth that there was little room for further limitation of capital punishment short of abolition.

One of the Americans who advised the Royal Commission was Professor Herbert Wechsler of Columbia Law School, a prominent constitutional lawyer. He was the chief draftsman of the Model Penal Code being prepared by the American Law Institute (ALI), a group of eminent lawyers and judges, in the hope that it would stimulate revision of the criminal law by state legislatures. Although the ALI was almost totally unknown to the public, its recommendations for changes in the law carried substantial weight within the profession.

In 1959, after the ALI advisory committee supported abolition by a vote of 18 to 2, Wechsler presented a recommendation to the council of the Institute that the Model Penal Code exclude capital punishment. For those jurisdictions that chose to retain the death penalty, Wechsler's draft contained restrictive procedures for applying it. A death case would involve a two-stage trial of the sort that California had enacted in 1957 to mitigate the harshness of existing capital case procedure. Under the proposal, the jury first determined whether the defendant was guilty or not guilty and, if the former, then reconvened to hear evidence on the question of sentence. At this hearing, the jury could sentence to death only if it found—a Wechsler innovation—an absence of enumerated mitigating circumstances and the presence of one or more specified aggravating circumstances.[3]

Before the capital punishment issue was put to the annual meeting of the ALI—attended by some four to five hundred lawyers and judges in Washington, D.C.—the views of the Institute's entire membership of approximately twelve hundred were surveyed by mail on several of the questions raised by the Wechsler proposals. Members were asked whether they thought the ALI ought to take any position on capital punishment, and secondly—assuming adoption of the two-stage trial and aggravation-mitigation formulation—whether they favored abolition or retention of the death penalty. An overwhelming majority responded that the Institute should not take a position on the death penalty; a smaller majority favored retention, if the new procedures were adopted.

Still, a floor fight over the abolition proposal was expected. Wechsler had commissioned another Royal Commission consultant, criminologist Thorsten Sellin, to collect available data on the relationship, if any, between the death penalty and homicide rates. After an extensive investigation, Sellin had concluded that execution was a statistically rare event and that there was no quantitative evidence relating capital punishment to murder rates. Wechsler was not surprised. Murders, he thought, were generally "either crimes of passion, in which a calculus of consequences has small psychological reality, or crimes of such depravity that the actor reveals himself as doubtfully within the reach of influences that might be especially inhibitory in the case of an ordinary man."[4]

Supreme Court Justice Robert H. Jackson, one of the most powerful and respected advocates of the day, offered to argue that the model code should ban capital punishment. The death penalty, Jackson told Wechsler privately, "completely bitches up the criminal law," by which he meant not only that it unnecessarily multiplied trials and appeals but that the entire judicial process was sentimentalized and sensationalized by injection of life-and-death questions. He promised to lead the abolition forces at the annual meeting.

It would take something spectacular, like a dramatic appearance by a Supreme Court Justice at the meeting, to overcome the unfavorable results of the membership survey. Wechsler was not optimistic. But he did think that if anyone could persuade the ALI to go on record against the death penalty it was Robert H. Jackson. Ironically, Jackson died before the meeting took place and the membership approved the new bifurcated trial procedures without taking any position on abolition.

Over the years, the arguments for and against capital punishment had focused on its wisdom, or lack of it, not its essential legality. Abolitionists devoted their energies, with slight success, to persuading state legislatures to end capital punishment. In 1961 a Los Angeles antitrust lawyer named Gerald Gottlieb suggested a different route. Gottlieb published an article in the *University of Southern California Law Review* contending that the death penalty was of dubious constitutionality. Whether or not it deterred certain crimes, Gottlieb thought that capital punishment was inconsistent with contemporary standards of decency and, therefore, violated the Eighth Amendment of the federal Constitution, which prohibited cruel and unusual punishment.

Intellectual and moral leaders, he argued, consider it unnecessary and no less barbaric than other punishments society has repudiated:

The phrase [cruel and unusual punishment] is . . . dynamic . . . and the courts must notice and consider . . . changed standards of decent conduct marked by our great penologists, wardens, social philosophers and psychologists.[5]

If Gottlieb was right in identifying a basis for constitutional challenge, the next step was action in the courts, rather than the legislatures.

Criticism of the administration of capital punishment suggested litigable issues other than the ultimate power of government to kill. The same year that Gottlieb's article appeared, Professor Walter E. Oberer of the University of Texas Law School wrote a critique of a century-old American legal procedure peculiar to the capital trial.[6] The practice—called "death qualification" or "scrupling"—permitted the prosecution to excuse potential jurors who expressed sentiments against capital punishment on the theory that the state was entitled to an impartial jury on the question of penalty. Oberer concluded that the practice purged the jury of its more humane members and that the jurors who remained after "death qualification" were more likely to convict. In order to give the state a jury willing to bring in a death sentence, the law had stacked the deck against the defendant's claim that he was not guilty.

In another day, scholarship of the sort produced by Wechsler, Sellin, Oberer, and Gottlieb, among others, would have served merely as the source or the justification for proposed legislation. The Supreme Court, as Yale law professor Alexander M. Bickel commented, had "missed" or "wilfully passed up" postwar opportunities to restrict capital punishment by refusing to interfere with Louisiana's "second (and successful) execution of the same man" after the first attempt had been thwarted by a mechanical failure (1947), the federal government's killing of atomic spies Julius and Ethel Rosenberg (1953), and California's gassing of Caryl Chessman after eleven years on death row (1960).[7] But now the Supreme Court was brewing a "due process revolution," handing down rulings on reapportionment, loyalty-security programs, public school Bible reading, juvenile courts, legislative investigations, and obscenity, as well as race relations and criminal procedure. And with activist decisions reaching into the crannies of daily life, it was not far-fetched to think that the Court might turn to capital punishment.

Lawyers go about their business of resolving disputes in many places other than the courtroom—in the board room, across the bargaining table, before administrative agencies, and legislatures—but during the 1960's law reformers showed an unmistakable preference for the courts, especially the federal courts. In part, this emphasis on litigation was a response to the Supreme Court's willingness to redraw America's ethical and legal map, a task state houses and executive mansions were slow to tackle. At times, the lawyers had no choice. Southern school boards, state welfare officials, and politicized district attorneys had little common ground on which to negotiate with the representatives of those who wished drastic changes in the traditional way of doing things. Nor do people with power have to negotiate with the powerless unless they are hauled into court. Reform through legislation requires an overwhelming public consensus or a powerful minority lobby. To modify the conduct, much less the attitudes, of large groups the executive branch usually requires massive commitment of new money and new workers which the legislature must authorize. Both executive and legislative branches react slowly except when pressed by crisis and confrontation.

Test cases, however, have their disadvantages. Reform through the courts is time-consuming, expensive, and frustrating. The victory won is often but a watered-down promise that legislators and bureaucrats will or will not do something in the future. Rarely does litigation accomplish a redistribution of political or economic power. Nevertheless, lawyers attempting to thrust egalitarian or humanitarian reforms on a reluctant society prefer to use the courts because lifetime-appointed federal judges are somewhat more insulated from the ebb and flow of political power and public opinion than legislators or executives. Consumer advocate Ralph Nader can concentrate on administrative agency rule-making, congressional politics, public relations, report writing, and book publishing because making capitalism honest commands far broader public support than does adding to the power of ethnic or political minorities. Nader is free to call for "citizen action," but the civil rights, criminal, and poverty law bars seek results that are viewed with hostility by a substantial portion of the public. They can succeed only in a forum where ideas—as well as power—count.

In the United States much of this law reform is accomplished in the name of those general principles of equity that are locked into the federal Constitution. The legal reformer attempts to market new constitutional protections to judges—who are merely other lawyers with the power to adopt and to implement. This is done successfully only if the ideas being promoted are acceptable in the first place to at least an influential minority and are reasonably deducible from prior decisions. The power of the courts is great when accommodating the newly accepted or refuting the outworn, but even liberal judges and radical attorneys, despite their protestations to the contrary, are uncomfortable with novelty.

Any court challenge to the death penalty was destined to travel at deliberate speed. It was back in 1932, as *New York Times* newsman Fred Graham has observed, "that the Supreme Court first focused upon the right of criminal defendants to have lawyers. The Court took the smallest possible bite," saying that at a capital trial a lawyer is required.[8] In the famous 1963 case of *Gideon v. Wainwright*[9] the Court took another bite. It reversed an earlier ruling and held that the states must provide counsel to the poor in serious criminal cases, but by then only thirteen states remained where lawyers were not regularly being appointed in felony cases. Significantly, the Court refused for nine more years to make the *Gideon* decision expressly applicable to the misdemeanor offenses[10] which constituted the overwhelming majority of criminal adjudications and, therefore, the locus of the greatest practical problems involved in giving every poor defendant the right to a lawyer.

One of the first cases to reflect a new attitude toward judicial abolition of capital punishment involved the appeal of Joseph Frady and Richard Gordon, two young Negroes convicted in 1963 of murder and robbery in the District of Columbia. Anthony G. Amsterdam, a former assistant

United States attorney in the District, then teaching at the University of Pennsylvania, was appointed amicus curiae, or friend of the court, in the case by the United States Court of Appeals. In 1964 Amsterdam urged the court to find that the death sentences imposed on Frady and Gordon were unlawful because accomplished by use of the single-verdict trial—a trial at which the jury determines guilt and sentence simultaneously—that Wechsler had successfully eliminated from the ALI model code.

When the case was decided, the court's brief opinion did not mention Amsterdam's argument that fairness required that a capital case defendant be accorded a separate hearing on sentence; the court of appeals—by a 5 to 4 vote—simply reduced the death sentences to life imprisonment because of technical errors in the conduct of the jury trial.[11] Concurring and dissenting opinions, however, spoke to Amsterdam's suggestion at length. One dissenting opinion, by then Circuit Judge Warren Earl Burger, praised the argument of amicus as "brilliantly advanced," but found it inappropriate for the federal courts to require a separate proceeding to consider penalty in the absence of express congressional authorization. Burger also wrote that he had "grave reservations" about capital punishment, but told his fellow judges "to uphold the law, not engage in sophisticated nitpicking in order to implement our disagreement with the decisions Congress has made on capital punishment."

At about the same time that Amsterdam was preparing his argument in the Frady and Gordon case LDF lawyers were beginning to explore potential challenges to capital punishment based on claims of racial discrimination. In rape cases, Southern juries often sentenced to death blacks who raped white women, while white rapists or blacks whose victims were black went to prison. It had long been thought that this pattern could be declared unconstitutional—if sufficient proof were massed to persuade a court that it was the product of discrimination, rather than nonracial factors. Civil rights movement legal victories demonstrating that lawyers could persuade courts to look through seemingly neutral-looking practices of Southern officials to see the racially biased realities behind them strongly suggested that it might be possible to collect the necessary evidence.

But no one seriously considered making the enormous effort that would be required until an October 1963 opinion by Supreme Court Justice Arthur Goldberg, concurred in by Justices William J. Brennan and William O. Douglas, jolted Fund lawyers into action. Goldberg seized upon obscure Alabama and Virginia rape cases, *Rudolph v. Alabama* and *Snider v Cunningham*,[12] to announce, in dissent from a decision by the Court not to review the two appeals, that he thought the Justices should determine whether the death penalty for rape was unconstitutional.

Despite the fact that the condemned men's lawyers had not challenged the constitutionality of the death penalty, Justice Goldberg listed three questions "relevant and worthy of argument and consideration by the Court":

1. In light of the trend both in this country and throughout the world against punishing rape by death, does the imposition of the death penalty by those States which retain it for rape violate "evolving standards of decency that mark the progress of [our] maturing society," or standards of decency more or less universally accepted?

2. Is the taking of human life to protect a value other than human life consistent with the constitutional proscription against "punishments which by their excessive . . . severity are greatly disproportioned to the offenses charged"?

3. Can the permissible aims of punishment (e.g., deterrence, isolation, rehabilitation) be achieved as effectively by punishing rape less severely than by death—e.g., by life imprisonment; if so, does the imposition of the death penalty for rape constitute "unnecessary cruelty"?

Racial discrimination in sentencing rapists was not one of the grounds mentioned by Goldberg—an omission which lawyers close to the Court took to mean that in 1963 it was still too early for many to accept that an interracial rape was not a more serious crime than an intraracial rape, and thereby worthy of more severe punishment. But careful readers of the dissent readily concluded that, *if proven,* a claim that the Southern states reserved the death penalty for blacks who raped whites was an even more compelling constitutional argument against capital punishment for the crime of rape than those mentioned by Goldberg.

The opinion awakened interest in the constitutionality of capital punishment, but Goldberg's position did not go unchallenged. Abolitionists immediately pointed out that the risk of forbidding death as a punishment because the criminal act did not involve taking life was to legitimize the death penalty for an act that *did* take life, and that the death penalty for murder was a far more serious problem than for rape. Despite his fierce opposition to the death penalty, Professor Herbert Packer of Stanford, an influential law professor, took Goldberg to task in the *Harvard Law Review.* Packer criticized Goldberg for assuming that the Constitution requires a proportion between crime and punishment, for implying that sexual attack does not endanger life, and for intimating that the death penalty for rape violated society's "evolving standards of decency"—the proper test, according to a 1958 Supreme Court decision, of whether a punishment was unconstitutionally cruel.[13]

The Supreme Court of Georgia took advantage of a capital case pending before it to ridicule the notion that rape does not deserve the death penalty:

No determination of this question is either wise or humane if it fails to take full account of the major place in civilized society of woman. She is the mother of the human race, the bedrock of civilization; her purity and virtue are the most priceless attributes of human kind. The infinite instances where she has resisted even unto death the bestial assaults of brutes who were trying to rape her are eloquent and indisputable proof of the human agonies she endures when raped. . . . Even a cur dog is too humane to do such an outrageous injury to the female.[14]

Regardless of whether Goldberg's suggested theories for challenging capital sentencing in rape cases were persuasive, his dissent was a timely exposure of the issue to the bar and public—probably its aim, for Justices rarely dissent publicly from a decision not to review a case. No longer did a direct attack in the courts on capital sentencing seem doomed to failure. Lawyers need authority to defeat the idea—often unpleasantly raised by their adversaries—that their legal arguments are departures from accepted doctrine. Now they could point to *Rudolph v. Alabama.* The words of three Supreme Court Justices, even in dissent, offer a strong foundation for the eventual acceptance of change.

One afternoon, several months after announcement of the Goldberg dissent, Frank Heffron and Leroy Clark, both LDF staff lawyers, and I, left the Fund's 10 Columbus Circle offices, bought sandwiches from a delicatessen take-out counter, and sprawled on the thin Central Park grass to discuss the implications of the opinion for the Fund. Tall and lean, Clark had the looks of a professional basketball player. He saw white society through unsentimental eyes, like a man who had settled in a country without having abandoned allegiance to the land of his birth. With characteristically mordant humor, Clark called Heffron "straight arrow." The label fit; a New Englander, Heffron had become an editor of the *Columbia Law Review,* graduated near the top of his class, and then married a hometown girl. Self-reliant and skeptical, he expressed his opinion on legal matters only after holding a conference with himself; the result was always as clear and clean as a printed page. The three of us were joined by ambition and a common habit of converting restless energy into the stuff of litigation.

Clark was bitter that Goldberg had not enumerated racial discrimination in rape sentencing as a ground "relevant and worthy of . . . consideration." I worried about the difficulty of proving discrimination. We tossed both problems around for an hour until Heffron reminded us that the Fund received several requests each month to represent black defendants under sentence of death. Legal assistance was always hard to refuse, despite the fact that these cases displaced others that involved significant civil rights issues. Staff lawyers strained to find grounds for appeal. Heffron concluded, "If we aren't able to turn these cases away, we might as well focus on the real issue—capital punishment."

Perhaps life was simpler in those days, or perhaps we were blinded by the long string of civil rights victories the Fund had accumulated, but Heffron's remark set our course. A week later we persuaded Greenberg that a staff attorney should be assigned to investigate the possibility of proving the existence of racial sentencing in rape cases, a task which ultimately fell to Heffron.

Years later, it became known that the *Rudolph* opinion was merely the remaining shard of a far more elaborate work which Goldberg had prepared in the hope of persuading his fellow Justices either to restrict capital punishment or to abolish it outright. Goldberg believed that constitutional guarantees of personal freedom and equal treatment were meant to inspire the Justices to deal imaginatively with the great social problems of each era. After John F. Kennedy appointed him to fill the vacancy on the Court caused by Felix Frankfurter's resignation in 1962, he soon confronted a batch of troubling capital case appeals. In several of the cases, racial discrimination seemed the only explanation for imposition of the death penalty; in others, there was evidence of mental illness; in still others, he was shocked by the performance of defense counsel. Goldberg was also disturbed by the fact that lawyers for the condemned men had not challenged the constitutionality of the death penalty.

A deeply religious man, Goldberg personally believed that the death penalty was an abomination. He was fond of pointing out that while the Old Testament often commanded death as the punishment for wrongdoers, the rabbinical judges who applied Jewish law rarely passed a death sentence. Capital punishment had been so hedged about by rigorous and confusing proof requirements that ancient Israel had abolished it in fact, if not in theory. But it was his oft-expressed view that the Constitution had to be interpreted dynamically, if it was to remain a continuing instrument of government, that led him to act.

In the summer of 1963, Goldberg began his first full term on the Court. At the time, his law clerk was Alan Dershowitz, who shortly thereafter became a Harvard Law professor. When Dershowitz arrived to take up his clerkship, Goldberg immediately set him to work searching out precedent to support an argument that the death penalty was cruel and unusual punishment in violation of the Eighth Amendment. Dershowitz was the right man for the job, for he was intensely interested in criminal law. After gathering a fistful of academic awards at the Yale Law School, he had spent a year clerking for David Bazelon, the Chief Judge of the Court of Appeals for the District of Columbia Circuit and an ardent criminal law reformer. As Bazelon's clerk, he had engaged in extensive research for an important capital case, one with Eighth Amendment overtones.

Assisted by Dershowitz, Goldberg drafted and redrafted a memorandum urging the Justices to consider seriously a grant of review in six pending capital case appeals (four murders and two rapes) in order to decide whether, and under what circumstances, the death penalty was unconstitutional. Although lower courts had not passed on the question and none of the condemned men had explicitly asked the Supreme Court to rule on the constitutionality of the death penalty, Goldberg argued that to permit the lower court judgments to stand was tantamount to upholding the legality of capital punishment: with life at stake, the Court itself should feel free to raise the issue. Eminent counsel presumably would be appointed to represent those men who did not have lawyers. One draft of the memorandum suggested that the Court order attorneys for the six to file legal briefs addressed to a set of specific legal questions about the death penalty, a technique used in the School Desegregation Cases.

After reading briefs and hearing oral argument, the Court would have a number of options. If it did not wish to rule that deliberate taking of human life violated community standards of decency, it might still find that the death penalty was unconstitutionally excessive because the states could achieve the legitimate ends of the criminal law by less severe punishment. Or the Court might limit its initial assault on the death penalty to cases where there was psychiatric evidence that the defendant simply could not control himself and conform his conduct to the law.

The Court could also postpone resolution of the constitutionality of the death penalty for murder by merely ruling that if sexual crimes could be deterred at all they could be as effectively deterred by imprisonment as by capital punishment. The Justices might focus on the fact that in rape cases life was being taken to protect a value other than life or on the pattern of racial sentencing. Even a narrow decision limited to the death penalty in rape cases would mold public opinion and hopefully nurture support for abolition.

But Goldberg's proposal to conduct a far-ranging inquiry into the constitutionality of the death penalty did not win approval from a majority of the Court. Apparently he was even unable to persuade Brennan and Douglas to do more than join a dissent which did not directly refer to racial discrimination in rape sentencing.

Suppose that a majority of the Justices disagreed with Goldberg's stance. Then why did they not agree to grant review in the six cases in order to uphold the death penalty as constitutional? The answer is that even those Justices who thought it constitutional intensely disliked capital punishment. Express judicial approval would make the death penalty even more difficult to eradicate in state legislatures and in Congress.

In the unlikely event that a majority of the Court agreed with Goldberg, there were still plenty of good reasons to postpone a campaign against the death penalty. The Court was in hot water because of its role in the civil rights revolution. Many controversial race relations issues remained undecided, including the legality of the sit-in as a device to integrate restaurants and places of recreation and the constitutionality of anti-miscegenation statutes. "Impeach Earl Warren" billboards covered Dixie like the dew. The Court faced rising criticism for restricting police interrogation practices and was in the midst of grappling with the thorny and politically explosive matter of reapportionment. Even a Justice sympathetic to Goldberg's views might have thought them too bold and adventurous to act upon.

In 1963 the Justices were unwilling to tackle the death penalty, but perhaps a well-prepared lawsuit would induce them to change their minds. A month after he got the green light from Greenberg to look into such a suit, Heffron reported back. A preliminary survey of the available data on racial disparities in rape sentencing was inconclusive. While 90 percent of those who had been executed since 1930 in the seventeen Southern and border states which at the time punished rape with death were black, Southern prosecuting attorneys could claim that this result was the product of factors other than racial discrimination. Condemned Negroes may have had longer criminal records than whites who were sentenced to life; they may have used more violence or employed weapons when whites did not.

So long as plausible nonracial explanations of the high

proportion of blacks sentenced to death were available, it would require new research to prove to the satisfaction of federal judges that these explanations failed to account for the striking disproportion between Negro and white death sentences. There was no way, Heffron warned, to predict the outcome of such research. If a study was not rigorous and objective enough to convince social scientists of its validity, success in court would be impossible. Such an investigation was feasible, he concluded, but the necessary work required the talents of specialists, and it would be costly.

Lawyers attempting to reconstruct the legal system through litigation need large doses of money to pay for printing bills, airplane fares, and expert assistance, since without briefs, mobility, and witnesses, the limits of reform are narrow. With an enormous civil rights legal program to support, Greenberg first attempted to finance research into capital sentencing in the South by approaching the few foundations which contribute to civil rights organizations. One refused because its chief executive officer thought that Fund-supervised research into racial discrimination was similar to tobacco-industry research into lung cancer. The death penalty, even racial sentencing patterns, simply did not interest others. Ultimately, Greenberg decided to take the money from the LDF general budget—taking a gamble, worthy of the most intrepid businessman, that increased contributions would offset the expense.

Some years later a friend surveyed what had followed from these beginnings and asked, "Why did you devote so much time and money to this human trash?" Questions of this sort cannot be answered, if they are answerable at all, by simplistic moralism or appeal to the sanctity of life. The death penalty is ugly, cruel, and violent, but then so is narcotics addiction, so is a rat-infested slum, so are many things.

Fund lawyers did not lack worthy claimants for their professional services; the money and men could have been spent on other valuable projects.

Why then was a choice made to preserve the lives of death-row inmates, if it could be done? Racial discrimination in capital sentencing was apparent, and its elimination was the lawyers' business. They came to believe that it was impossible to separate racism from the death penalty; that the only remedy for discrimination was to ensure that the opportunity to execute blacks simply did not arise.

But even this calculus, so compelling in a nation of double standards for black and white, rich and poor, powerful and friendless, does not explain why so few did so much with so little. One suspects that, at bottom, the lawyers who decided to challenge the death penalty acted as much for themselves and for the order of things they wished to call into being as for the condemned. Caryl Chessman had said that the only way he could cope with the fear of death was to think of himself as the lawyer for a man facing execution. Perhaps a similar psychological process enabled these lawyers to identify with men condemned to death. In any event, if the question of motivation is answerable, neither the wrongness of the death penalty, nor its arbitrary application, nor its failure to pass a cost-benefit test, is the whole story.

Professional pride, however, was a force in the decision to proceed. By 1965, when a litigation strategy took shape, the long golden days of the civil rights movement had begun to wane. A rash of urban riots shifted attention from the courtroom to the streets, and no one feels so irrelevant as a lawyer in a shoot-out. I had received a phone call from an exhausted NAACP official during a turbulent riot. Snipers and police were exchanging shots only two blocks from his office and he had bawled into the phone: "You must stop this thing. Can't you got to court and stop this thing?" Stokely Carmichael, H. Rap Brown, Malcolm X and their followers had center stage. The success of the civil rights movement in sweeping away the formal structure of articulated racism had made it possible for them to finger the tangled feelings and institutionalized inequality which undergirded explicit racial discrimination. With the rhetoric of revolution and a flair for publicity, they goaded the black man not to settle for the "equal opportunity" goals of the movement when he had been denied the means to compete equally.

When people begin to speak for themselves, lawyers are left behind or given a small part, a character role. But, again to quote De Tocqueville, lawyers have notions of superiority based on their "habit of directing to their purpose the blind passions of parties in litigation . . ."[15] So if one asks why talented men devoted their energies, amidst a time of civil disturbance and beastly war, to eradication of a penalty which probably carried off yearly but a few of the vicious or the moronic, persons as a class unlikely to contribute a jot to their families, much less the world around them, perhaps it was that tools had been developed which now threatened to collect dust. No court was ready to declare the war in Vietnam unconstitutional or to eliminate the causes of civil disorder. But ending "judicial homicide," to use Jacques Barzun's phrase, seemed a realizable goal, one which, if achieved, might counteract what Anthony Amsterdam later described as "our terrible propensity to deal with complex social problems with violence—by the simple expedient of gassing the guy who is the problem."

There was more to it, of course, though here the speculations so outnumber the facts as to make one hesitate to share what likely amounts to little more than personal vision. In my judgment the unmasking and delegitimizing of American racism undermined the public's sense—already subject to attack from other quarters—of the culpability of criminals. Public consciousness was force-fed knowledge that the negative traits Americans ascribed to blacks, most prominent of which was "black criminality," were the product of a particular environment—made in the U.S.A. This was not a new idea, but very new indeed was the daily demonstration —often through confrontation politics—of the details. No longer could the black criminal—or any criminal handicapped by the culture of poverty or taught that he deserved a life of deprivation—be shrugged off as willful, acting out of malice or greed, or simply not thought of at all. If Americans had not solved the crime problem with supermarkets full of goods and "know how," they had to come to terms with their responsibility for it.

A nation's criminal law is a subtle barometer of its fears and confidences. Winston Churchill merely summed up a common observation of lawyers, philosophers, and statesmen when he wrote that "The treatment of crime and criminals is one of the most unfailing tests of the civilization of any country."[16] Why? One reason is that the criminal always tempts us to use him as a scapegoat. We are exculpated as he blots out our feelings of guilt: "Along with the stone, we cast our own sins onto the criminal."[17] Whatever it may have been in the past, maturity in nations now resides in their capacity to distinguish between the actual threat posed by the criminal (the outsider, the enemy) and the distorted perception of that threat yielded by man's chaotic mental life.

If the criminal act is felt as an alien, although familiar, occurrence, a nation can deal with it by measured remedies: plotted carefully, imposed with humanity, pointed to future avoidance of the evil in question. But what happens when the punisher empathizes with the punished; when he begins to think of the criminal and his disturbing act as an all-too-understandable response to the pressures and passions of the society which both inhabit? Such an identification, if left unknown and unexamined, is pregnant with danger. It may stir a blind punitiveness (so as to deny the bond between law-abiding and law-breaking) or a sentimentalizing of the criminal (because if he is not guilty no one need be punished). Or one hand can remain ignorant of the other: the first imposes vindictive penalties while the second passes out promises of fairness and help. This latter course dominates the American way of punishment.

What catches the eye is not so much that our system of punishing criminals is so very cruel—though it has much inhumanity—or that the cruelty is unnecessary—which is debatable—but that so little of its severity is acknowledged. The parallel to Vietnam, where villages were bombed in the name of "pacification" and "protective reaction," is compelling. At home, men are jailed "to deter other criminals" (even those who never weigh the risks of being caught) after judges have "carefully weighed many factors." They are held in prison until they have "adjusted satisfactorily" or "completed a successful rehabilitation." Behind the jargon is sophistry and misery in abundance.

Marvin Frankel, an experienced United States judge, has written[18] with great wisdom of this unacknowledged punitiveness in our system of criminal sentencing. A man rarely given to exaggeration, Frankel views American criminal sentencing as "a wasteland in the law," a "bizarre 'nonsystem' of extravagant powers confided to essentially unregulated judges, keepers, and parole officials."

Sentences are imposed regularly with "feckless cruelty," uncritically, on the basis of vague speculations. Penalties are accepted without inquiry, review, or reevaluation—although among the harshest in the world. American judges and parole boards are often vested with "an enormous range of choice" to incarcerate a man in a grim prison environment from one day to the greater portion of his productive years; such powers are conventionally exercised without guidance "about the factors to be weighed in moving to either end of the spectrum or to some place between."

The individuals who make these decisions receive little training in what they are about other than "fleeting, random, anecdotal, and essentially trivial shop talk" with their colleagues. They are rarely provided with assistance from experienced students of human behavior. Judges and parole officials are not forced to explain why they have chosen a particular sentence either to the man who must serve it or to appellate courts.

In the years that the legal movement to abolish capital punishment gathered momentum, only the prisoners themselves and a few lawyers and scholars protested these vices. Their voices could only be heard after a spate of tragic prison riots attracted a larger audience. But there was no mistaking the outward signs of a crisis in crime and punishment. The level of violence was excessive and probably increasing. Crime was a front-page story. Relatively settled social arrangements between the races and the generations were coming apart and playing an undeniable role in intensifying both its rate and visibility.

In response, many mouthed, as Marvin Wolfgang and Bernard Cohen put it, "the easy political rhetoric," focusing on "increased 'law and order'—stricter punishments, longer sentences, the need to 'unhandcuff' the police and the courts in their dealings with suspected criminals." Others felt that "such emphasis, by stressing a punitive approach and ignoring the vital social change needed to get at the root causes of crime, tends to delay, rather than contribute to, a reduction in the crime rate."[19]

A debate between the proponents of these two views of the world raged through the 1960's. Scholars, commission reports, and the political pitchmen behind the "war on poverty" blamed ghetto living conditions and a culture which emphasized material success and immediate gratification. But Americans elected Richard M. Nixon in 1968 after he campaigned against permissiveness and a Supreme Court—the same Court that had challenged racism—which had "seriously hamstrung the peace forces" and encouraged the criminal. The conflict surfaced in many guises—over welfare payments, no-knock laws, longhaired hippies, habeas corpus, judicial candidates, warnings to suspects, drug laws—but underneath the different issues was the common question of how much responsibility America could stomach for what America had made.

The dilemmas involved in administering a system of penalties when the society which does the punishing feels itself implicated in the crime found their way, as do so many questions of moral ambiguity, to the Supreme Court of the United States—our secular version of the College of Cardinals or the Rabbinate of old.

Coextensive with the civil rights revolution, the Court announced a series of landmark criminal procedure decisions. These decisions worked great changes in the law, but not nearly so many as their friends or their foes claimed. The Court ruled, for example, that state courts could not receive evidence wrongly seized by the police.[20] It guaranteed the poor an opportunity to defend themselves reasonably consistent with that available to the rich;[21] and tightened rules governing the admission in evidence of involuntary confessions.[22]

But the new rules were often merely transplants that had worked well for years in federal courts. Critics failed to notice that while constitutional rights were extended from the federal sphere to the states, the rights themselves were often afterward redefined in a fashion less favorable to defendants. For example, the Court required the states to honor requests for trial by jury but later permitted them to offer juries with fewer than the traditional twelve members.[23] The Court held to its 1961 decision, *Mapp v. Ohio,* that the Fourth and Fourteenth Amendments required exclusion of unreasonably seized evidence, but in 1968 watered down its protection against unlawful searches by authorizing the police to "stop and frisk" pedestrians on bare suspicion of illegal conduct.[24]

Like men stripping off their coats for a fight, the more vocal contestants were not interested in the particulars. It was widely believed that the Court's decisions thwarted the police and frustrated the justifiable zeal of local courts. In the eyes of a growing segment of the public, tinkering with the tried and true punitive methods encouraged crime and moral laxity. And there was a grain of truth in this untutored view, for the Court imposed new demands on relatively impoverished institutions. Perhaps the resulting strain slightly impaired law enforcement at a time when population growth, urbanization, and social conflict already asked too much of police and judges.

It is important, however, to recognize that the Court's decisions had little demonstrable effect on crime (One wished they had. If "bad" decisions encouraged crime, presumably "good" ones could deter it). The Supreme Court did not even much change the conduct of police, prosecutors, or criminal courts—the agencies of government that deal with crime after the fact. All but a handful of the innovative decisions had turned on the admissibility of evidence, not the right to try criminal defendants. Left virtually untouched were plea bargaining practices which determined the fate of most criminal defendants, the money bail system which only incarcerated the poor, lawlessness in sentencing, warehouse-like prisons, availability of legal services for the middle classes, the quality of criminal justice system personnel, and other critical areas the Court did not wish, or was not able, to reach.

Even when the Supreme Court speaks directly to an issue, its pronouncements trickle down to the local level in a highly diluted form. Lower courts discount the constitutional niceties; their primary job is to keep the wheels of criminal justice constantly grinding. The Court has but a small supervisory power over police, prosecuting attorneys, and state judges, and exercises even these limited powers only when cases are brought to it for review. The Supreme Court decides roughly a hundred and fifty cases a year, only a portion of which involve criminal law. Most importantly, it is a court—and an appellate and constitutional court at that—not an inspector-general or ministry of justice.

What seemed to anger critics of the "criminal law revolution" most was not the debatable practical effects of the Court's decisions, but that the Justices had elevated scrupulous fairness for the criminal to an ideology. Anthony Amsterdam ironically compared the Court to the Delphic oracle whose piercing cries—after priestly interpretation— were taken as the word of the gods but were, nevertheless, of little practical value: "The significance of the Court's pronouncements—their power to shake the assembled faithful with awful tremors of exultation and loathing— does not depend on their correspondence with reality."[25]

Because many stubbornly viewed the Court's criminal procedure decisions as excuses for criminality and encouragements to leniency, the public conflict about the criminal law emerged from the shadows. One side blamed the outcasts and called for "law and order"; the other pointed "fingers of accusation," as Telford Taylor wrote of Vietnam, not at those "for whom we have felt scorn and contempt, but at ourselves."[26] "Fingers of accusation" were pointed, as what white Americans had done to blacks became less of a textbook principle, an item of liberal rhetoric, and more a yelping reality—exposed first by the backlash that civil rights activity generated, then by ghetto riots. But for every ounce of guilt, Americans contended with a pound of grim reality. Crime and the fear of crime pressed too close for comfort. "Rip off" moved from the Harlem argot to middle-class usage; dinner parties often featured harrowing tales of muggings and burglaries. Regardless of who or what was responsible, there was too much crime.

At issue was whether American society would use punitiveness to evade the uncomfortable consequences of learning how it had created its victims. The alternative was to accept the contradiction of guilt and self-preservation, to seek protection against the criminal while attempting also to remove his reason to be a criminal. Vacillation between the two courses characterized the 1960's. Abolition came to symbolize a part of the inner struggle: a tug of war over the national soul between merchants of "law and order," on the one side, and promoters of social change, on the other, with the criminal process—which ultimately means the Supreme Court of the United States—in the middle.

3

The Facts of Death

It would be some time, however, before the Supreme Court was ready to speak to the constitutionality of the death penalty. Constitutional law develops slowly. Its larger issues emerge only after a case-by-case dialogue between the Court and lawyers, legislatures, lower courts, and public opinion signals that they are ripe for resolution. Writing about the Supreme Court and capital punishment in 1962, Professor Bickel unhappily concluded that "no sort of colloquy can be said to be in progress, and barring spectacular extraneous events the moment of judgment is therefore a generation or more away."[1]

But "a generation or more" is only a short time in the history of the death penalty. Although its origins are lost in obscurity, imposition of death as punishment for violation of law or custom, religious or secular, is an ancient practice. We do know that men killed to avenge themselves and their kin long before the conduct which provoked retaliation was considered a wrong to the community; and that initially the criminal law was used to compensate for a wrong done to a private party or his family, not to punish in the name of the state.

The idea of crime as an injury to the interests of the society came later and implied a general interest in regulating private retaliation—to the public benefit. The command of Exodus ordering that "life for life, eye for eye, tooth for tooth"² be taken as punishment was in its day an ethical advance, teaching that excessive penalties were not in the interest of the community. The Talmudic decree required that vengeance be proportioned to the crime: if by only taking "measure for measure," God exercised self-restraint, "*a fortiori* must the victim of the offense, the blood avenger, exercise it and never take vengeance beyond the measure of the damage or mischief caused to him."³

Despite the Biblical principle of proportionality between crime and punishment government used the death penalty to punish a variety of antisocial acts other than homicide. The Scriptures themselves authorized execution for a dozen or so offenses, including bearing false witness, adultery, sodomy, and blasphemy. Egyptians were killed for revealing the burial place of the sacred bull; a Roman who slandered the republic could be flogged to death. Henry VIII condemned imagination of the death of the king; the Turks have executed for the use of tobacco. The English of the seventeenth and eighteenth centuries developed a "Bloody Code" that punished with death over two hundred offenses, including the theft of five shillings, forgery, consorting with gypsies, stealing from bleaching grounds, and pocket picking. In 1967, Georgia made a second conviction for sale of narcotics to a minor a capital offense.

The list of crimes—odd to obvious—which men have considered worthy of capital punishment is as long as the list of cunning methods devised to kill—hanging, axing, burning, garroting, pressing with weights, stoning, impalement, crucifixion, starvation, boiling in oil, burial alive. At times, death was alternated with other serious penalties—mutilation, torture, flogging, banishment, branding, confiscation of property—but capital punishment has always been a part of the heritage of Western man.

The first American colonists were not exempt from this tradition. They inherited from the English a considerable number of capital offenses—murder, arson, robbery, treason, and burglary, to name a few—and added several quaint ones of their own—idolatry, witchcraft, stubbornness in a child—from Biblical sources. But neither the list of offenses nor the number of executions compared to British or Continental practice. According to philosopher (and historian of capital punishment in America) Hugo Adam Bedau, "ambitious efforts" were made "to reduce the number of capital crimes" which were defeated early in the eighteenth century when the British Crown forced the colonists to adopt harsh penal codes.[4]

Early Americans were also heirs of the European Enlightenment and its trenchant criticism of vengeful criminal laws and capital punishment in particular. By far the most influential European critic of capital punishment was the Italian jurist Cesare Beccaria. In his book *On Crimes and Punishments,* published in Italy in 1764 and translated and published in New York in 1773, Beccaria spelled out a position that dominated abolitionist thought for a century. The death penalty, he argued, was too quickly administered and too momentous in its consequences to be effective; it instilled compassion, rather than fear, in the observer. Crime was not curbed by the "terrible yet momentary spectacle of the death of a wretch" but by "the long and painful example of a man deprived of liberty, who, having become a beast of burden, recompenses with his labors the society he has offended."[5] The lesson was plain: hard labor and confinement should replace the scaffold.

Beccaria's application of Enlightenment rationalism to the criminal law attracted the interest of Voltaire, Jeremy Bentham and English law reformer Sir Samuel Romilly, as well as the Grand Duke of Tuscany, who abolished capital punishment in 1765. In America, Dr. Benjamin Rush, a Philadelphia physician, William Bradford, an Attorney General of Pennsylvania and later of the United States, and Edward Livingston, a lawyer and future Secretary of State, popularized Beccaria's approach: that the use or abandonment of capital punishment was a matter of social policy that could not be decided by blind adherence to scriptural command or to a "natural right" of retribution. The abolitionist efforts of Rush, Bradford, and Livingston roughly paralleled a growing acceptance of the idea that society's first line of defense should be to remove the offender from the corrupt influences of the outside world by imprisoning him. The miscreant should be housed in the penitentiary—a new institution, which unlike jails of the period was designed to isolate the convict from his fellow inmates—until he learned the error of his ways.

In 1787, the same year he helped found the Philadelphia Society for Alleviating the Miseries of Public Prisons, Rush delivered a paper to a gathering at Benjamin Franklin's home, which argued that reformation of the criminal was both possible and desirable: "I hear the inhabitants of our villages and townships counting the years that should complete the reformation of one of their citizens. I behold them," Rush declared optimistically, "running to meet him on the day of his deliverance."[6]

In 1792, Rush expanded on this theme in his most famous tract: *Considerations on the Injustice and Impolicy of Punishing Murder with Death*. Life imprisonment, he urged, should supplant the death penalty because it holds out the prospect of rehabilitation. Capital punishment lessens the horror of taking human life and influences the suicidal to kill in order to end their lives by hanging. Writing at a time when a murder conviction meant an automatic death sentence, he complained that when jurors were loath to see a capital sentence imposed, they let murderers go free. Prison avoided such problems: "If the punishment of murder consisted in long confinement and hard labour, it would be proportioned to . . . our feelings of justice, and every member of society would be a watchman or a magistrate to apprehend a destroyer of human life, and to bring him to punishment."[7]

William Bradford also thought that capital punishment

was an ineffective deterrent because the hope of acquittal or pardon weakened the terror of death. The important thing about a punishment, he argued, was not so much its severity as the certainty that it will be imposed. He agreed with Montesquieu "that the source of all human corruption lies in the impunity of the criminal, not in the moderation of Punishment."[8]

But Bradford was not a total abolitionist. Although skeptical of the deterrent power of capital punishment, he thought that murder deserved death because the killer trampled on the sanctity of life. If the prospect of death had not effectively deterred murderers in the past, this was only because they hoped to escape. The death penalty would preserve life only if it were to stand out as a certain punishment for the crime of murder, and for no other. In order to eliminate from the category of capital offenses those homicides that jurors did not wish to see punishable by death, Bradford recommended introduction of two degrees of murder, with only the first degree—deliberate, intentional murder—warranting the death penalty, a proposal that the Pennsylvania and Virginia legislatures adopted in 1794. Several years later Pennsylvania eliminated capital punishment for all crimes but murder, a step which Kentucky took in 1800.[9] But most of the new states remained unaffected by the ideas of the two Pennsylvanians. North Carolina, for instance, had over twenty capital crimes; throughout the South, slaves could be executed for any number of trivial offenses.

During the religious revival of the 1830's and 1840's, opponents of the death penalty began to have a practical impact on the administration of the criminal law. In 1824 Edward Livingston had built on the foundation laid by Rush and Bradford when he drafted a new penal code for Louisiana which substituted imprisonment for the death penalty. Although Livingston's code was too far ahead of its time to be adopted, it became a symbol to the growing ranks of abolitionists that their demands might be translated into legislation. Quaker, Universalist, and Unitarian religious leaders of the period, along with editors like Horacc Greeley and writers like John Greenleaf Whittier and William Cullen Bryant, aimed fiery sermons, pamphlets, and evangelist poetry at clergymen of Calvinist persuasion who favored the death penalty.[10] Appeals to sentiment and Scripture replaced the utilitarian calibrations of the Enlightenment—did moderate and certain penalties deter criminals more effectively than severe and excessive ones; did the public safety require the extermination of criminals?

Opponents of capital punishment were often antislavery activists. William Lloyd Garrison and the Reverend Henry Clarke Wright exhorted Americans to end war and slavery by eliminating the "man-killing principle" from society and substituting Christian love in its place. Anti-capital punishment societies, often organized by foes of slavery, conducted intensive lobbying campaigns in many states and had an influence far exceeding the number of their adherents in the general population.[11] The reformers pressed their efforts, especially in the New England and mid-Atlantic states, but it was the territory of Michigan which capitulated first, by eliminating the gallows (for all offenses but treason) in 1846.

The movement to abolish the death penalty began to slacken with the advent of the Civil War. Its advocates had eliminated capital punishment in only a few states but they had made it more difficult to impose everywhere. As a result of mid-nineteenth-century abolitionist activity, the number of capital crimes was dramatically reduced. Three-fourths of the states made robbery and burglary non-capital. Many followed the lead of Pennsylvania and Virginia by dividing murder into capital and non-capital degrees. Juries were also given the power to convict men who were charged with murder of the lesser crime of manslaughter, a non-capital offense. Tennessee, Alabama, Louisiana, Texas, and Georgia authorized juries to set life sentences for capital offenses; before the turn of the century the federal government and eighteen more states and territories passed such laws[12] as a means of both limiting the use of the death penalty and avoiding the practice called "pious perjury" that had troubled Rush and Bradford—acquitting a guilty man whom the jury did not wish to condemn to death.

Increasingly, courts also accepted claims of extenuating circumstances because of age, incapacity, mental illness, duress, and self-defense as grounds for avoidance of a death sentence. The introduction of the right to appeal in criminal cases made it more likely that capital sentences would not result in actual execution. In 1837 Maine changed its laws in a way which successive governors interpreted as permitting courts to sentence to death but not permitting the executive to enforce the sentence. Several other states followed Maine's lead and simply retained the penalty in name only; a few followed Michigan's and abolished outright: Rhode Island (except for murder by a life-term convict) in 1852[13] and Wisconsin in 1853,[14] to name two of the earliest.

In short, by the time Fund lawyers began to consider a serious legal challenge, the use and availability of capital punishment had been dwindling for more than a hundred years but, paradoxically, total abolition was no more likely than it had been in the nineteenth century. The steady erosion of the state's power to impose the death penalty removed executions from common experience and made them a more difficult target for reformers. Whatever guilt feelings capital punishment evoked were further reduced by the introduction of supposedly more humane methods of execution to replace the gallows: electrocution (1890) and lethal gas (1924).

By 1965 six states were counted in the abolitionist column in addition to Michigan, Maine, and Wisconsin: Minnesota (1911), Alaska (1957), Hawaii (1957), Oregon

(1964), Iowa (1965), and West Virginia (1965). In addition to Rhode Island, North Dakota (1915), New York (1965), and Vermont (1965) drastically limited its application. But few of the remaining states were ready to join them.

In no region was this plainer than in the South. Half of the men subject to execution were held in Southern prisons. Of the 3,859 persons executed in the entire nation since 1930, when the federal government began to keep statistics, 2,306 were executed by sixteen Southern states and the District of Columbia.[15] The figures for the 191 executions held between 1960 and 1965 told the same tale: Southern states and the District of Columbia accounted for 103.[16] And there was a more sinister side to the statistics. Between 1882 and 1946 over 4,000 Americans (three-quarters of them black) were lynched in the Southern states.[17] Many of these men would have been executed if they had gone to trial.

The Legal Defense Fund lawyers who pondered the decline in executions were impressed by the fact that it had taken place despite a general belief that the rate of violent crime had increased and a clamor for measures to reduce it. Apparently, the public fear of murder, robbery, and rape was not so strong that it demanded greater use of the death penalty. This was surprising when one considered that executions could be ignored easily because they took place behind prison walls, and that the death penalty was still legitimized by law and still supported by periodic police claims that it was a unique deterrent. Abolition movements could provoke intense feelings and passionate polemics, but capital punishment in America in fact meant only a few killings a year.

This unwillingness to kill was the product of a prosperity which operated as a liberalizing force; of the brutality of state-imposed death, which had disgusted men who had seen or imagined it; and of the increasing awareness of the fallibility of the criminal law. But while Americans seemed to need, or to tolerate, less capital punishment than their ancestors, they were not significantly more willing to abandon it. Although several plebiscites had been held, abolition only succeeded once at the polls: in Oregon in 1964.[18] Massachusetts had not executed anyone since 1947, but each year an abolition bill died in legislative committee. "In Massachusetts," Hugo Bedau remarked, "we can go for a generation without a legal execution in our . . . prisons [but] cannot go one day without the death penalty on our statutes."[19] In other states the results were the same. Legislators usually permitted abolition bills to languish in committee or defeated them by large margins.

Perhaps the recurring incidence of violent crime confronts and defeats the impulse to abolish because it arouses terror, which leads to rage, and in turn to revenge. The powerful emotions inflamed by vividly reported vicious crimes cancel guilt feelings about legal killing. Killers like Lee Harvey Oswald, Sirhan Sirhan, Richard Speck, and Charles Manson are only current examples of criminals who evoke, even in people who dislike the death penalty, a strong wish for counterviolence—and thus a need to keep capital punishment theoretically available. Any newspaper reader may experience this reaction to the horrifying murders that America has spawned—making it difficult for him to keep in mind that thousands of years of capital punishment have not decreased man's aptitude for murder. As a result, while polls show that a substantial portion of the population opposes the death penalty, public opinion fluctuates madly between humanist sentiment and calls for revenge.[20]

In 1917 Pennsylvania was on the verge of abolition; the Harrisburg *Evening Bulletin* predicted that the electric chair would soon join the rack as an historical curiosity. But World War I intervened. An ammunitions plant exploded near Chester and many young women died. Suspecting sabotage, lawmakers decided to keep the ultimate punishment. Truman Capote concluded that Kansas, which had abolished the death penalty in 1907, reinstituted it in 1935 "due to a sudden prevalence in the Midwest of rampaging professional criminals (Alvin 'Old Creepy' Karpis, Charles 'Pretty Boy' Floyd, Clyde Barrow and his homicidal sweetheart Bonnie Parker)."[21] After studying reintroduction of the death penalty in states which had once abolished— Washington, Tennessee, Kansas, South Dakota, Iowa, Colorado, Arizona, Oregon, Missouri, and Delaware— Bedau found fragile majorities for abolition overwhelmed by "one or two particularly violent and revolting crimes" and "hysterical demand for restoration of the death penalty."[22]

As Legal Defense Fund lawyers assembled the facts of state-imposed death, their resolve to challenge it in the courts stiffened. Political action to abolish the death penalty was not in fashion. Only a few maverick moralists (like Bedau, Jerome Nathanson of the Ethical Culture Society, and Sara R. Ehrmann of the American League to Abolish Capital Punishment), professional organizations (like the National Council on Crime and Delinquency), lawyers (like New York University Law Professor Norman Redlich and Delaware attorney Herbert L. Cobin), and a rare public official (like Senator Philip A. Hart (D., Mich.), Attorney General Ramsey Clark, or Ohio Governor Michael V. DiSalle) considered the continued existence of the death penalty in the 1960's an issue worthy of a public commitment. Abolitionist campaigns mounted by ad hoc citizens' groups, some of them barely able to afford a mimeograph machine, had forced legislative votes on abolition bills in many states, but success was infrequent. The election defeats of several governors (Robert Holmes of Oregon in 1958, Endicott Peabody of Massachusetts in 1964, and Edmund G. "Pat" Brown of California in 1966) were to some extent attributable to their stated reluctance to employ the death penalty.

Until 1965, the official position of even the American Civil Liberties Union was that capital punishment did not present "a civil liberties issue." In that year the Union's Board of Directors—after prodding from New York University law professor Norman Dorsen, University of Pennsylvania law professor Caleb Foote, and Gerald Gottlieb—for the first time authorized ACLU lawyers to enter cases where it was claimed that the death penalty had been imposed on the basis of race or class, "provided that a factual study has been made which seems to justify this conclusion."

Organized religion, on the other hand, notably Protestant denominations, demonstrated consistent interest in abolition, but their press releases were buried beneath the tons of newsprint used to report sensational homicides. An imminent execution, especially of an articulate and charismatic inmate such as Caryl Chessman, could capture public attention and stimulate a flurry of abolitionist activity, but the interested constituency had a short memory. Capital trials made good copy, especially when violence was mixed with sex and crossed class or racial lines, but once the death sentence was pronounced indifference set in. In a nation increasingly consumed in the 1960's by the politics of war and peace, group disorder, criminal violence, racism, and backlash, no politician stepped forward, as had Labor M.P. Sidney Silverman in England, to dramatize the issue.[23] There was no national organization, like Britain's National Council for the Abolition of the Death Penalty, that refused to let the public forget that some men and women would still be gassed or electrocuted and hundreds of others would live for years under the threat of momentary execution.

Another factor devastating to reformers trying to work up public interest in the issue was that even proponents of capital punishment rarely thrust it forward as an effective cure for social ills, confining themselves instead to but an occasional, reflexive rebuttal. The most J. Edgar Hoover could muster in the early 1960's was the cautious opinion that "when no shadow of a doubt remains relative to the guilt of a defendant, the public interest demands capital punishment be invoked where the law so provides"[24]—hardly the sort of statement calculated to incite the bloodthirsty.

Nor were governmental agencies charged with serious consideration of abolition able to make up their collective minds to abandon a sanction that was used so rarely that it could no longer be said to deter. The Presidential commission (The President's Commission on Law Enforcement and Administration of Justice) which in 1967 made recommendations concerning every aspect of the administration of criminal law was typically divided and uncertain—although the commission staff overwhelmingly favored abolition:

Some members of the Commission favor abolition of capital punishment, while others favor its retention. Some would support its abolition if more adequate safeguards against the release of dangerous offenders were devised.[25]

The psychological and ethical dimensions of state-imposed death are such that most study groups split among hawks and doves. Policy choices are made "between competing values on the basis of imperfect data"—as a New York State commission[26] put it in 1965—and reflect moral training and personality as much as rational analysis. A New York commission majority of nine, which included Professor Wechsler, recommended abolition, after deciding that death exerted no greater deterrent effect on murderers than life imprisonment. Capital punishment, the majority found, adversely affected the court system, sensationalized the administration of justice, and inevitably led to erroneous convictions and arbitrary selection of victims.

But a minority of four commissioners refused to recommend abolition because they were not satisfied that the death penalty was totally undesirable: no one had proved that it did not deter homicide. Other rejoinders to the commission majority included arguments that there was no such thing as a life sentence (because of the availability of parole); that given the few executions carried out, innocent lives were not in danger of extinction; and finally an ominous expression that the "nature and complex makeup of our population, the ugly moods and attitudes which now appear to prevail among varying ethnic and social groups in this State, the boldness with which atrocious crimes are committed, with less and less effort at concealment, the frequently appalling lack of regard for the rights and sensitivities of others, make it entirely possible that movement toward abolition of capital punishment in the State at this time may be taken by the lawless masses as a signal for even further threats of lawlessness."

The arguments for—and against—the death penalty are numerous; one observer has counted 65 pro and 87 contra. So many considerations are advanced on both sides of the question that one suspects few people undertake the demanding task of sifting the evidence before taking a position. Library shelves heave from the weight of volumes devoted to the history, morality, and utility of capital punishment. Although the arguments can be evaluated and then balanced in an effort at rational decision making, support, opposition, or indifference seems to come as much from the gut as the head.

Opponents stress that execution makes it impossible to rehabilitate the offender (but how often does a long prison sentence?); or to provide restitution to the victim or his family (neither do most criminal penalties). They point out that there is no evidence that the death penalty is a greater deterrent than life imprisonment. But we know little about deterrence. There is, for example, little hard evidence that harsher criminal penalties deter crime more than light punishment. It is said that crime rates are no higher in states without the death penalty, and that homicide rates are, in fact, somewhat lower. But such comparisons only take into account those who have committed homicides; not those who have been deterred. Does an absence of proof either way—that the death penalty deters murder more effectively than a prison sentence, or that it does not—imply that society should retain or abolish capital punishment?

Some researchers have found that policemen and prison guards in abolition states are no more likely to be murdered than are policemen and prison guards in death penalty states, but of all groups in our society, with the possible exception of judges responsible for having sent men to death, law enforcement officers most vocally favor the death penalty. Many cite personal experiences of robbers who carried toy guns or kidnapers who spared their victims to avoid the "hot seat" or San Quentin's "green room."

It is claimed that the high suicide rate, almost double that of murder, suggests that a number of persons court death, and that some do so by committing capital crimes. But the evidence here is inconclusive—as evidence almost always is when a question arouses passionate division.

Abolitionists contend that a substantial portion of all murders are committed under the influence of emotions— fear, anger, jealousy, love, depraved sexuality—which overcome any rational balance of penalty with risk. While roughly one-third of all murders take place in domestic and other situations where passions are high, a significant proportion do not.

Retentionists have argued that there are vicious brutes who must be "put out of the way" not for the sake of punishing them or to make an example of them for others, but to ensure that they never again have the opportunity to kill. Murderers, however, have an extremely low rate of recidivism; many become "model prisoners" and excellent prospects for rehabilitation. Additionally, it has never been established that murderers are any more likely to kill if released from prison than other criminals. If society must eliminate potential killers by killing them first, it will have to put to death most men convicted of felonies.

Capital punishment is also thought to represent the brutality and irrationality of our society (but then so does violent crime); to squander the time of courts, lawyers, and jurors (but this is a general characteristic of our judicial system); and cost the government millions simply to kill a man (but if it reduced crime rates many would gladly pay the price).

There are additional arguments from the abolitionists and appropriate rejoinders from retentionists; rebuttal and surrebuttal—ethical, legal, polemical, theological, speculative, statistical. Fund lawyers considered them all, surveying the vast literature of capital punishment to search out the most compelling. But they were only secondarily concerned with the undesirability of the death penalty—of that they had no doubts. They contemplated not whether to abolish, but how.

4

The Strategy Unfolds

When the current was turned off my father's rigid body suddenly slumped in the chair, and it perhaps occurred to the witnesses that what they had taken for the shuddering spasming movements of his life for God knows how many seconds was instead a portrait of electric current, normally invisible, moving through a field of resistance.

—E. L. DOCTOROW, *The Book of Daniel*

The initial plotters of the Fund's strategy—Heffron, Clark, and myself—concluded immediately that neither politicians nor judges would welcome LDF's challenge to capital punishment, for the most prominent characteristic of the legal apparatus that did the condemning was general refusal to confront what it was doing. Legislators did not feel responsible for the death penalty because the law rarely required it; selection of the condemned was left to juries and judges. Prosecuting attorneys told themselves that they only presented the state's case in the courts. Jurors often believed that trial judges would correct matters if they acted improperly. The trial judge, on the other hand, felt that the life-death decision was in the hands of the jury. If he did make an error in handling the case, surely the appellate courts would set it right. Courts of review conventionally complained that they had limited power and capacity to upset the verdict of a jury or the rulings of a judge who had observed the trial testimony. At any rate, executive clemency was available. But governors pointed to the jury verdict, the trial judge who could have set it aside, and the appellate courts that had declined to interfere; jurors and judges had agreed on a death sentence, and the power to commute was narrow. The warden, of course, was only doing his job. When the time came to pull the switch there might be several switches so that the executioner was unknown even to himself.

Here then was a process of exquisite irresponsibility, one which escaped debate and eluded scrutiny.

Concealment of the execution from public view reinforced this lack of accountability. Although men were supposedly killed as an example to others, public executions had almost vanished from the American scene in the nineteenth century. The carnival-like atmosphere of drunks, beggars, prostitutes, fights, "brutal jokes, tumultuous demonstrations of indecent delight when swooning women were dragged out of the crowd by the police with their dresses disordered,"[1] gave way to the silence of the prison-yard scaffold and then to the electric chair and gas chamber.

Most American states had eliminated public execution in response to abolitionist claims that they corrupted public morals and cheapened life. But there was something as disturbing as gallows ribaldry and mirth in the "gruesome" prospect of a "more lonely, mechanical and dehumanized"[2] modern death. In 1928 a New York *Daily News* photographer smuggled a miniature camera into the Sing Sing death house and recorded for all the world the moment of murderess Ruth Snyder's death. The *News* published a blown-up photograph of the dying woman, strapped to the fearsome electric chair, straining as the current coursed through her body. A storm of criticism from civic leaders led to new restrictions on the witnesses permitted to attend executions.

"The man," wrote Albert Camus, "who enjoys his coffee while reading that justice has been done would spit it out at the least detail."[3] If twentieth-century executions were carried out as public spectacles, the "details" might have demanded the public's attention and perhaps stimulated political pressure for abolition. A favorite story of abolitionists makes the point by telling of a 1906 hanging witnessed by a St. Paul, Minnesota, newspaperman. Because the rope was too long, death was prolonged by a fourteen-and-a-half-minute agony of strangulation. Reported graphically, under the headline "Displayed His Nerve to the Very Last," the execution resulted in a controversy which led Minnesota to abolish capital punishment in 1911.[4]

But the public does not want to know that in the silent mingling of sulphuric acid and cyanide observers see "extreme evidence of horror, pain, and strangling. The eyes pop, they turn purple, they drool. It is a horrible sight."[5] During the hundred and fifteen occasions Warden Lewis E. Lawes had applied two minutes of high-voltage electric current—generating enough heat to melt copper—he had often smelled a "faint odor of burning flesh. The hands turn red, then white, and the cords of the neck stand out like steel bands."[6]

No greater interest is shown in the life of the condemned man awaiting execution. When Tom Murton took over as superintendent of Arkansas' Tucker Prison Farm in 1967, he found death-row inmates had "no reading material. No radio. A single television. No recreation. No exercise." The prison kitchen did not serve death row; inmates were dependent upon supplies brought in from the outside by visitors which they cooked on hot plates. Luther Baily, a black who had survived fourteen years confined to a death-row cell, died of peritonitis as a result of neglect by the prison doctor.[7]

Perhaps death is too terrifying for contemporary Americans to deal with in a systematic and open way. Men once died in their own beds surrounded by relatives and friends. If dying was no less terrible than it is now, family members at least encountered it directly and came to think of death as a "normal" part of the life process. Today, the hospital or the institution has replaced the home; doctors and nurses who have no personal relationship to the patient are the likely witnesses to his demise. Drugs prolong life but often destroy the faculties that distinguished the individual's life. Modern medicine saves many lives, but it does so at the price of making the actual experience of death remote and unfamiliar.

As a consequence, the idea of death is even more fearsome than it was. Dying is taboo, its likelihood to be kept from the patient and discusssed only in euphemisms. At the same time that dying is removed from sight, civilian as well as soldier "has to anticipate weapons of mass destruction which offer no one a reasonable chance . . . science and technology have contributed to an ever-increasing fear of destruction and therefore fear of death."[8] Whatever the cause, psychologist Herman Feifel's observation that "The individual face of death has become blurred by embarrassed incuriosity and institutionalization"[9] applies with particular force to capital punishment.

One consequence of the general public's lack of interest in the facts of legal death is that those few people who have made a commitment to abolition a part of their professional lives perceive themselves as a small embattled band with a special gift of moral superiority. After all, they live with unpleasant realities which others ignore, and he who has set himself up against death, is he not among the righteous? Such attitudes are not always conducive to winning friends or influencing people. Abolitionists could tap considerable support when they organized, as in Oregon in 1964, a broad-based coalition of civic, social, and religious groups. But too many have lacked the political savvy to reach the grass roots. Accordingly, LDF lawyers concluded that if the death penalty were to wither away it would be necessary to set in motion forces other than those generated by organized abolitionists.

The New York experience was instructive. The small membership of the New York Committee to Abolish Capital Punishment had for many years rendered great humane service representing death-row inmates in court and at clemency hearings before the governor. Clever lobbying in Albany by Committee lawyers and clergymen attracted several influential legislators to abolition. The stage was set, but prospects were remote for a bill to clear committee, much less the full legislature. Although a blue-ribbon commission, chaired by Richard J. Bartlett, had recommended that the death penalty be purged from the penal code, public opinion showed not the slightest interest in eliminating electrocution from the state's arsenal of criminal sanctions. The New York Committee's occasional meetings at the Ethical Culture Society building on Central Park West were sparsely attended, and its treasury was nearly empty.

In 1965 abolition came suddenly to New York in the wake of a sensational murder case. On August 23, 1963, Janice Wylie and Emily Hoffert, two young white girls who lived in an expensive East Side apartment building, were brutally stabbed and murdered. The Noxema-smeared body of one was found unclothed, and showed signs of sexual assault. The police announced that George Whitmore, Jr., a nineteen-year-old unemployed Negro, had confessed to the murders; the press and the public eagerly accepted the story. When the "confession" was ultimately exposed as the product of police suggestion and the apparently boundless capacity of Whitmore's interrogators to deceive themselves as to what he knew of the crime, many were shocked—after all, Whitmore had been convicted in their minds. Another man, Richard Robles, was eventually convicted of the murders.

Coming as it did in the midst of civil rights agitation, the Whitmore case was more than an egregious example of what can happen when police and prosecution fail to abide by the constitutional rights of suspects. The collapse of Whitmore's "confession" exposed the deadly dangers of an entrenched public fantasy—white innocence besmirched by black violence—and confirmed what blacks had always said lurked behind the face of white justice. It was not accidental that the urban riots of the 1960's were most commonly ignited by a police shooting of a black man, a form of instant capital punishment which the white community tolerated, even if it had not approved, by not doing anything about it.

New York Committee lobbyists and lawyers had been resourceful in rounding up support of key state legislators and keeping abolition afloat as an issue during the dry years. But it took the fresh memory of the potentially fatal mistake in the Whitmore case to induce the New York legislature to restrict the death penalty to murder of a police officer in the line of duty or of anyone by a prisoner under life sentence.

Despite Whitmore's phony "confession" the margin of victory was slim. When the abolition bill was presented to Governor Nelson Rockefeller, it was rumored that he would veto it. At least one close associate of the Governor argued that signing the bill would damage his future chances for a Republican Presidential nomination. But several influential lawyers let Rockefeller know through an intermediary that no New York governor had ever permitted so many executions as would take place if the bill were vetoed. Aside from the merits of the abolition bill, they inquired, did Rockefeller wish to go down in history as the governor of New York who had sent the most men to the electric chair? Shortly thereafter, Rockefeller signed the bill into law.

The abolitionist victory in New York showed that even a poorly financed campaign by a small group could succeed if the times were auspicious. But no one can plan a Whitmore case. The only way to duplicate on the national level the "spectacular extraneous events" Professor Bickel had predicted necessary for judicial abolition was to reduce the number of executions to the point where the condemned man seemed the loser in a ghoulish national lottery. If capital punishment became increasingly rare, it would be demonstrated that society did not actually use it for self-protection; claims that it was necessary would ring hollow.

Observers of the Warren Court would have been surprised by a decision in the mid-1960's that the death penalty was unconstitutional; the Supreme Court had not taken even its first step toward abolition. By analogy, in 1938, sixteen years before *Brown v. Board of Education* doomed the "separate but equal" doctrine, the Court had chipped away at the legal foundation of racial segregation when it ordered Missouri either to place a black graduate student in an all-white university, or to set up a black school for him.[10]

A challenge to legal procedures employed in capital cases was less controversial than an attack on the death penalty as cruel and unusual punishment, offering the Court claims that were reasonable extensions of recent decisions adopting rules favorable to criminal defendants. Litigation over procedural rights would force the states to extended judicial proceedings in order to make a death sentence stick. If the condemned men won some of these cases, state legislatures might have to pass new laws changing criminal procedures in order to retain the death penalty. In this case, it would be easier for abolition-minded legislators to block passage of such new legislation than it had been for them to pass laws for abolition. No one convicted under rejected procedures could be executed without retrial or resentencing—unless decisions requiring changes in procedure were expressly declared nonretroactive—and this would mean years during which the United States would manage to survive without legal killing. If procedural challenges halted executions, the resulting moratorium might make it politically unprofitable for state governors to support a resumption. The electorate was not "for" abolition, but it was not "for" mass killings either.

Measured by what they did, the American people seemed to be unable to use the death penalty in a systematic manner *or* to disavow it completely. Both executive and legislative branches were prisoners of the contradiction, one which apparently reflected fear of either course. As a result, frequent executions were a thing of the past, but a small group of arbitrarily selected men were still in jeopardy.

By the 1960's this pattern was no more ripe for assault in most state legislative chambers than it had been in previous years. But the federal courts, under the prod of the Warren Court, were attempting to square the fact that the Constitution says so much about criminal law with the miserable condition of the criminal justice system. Influential judges felt that inquiry into the sources of crime was unlikely so long as a punitive criminal law held out the illusion that social problems might be solved by punishment. They believed that it was exceedingly difficult to fashion a humane criminal law so long as capital punishment mocked the ideal of rehabilitation. Some judges would welcome an opportunity to restrict the death penalty. LDF's task was to present them with sensible legal arguments in favorable settings. One route was to attempt to prove racial discrimination in the selection of the condemned. In addition, there were three capital case procedures that presented obvious occasions for judicial intervention.

First. Although the American jury supposedly reflected a microcosm of the community at large, persons who had scruples against the imposition of capital punishment were, by the rule that Professor Oberer had criticized, conventionally excluded from the trial jury in capital cases. The idea behind the exclusion was that such jurors could not reasonably consider a penalty authorized by law, and were partial to the defense to an extent which might even make it impossible for them to vote for a conviction warranted by the evidence. But the result of exclusion was a dearth of jurors opposed to the death penalty. The definition of justice in a capital case was turned over to an unrepresentative subgroup of the community comprising those who were more likely to impose a death sentence and those who many thought were more likely to convict.

Second. In most criminal cases, the trial judge imposed sentence after a guilty verdict. In capital cases, this task fell to the jury and, except in a handful of states, the jury decided guilt and sentence simultaneously, fixing the punishment of the guilty as death or a prison term. Since there was no separate hearing on the question of sentence, there was no opportunity—other than at the guilt trial—to present to the jury evidence of the defendant's character, background, attitude, and health—although this information obviously might affect the jury's life-death decision. In most states the rules governing the admissibility of evidence at the single-verdict capital trial limited such evidence to that relevant to guilt; if the jury heard any evidence relevant to penalty that was fortuitous. Of course the defendant could choose to waive his Fifth Amendment right not to testify and take the witness stand in order to bring this information before the jury or to plead for mercy, but once on the stand he might convict himself out of his own mouth. The prosecution was free to bring up prior criminal convictions and, if the defendant put his character at issue, past misconduct. Much evidence that might persuade a jury to leniency at sentencing—like drug use or mental instability—could be devastating to the defendant's hopes for a not guilty verdict.

The American Law Institute had characterized this "single-verdict" procedure as one which forced the capital case defendant to a "choice between a method which threatens the fairness of the trial of guilt or innocence, and one which detracts from the rationality of the determination of the sentence."[11] The Fifth Amendment right not to testify clashed head on with the defendant's interest in having the jury learn evidence that would help him at sentencing but not hurt him before conviction. As a result of single-verdict procedure, capital sentencing was frequently done by a jury that knew next to nothing about the defendant, and did not even hear him speak in favor of his life. Unable to make personal contact with the jury, because to do so would give the prosecution an opportunity to bring out unfavorable evidence, he was all the more readily cast out and doomed.

Third. The jury which was selected by a culling out of anyone who indicated opposition to the death penalty and which was deprived of factual information essential to a reasoned sentencing decision by the single verdict was also forced to decide whether or not to condemn without the benefit of any legal standards. A juror deciding whether to impose money damages on an allegedly negligent truck driver is given an extensive briefing by the trial judge. When considering the issue of *guilt* in a criminal case, the jury receives instruction in the governing legal principles—such as the elements of the crime and the standard of proof—and how to apply them. But when the jury is given the responsibility for *sentencing*—as is usual in capital trials—it is informed of its obligation to impose sentence and nothing more.

This momentous human decision was made pursuant to no rules of law or generalized doctrines or principles. Each juror exercised an absolute discretion which was unguided and unfettered, according to whatever whims or urges might move him. Each juror was left to his "prejudices and his subconscious for the keys to decision."[12]

A consequence of this lack of standards was that the defendant and his lawyer had absolutely no guidance as to what the law-abiding juror would deem worthy of capital punishment. Would it help or harm a defendant's chance to live that he had a record of mental illness or a deprived boyhood; that he was drunk or did not testify in his own behalf; or that his lawyer subjected prosecution witnesses to vigorous cross-examination? The defense was in the dark. Every lawyer knows that jurors do not always follow instructions, but they do not always ignore them either. When a jury is told that it may sentence to death but is not told what principles it should follow in deciding *whether* to sentence to death, a defense attorney has about as much capacity to help the defendant as his minister does.

Another set of legal rules—though not peculiar to death cases—magnified the unfairness of these jury selection and sentencing procedures. Defendants have a right to appeal their *conviction* to higher courts, but appellate judges generally are not authorized to review the *sentence* imposed by trial courts, a practice all the more prejudicial in a death case because so much more is at stake. Even those few courts empowered to review death sentences were hindered because there was little to review in a decision which did not respond to any legally required standards; appellate judges rightfully felt they were being asked to review the merits of a judgment based on intangibles. And while a death sentence was subject to correction by the exercise of executive clemency, governors administered this power in haphazard fashion. Scholarly evaluations of the gubernatorial commutation power turned up crazy-quilt patterns, with similar cases treated differently for no discernible reason.

There was, therefore, good cause to believe that those who were selected to die seemed chosen by a roll of the dice. "Experienced wardens," Attorney General Ramsey Clark told a United States Senate subcommittee, "know many prisoners serving life or less whose crimes were equally, or more, atrocious than those of men on death row."[13] Clark's opinion was difficult to refute in a nation which held infrequent executions but each year imprisoned 200,000 men. The few men who were selected to die had impressed many a warden, prison chaplain, and penologist as poor, uneducated, friendless, and disproportionately black. Former San Quentin warden Clinton T. Duffy stated flatly that he had never known a person of means to be executed.

But to identify legal procedures that leave too much room for arbitrariness, or even vindictiveness, is not to prove new rules will work any better. Even if jurors were instructed to employ certain principles for selecting the condemned, they could not be forced to obey. For example a jury which learned more about certain defendants or was told to consider a specific set of factors before sentencing (such as criminal record, capacity to be rehabilitated, violence of the crime) often would be more, not less, likely to sentence to death. Reasonable men differed about the wisdom, and the constitutionality, of requiring legal standards, split verdicts, and other supposedly protective procedures. Additionally, it was debatable whether workable standards could be drafted.

The abolitionist lawyers discounted such doubts—not because they were unreal but because the procedural reforms they would press on the courts were not sought for their own sake. The criminal law might be better off with them, but it might not. If the reforms were accepted, however, several hundred lives might be saved. Procedural disputes also bought time—time to dramatize the plight of death-row inmates, to expose society's ambivalence toward capital punishment, to develop the law, and most important, to demonstrate that the death penalty was so rarely used that it could not possibly protect the public.

In short, the lawyers' primary obligation was to their clients. They represented individuals who each claimed that capital case procedures were unfair. Each defendant was willing to take his chances with different procedures (What could he lose, being already under sentence of death?). It was the lawyer's responsibility to keep him alive by raising every legal argument available, whether in the long run the new procedures improved the quality of criminal justice or worked like sand poured in a machine.

But a challenge to current procedural rules was not ingenuous, or a typical lawyers' resort to technicality. The fact was that juries did sentence by whim and caprice, without much information, and often without reflecting the entire community's sensibilities. Men were condemned who should have been given the chance to live; while others escaped who would have appeared most worthy of death, if anyone was. And "No matter how we amend or restate the legal test of criminal responsibility," as Edmund Cahn had concluded, "we shall never feel sure that we are not sending mentally defective, diseased or irresponsible persons to the electric chair."[14] If new procedures failed to evoke confidence that the men selected to die were receiving their due, the lesson was that a change in procedure was not enough: just administration of the death penalty was impossible.

By 1963 capital punishment in the United States was in good measure arbitrarily applied, infrequently employed, and of questionable utility. But so it had been for some time. Eventually the death penalty would be discarded, but this was unlikely, despite Justice Goldberg's dramatic attempt to put the Supreme Court on the road to abolition, until after it had taken a further toll from the inmates of death row. It seemed certain that many would die before the legislative process ground out abolition or the executive branch freely granted clemency. All this changed because the small group of Fund lawyers made common cause with the most versatile and talented lawyer of their generation.

5

The Race Factor

In the mid 1960's the Legal Defense Fund was ill-prepared to mount a systematic challenge to the procedures employed by the states to impose the death penalty. Its New York staff was still small, spread dangerously thin, and plagued by almost daily civil rights movement crises that required immediate action. What little lawyers' time was available for capital punishment was spent devising, but not implementing, a national abolition strategy or exploring means to prove that capital sentencing for rape was racially discriminatory. For a civil rights organization like the Fund, elimination of racial discrimination was the first priority. The problem that confronted the lawyers here was not changing the law, but assembling the facts so that existing law could be applied and enforced.

One of the purposes behind the Fourteenth Amendment guarantee, adopted in 1868, that the states not "deprive any person of life, liberty, or property, without due process of law," nor deny "the equal protection of the laws" was to ensure that all Americans would be subject to like criminal punishment regardless of race or color. While historians have long debated what Reconstruction Congresses thought about matters such as school segregation, the history of the Fourteenth Amendment shows with relative clarity a desire to eliminate the then-pervasive practice of subjecting blacks to uniquely harsh criminal penalties. Jacob M. Howard of Michigan, an influential Senate member of the Joint Committee on Reconstruction, put it bluntly: the Amendment "prohibits the hanging of a black man for a crime for which the white man is not to be hanged."[1]

Soon after the Civil War, states began to remove from the statute books criminal laws that punished blacks more harshly than whites, in token compliance with the federal will. Whites, however, abandoned little of their power to impose the punishment which they thought fit the race of the offender.[2]

The criminal law is honeycombed with important choice points: whether to arrest; whether to charge and, if so, with what offense; how much bail should be set; how much evidence should be disclosed to the defense prior to trial; whether to plea bargain and what sentence to offer a defendant in return for a guilty plea. To the offender, the most critical decisions pertain to sentence: will he be fined? placed on probation? sentenced to jail? If so, for how long? Or will he be condemned to death? Modern practice favors individualized treatment at each of these choice points. The law gives police, prosecuting attorneys, judges, and jurors great leeway to decide each defendant's fate on a case-by-case basis. In place of a dual set of laws, they exercise sufficient discretion to apply the same old double standard to blacks.

Much of the growth of this power in officialdom to decide important aspects of each case on its individual facts has taken place in the twentieth century, but replacement of explicit racial distinctions with broad ill-defined discretion was a striking characteristic of Reconstruction legislation. Blacks could vote and serve on juries only if minor public officials such as voting registrars and jury commissioners found them "upright," "intelligent," or of "good moral character." Blacks spent one or ten years in prison, lived or died, depending on whether judges or jurors found them worthy or unworthy. The enforcement of the Negroes' federal constitutional and statutory guarantees of legal equality hinged, therefore, on proof that a particular law or practice, though apparently neutral, was in fact discriminatorily applied.

Frank Heffron had concluded that historical evidence, available data on the results of Southern sentencing in rape cases, and such scanty research as had been done on the subject of discriminatory imposition of penalties for other criminal offenses, strongly suggested that race was associated with long prison sentences generally and capital sentencing in particular. The total number of persons executed between 1930 and 1967 broke down by offense and race in striking fashion:[3]

Executions in the United States by Race and Offense, 1930–1967

	MURDER	RAPE	OTHER	TOTAL
White:	1,664 (49.9%)	48 (10.6%)	39 (55.7%)	1,751 (45.4%)
Negro:	1,630 (48.9%)	405 (89.0%)	31 (44.3%)	2,066 (53.5%)
Other:	40 (1.2%)	2 (0.4%)	0 (0.0%)	42 (1.1%)
Total:	3,334 (100%)	455 (100%)	70 (100%)	3,859 (100%)

Although the evidence of discrimination was strongest in rape cases, research also raised suspicions of racial sentencing in murder cases from Northern states. A study of New Jersey records published in 1964 by Edwin L. Wolf was typical. From 1937 to 1961, sixty-six men were sentenced to death in New Jersey: thirty-eight were black (and three Puerto Rican), although blacks made up only about 8 percent of the state's residents. The probability that a white charged with a capital murder would receive a death sentence was three in ten; the probability for a black was close to five out of ten.[4]

Heffron thought that LDF could use such scholarly research as well as more impressionistic data to build a legal argument that capital punishment, at least for rape, violated the Equal Protection Clause of the Fourteenth Amend-

ment. Suits claiming racial discrimination might keep men
alive until more precise statistics were gathered, but it was
extremely unlikely, he concluded, that figures showing that
blacks received a high proportion of all death sentences
would persuade a court to eliminate the death penalty or
even to modify the procedures used to reach the life-death
decision.

What seemed self-evident to the civil rights lawyer had to
be established by scientific method and demonstrated in a
courtroom. There was no lack of evidence that the American Negro male was insulted and abused, arrested, as-
saulted by the police, detained on higher bail, excluded
from juries, convicted, sentenced more heavily, condemned
to die, and executed all out of proportion to his numbers.
Accounting for the verifiable proposition that the criminal
law treated blacks more harshly than it did whites presented
a different question. One man will write, as had Thorsten
Sellin, that the traditional poverty and discrimination of its
environment predictably makes the black race less "law-
abiding than the white, which enjoys more fully the advantages of a civilization the Negro has helped to create."[5]
Another will find the thread of racial animosity tightly
woven into all institutions and perceive a society which
consistently defines the black man as a criminal in order to
dehumanize him. A third will say that this is the way *those
people* are.

If Fund lawyers wished to have the courts find that capital sentencing in rape cases violated constitutional guarantees of equal treatment, they would be put to a grueling,
expensive, and tedious enterprise, with a high risk of
failure. A complicated factual inquiry would be required to
prove discrimination, although capital punishment of
rapists plainly reflected the exaggerated fear of sexual contact between black men and white women in a segregated
society. It could not be accidental that rape was a capital
offense only in Southern and border states, and the District

of Columbia with its Southern tradition, plus Nevada (which had not executed anyone for rape in over forty years).

A 1965 United Nations study of sixty nations underscored the point. In authorizing execution of rapists the Southern states were joined by only three jurisdictions: Taiwan, South Africa, and Malawi.[6] Available data suggested that only the Southern states and South Africa actually used the death penalty for rape; that in the overwhelming majority of the 455 American cases since 1930 where a rape conviction led to actual execution the victim was white, the rapist black.

Elaborate empirical research would be necessary even in states like Florida, one of the few where reasonably complete statistics had been gathered. According to a report leaked to the Fund from a confidential source, of 6 white men sentenced to death for rape since 1940, 5 had received clemency or had their convictions reversed by the courts. In contrast, of the 48 Negro rapists sentenced to death since 1940, 29 had died in the electric chair. Of those remaining, 12 were awaiting execution at the Florida State Prison in Raiford. The convictions of only 4 of the 48 blacks were reversed by the courts; only 2 of the 48 persuaded the Pardon Board to commute their death sentences; the forty-eighth was killed in custody by a white sheriff under mysterious circumstances. During this period, 132 white men and 153 Negroes had been convicted of rape. But while 45 of the 48 Negroes were sentenced to death for rape of white women, no white man had been sentenced to death for the rape of a black woman.

Striking as this evidence was, no court, said Heffron, would find it sufficient. In order to persuade tough-minded federal judges that sentencing decisions were the product of racial discrimination, one would have to learn not only the sentencing disposition made in a statistically significant number of rape cases, the race of each defendant and the race of his victim, but the background of each defendant and, most critically, the nature of judicial proceedings in each case which might have affected sentencing.

The research necessary to determine whether, and to what extent, race affected capital sentencing for rape was made possible by the willingness of two men to join the small group of lawyers working against the death penalty. Marvin Wolfgang, Chairman of the Department of Sociology at the University of Pennsylvania, was widely regarded as the leading criminologist in the United States. Wolfgang had conducted an extensive investigation into patterns of criminal homicide; he was president of the Pennsylvania Prison Society, an expert on capital punishment, and a prolific scholar. Wolfgang regarded the death penalty as a senseless and brutalizing sanction and he readily agreed to help the Fund after his colleague Anthony Amsterdam insisted that the study was impossible without him. Amsterdam himself was the other essential ingredient.

The Fund had an enormous interest in keeping the Southern black lawyer who was the source of its cases, and ultimately its power, well informed on dizzying developments in civil rights law, a legal specialty with its own technicalities, as complex as tax or copyright law. One means of doing this was periodic Civil Rights Institutes, held at Howard Law School in Washington. The front-line troops, most of them Howard graduates, were invited from the battle zone to hear three days of lectures and, not incidentally, to bivouac in the District's watering places. By 1963 these conferences had acquired prestige as the birthplace of many a civil rights strategy, but the assorted pleasures of liberty were a constant distraction, and so they were moved first to New Orleans, then to Atlanta, and finally to Airlie House, a pleasant and relatively isolated conference center in the Virginia hunt country.

It was at the 1963 New Orleans conference held at Dillard University that many Fund lawyers first became acquainted with Anthony G. Amsterdam. Several months earlier, Heffron had set up a meeting in New York to discuss strategy for the impending retrial of Charles Clarence Hamilton, an Alabama black. Hamilton's conviction and death sentence for breaking and entering a dwelling at night with intent to ravish had been overturned by the United States Supreme Court because he had been denied a lawyer at his arraignment.[7] One proposal under consideration was to argue that Hamilton could not be subjected to the death penalty if reconvicted because he had not actually harmed the victim of the crime. Amsterdam attended the New York meeting in place of Professor Caleb Foote, who was unable to come at the last minute, and he agreed to help Heffron with the case. Jack Greenberg was so impressed with what he saw of Amsterdam's work that he invited him to speak at the Dillard conference.

After Amsterdam had finished his lecture to LDF cooperating attorneys on the techniques of defending civil rights demonstrators, the lobby hummed with talk of him. Those who ventured to solicit the advice of the tall, athletic-looking young law professor soon found that they were not only dealing with a scholar but with an intensely practical man who talked of law, courts, police stations, and prisons as if he were a veteran of twenty years practice in a magistrate's court. The other lawyers at the meeting did not so much converse with Amsterdam as ask questions and listen to a dazzling display of erudition, memory, lawyer's cunning, and complicated sentence structure, all mixed with liberal amounts of humor, legal citations, and cigar smoke.

Amsterdam was born in 1935 in Philadelphia, the son of a prominent businessman and lawyer; A.B. summa cum laude, Haverford College in 1957; LL.B. summa cum laude, University of Pennsylvania, 1960; and editor-in-chief of the Pennsylvania Law Review. Apparently no one had ever passed through these schools with higher grades. In 1960 Amsterdam became the first non-Harvard Law

School graduate selected by Justice Felix Frankfurter as his law clerk, after—rumor had it—Jefferson Fordham, the Pennsylvania Law School dean, had told Frankfurter he feared that Amsterdam would leave the law to pursue another of his interests—art history—if the Justice did not choose him. In 1961 Amsterdam prosecuted cases for the government as an Assistant United States Attorney in the District of Columbia, and in 1962 he returned to the University of Pennsylvania Law School to teach.

At the time of the Dillard University meeting, Amsterdam's best-known contribution to the law was a long and complex article, "The Void for Vagueness Doctrine in the Supreme Court,"[8] written when a student at the University of Pennsylvania. Based on the character and frequency of its citation in Supreme Court opinions, Amsterdam's stunning analysis seemed to have influenced the Court to extend its use of the device of declaring state statutes unconstitutionally vague and over-broad as a means of protecting freedom of speech and assembly from harassment by state officials.

The stories told about Amsterdam were the raw material for future myths. While he was a government prosecutor in the District of Columbia, he had argued a criminal case before a three-judge panel of the United States Court of Appeals, and to illustrate a point of law which had arisen during the argument, called the court's attention to an old Supreme Court case, citing volume and page. A skeptical judge called for the book, whether to check on the young lawyer or to peruse the opinion is not known, and did not find the case on the page mentioned. Before Amsterdam finished his argument, the judge inquired as to the whereabouts of the case, implying that one does not mention cases by the page quite so freely, and perhaps that the lawyer's argument was not now so compelling. Amsterdam coolly replied that the volume must have been misbound. The astonished jurist examined the law book and found that this was so. The book, Amsterdam later told me when I asked him about this story, had been incorrectly engraved 211 U.S. on the spine by the binder; inside it was 210 U.S. The judge sent back for the real 211 U.S. and found the cited case on the cited page.

Another Amsterdam story involved an appeal before the same court in which the legal issue was whether District of Columbia police had hesitated long enough to permit the occupants of an apartment to open the door before barging in, a period of some twenty-five seconds. Representing the government, Amsterdam began his argument with the traditional "May it please the Court . . ." and then stood in respectful silence almost as if it were someone else's place to speak. The few seconds seemed an eternity. The judges quickly became fidgety and were about to intervene when Amsterdam finally spoke up: "That was the length of time that the police waited before they broke into the defendant's apartment." The police were upheld.

At the New Orleans meeting, Howard Moore, Jr., a young Atlanta lawyer and a militant mainstay of the Georgia civil rights bar, brought up a vexing legal issue. Amsterdam's reaction to Moore's problem was to determine for several years to come the strategy employed by civil rights lawyers in representing black demonstrators. The story is best told in the words of Melvyn Zarr, a Fund lawyer who soon became closely associated with Amsterdam in the defense of thousands of Southern black protestors.

"Moore had taken state criminal cases involving arrests of blacks for sitting-in at segregated lunch counters and removed them to federal court by resurrecting an old, moribund civil rights statute enacted by Congress in 1866. If applicable, the law would have given each defendant the right to have his trial in federal, rather than state, court—a result which would blunt the capacity of state prosecutors to interfere with the sit-ins. But an Atlanta federal district judge had laughed Moore out of court and promptly remanded the cases to the state courts.

"Undaunted, Moore asked the Fifth Circuit Court of

Appeals for a stay of the remand order pending appeal so that the applicability of the 1866 law could be authoritatively determined before his clients were tried in state court, and Elbert Parr Tuttle, a great liberal judge and at the time the chief judge of the court, granted the stay. Georgia indignantly sought a writ of prohibition from the United States Supreme Court and there the matter stood.

"Amsterdam was intrigued by the case—offering as it did a glimmer of hope, a better means of defending civil rights workers than appealing every case through the state courts to the Supreme Court of the United States. He agreed, under Fund auspices, to prepare a response to Georgia's petition. Amsterdam asked Jack Greenberg for help, and I was deputized.

"That involved spending the next three weeks in Philadelphia with Amsterdam. We would arrive at his office before nine and work at a feverish pace until after midnight. Initially, I thought that I could keep up with him. But after a few days, he did not stop. I did. For the remainder of my stay, I kept civilized hours and vowed never again to try to keep up with his pace. We turned out a sparkling one hundred-page document, and the Supreme Court denied Georgia's petition.

"At the next Fund lawyers' conference held in Atlanta in May, 1964, a call from Mississippi came shortly before we were to return North. A large number of civil rights workers—the advance guard of the fateful Mississippi summer of 1964—had been arrested. This was our chance to build a successful removal case from the ground up, so we flew immediately to Jackson, Mississippi. That night we worked in the old COFO (Council of Federated Organizations) office, ominously located on Lynch Street, turning out removal petitions and all the legal paraphernalia that went with them.

"At this time we were fighting a paper war and were grossly unprepared. We had no secretaries and only a beat-up typewriter and mimeograph machine to work with. But

Amsterdam rose to the occasion. Working semi-naked in the steaming one hundred-degree-plus heat, he typed the stencils, fixed the mimeograph machine, and ground out the papers. By 4 A.M., I decided to apply my hard learned lesson and sought an hour's rest. I took our rented car and drove around Jackson until I found a motel and spent the next hour in the pool. When I returned to the office, he had finished the job. We set off for Biloxi to find a federal judge, but we did not get ten yards before the Jackson police staking out the civil rights organization office stopped the car and questioned Tony about a fictitious traffic violation. He responded in true military manner: 'Yes, sir! No, sir! No excuse, sir!' Finally set free, we continued on our way."

Zarr's description captures Amsterdam's drive and versatility, as well as his skill, but the law is a rewarded profession in our society and attracts more than its share of gifted men and women. The adjective brilliant and the noun lawyer have acquired a contiguity which makes the combination a cliché but the phrase is truly apt to describe Amsterdam.

He was eager to put his knowledge to work in the service of lawyers representing criminal defendants or civil rights activists and protestors. A six-line letter to Amsterdam asking for general legal advice often resulted in a reply which the addressee needed only to turn over to a typist in order to have a complete brief ready for filing in court. To the overworked civil rights bar, Amsterdam was like the gift of a well-programmed legal computer; he vastly enlarged the Fund's capacity to go to court and win.

In the critical mid-1960's, when massive black protests seemed likely to lead either to repression and defeat or to a new level of the struggle for an America without institutionalized racism, he was rarely at home and often truant from his law school classes. He could be found commuting between Jackson, Atlanta, and New Orleans, munching hamburgers in an airport coffee shop, or banging away on a portable typewriter in a waiting room. In but two years as a government lawyer he had acquired a proficiency in the practical and technical aspects of his profession which complemented his intellectual ability, and he did not allow these skills to collect dust. Other lawyers, often veteran practitioners twice his age, would take second place to the intense law professor who sounded in court as if the opinions of the Supreme Court were his bedtime reading.

A legal case contains so many variables that mistakes are inevitable. Many times I have returned from court to office only to kick myself at the recognition of a question not asked or answered, an authority not cited. Amsterdam minimized such errors by a sometimes fanatical devotion to preparation, to plotting out of the consequences of an act or an idea. We all came to recognize a certain trancelike state that was prelude to creation. "He realizes in foresight," said a colleague, "what few approach in hindsight."

A man of this intelligence and force is rare in any age; our own teaches us to look for feet of clay. Those who heard of Amsterdam's reputation for the first time often assumed that his qualities were exaggerated, to which his admirers would offer a condescending smile and say, "Find out for yourself. Ask anyone who knows him." Many could not get over the fact that he was pleasant to be with, even though his feats led bright and ambitious colleagues to feel intellectually inadequate. He was self-effacing with his associates, but powerful and confident when dealing with the legal world around him. Amsterdam's participation in any venture meant unity and induced a nonsectarian atmosphere which was to become critical in the litigation of the capital punishment cases. When he was present, the internecine strife—seeming so necessary to the insider, so wasteful to the outsider—that plagues do-gooders, with no principle of profit and loss to settle all arguments, was replaced by true cohesiveness.

Thus Amsterdam became the guiding hand behind numerous lawsuits and projects supported by the American Civil Liberties Union, the Lawyers' Committee for Civil

Rights Under Law and the Lawyers' Constitutional Defense Fund, as well as the Legal Defense Fund. In the years to follow, he participated in controversial cases involving rioters and black militants, student activists, antiwar demonstrators, and school decentralization advocates. He was a key member of the legal team that represented the Chicago Seven in their appeal from the conspiracy conviction handed down in Judge Julius Hoffman's bizarre Chicago courtroom. Along with Fund lawyers Elizabeth Dubois, Eric Schnapper and myself, he forged the legal strategy that upset Hoffman's barbaric four-year sentence of Black Panther Party Chairman Bobby Seale for contempt.[9] And it was Amsterdam who almost revolutionized the law governing the refusal of journalists to turn information gathered from confidential sources over to government prosecutors. He represented Earl Caldwell, a black *New York Times* reporter who resisted Attorney General John Mitchell's attempt to force grand jury testimony of his interviews with California Black Panthers until a 5-to-4 Supreme Court decision rejected constitutional arguments for a newsman's privilege.[10]

During these years Amsterdam's assistance was also sought by the orthodox and official: The American Law Institute, the President's Commission on Law Enforcement and Administration of Justice (the National Crime Commission), the National Advisory Commission on Civil Disorders (the Kerner Commission), and the American Bar Association. He was a member of the commission, headed by former Solicitor-General Archibald Cox, which studied the 1968 disturbances that converted Columbia University into a battleground. It was said that he clung to Cox like a leech for a solid week before the commission's report went to press, lobbying, with ultimate success, for inclusion of passages which pointed an accusing finger at theretofore unmentioned failures of the university administration and police.[11]

After 1963, when he first became a Fund consultant,

Amsterdam was sought persistently to serve on boards of directors, to try cases, to write briefs, and to argue appeals. Lawyers from everywhere in the United States called him to discuss their most troublesome cases. As the months of his "part-time" work with the Fund turned into years, the rhythm of his life began to resemble that of the only doctor in a plague-ridden city. His body rebelled, and a perpetual weariness settled over him. Close associates conspired to regulate the flow of requests for his assistance. Fund lawyers were asked to check with me or Jim Nabrit whether a particular problem was "worth troubling Tony about." Ultimately, he stiffened himself to deny some of the less weighty demands for his time, slept more regularly—even if no more than four or five hours a night—and relied on his colleagues more readily.

That Amsterdam freed himself slightly from the role of advisor-at-large to hundreds of civil rights and civil liberties lawyers was good fortune for the inmates of death rows, for he became increasingly involved in, and finally came to manage, the Fund's growing docket of capital cases. Between 1965 and 1972 he spent no less than forty hours a week, every week of every year, representing capital case defendants. Whatever frustration he felt at having to refuse some of those who sought his assistance must have been eased by the knowledge that only he, and his associates, barred the door to the chamber of death.

In the spring of 1965, Amsterdam and Jack Greenberg requested that a student group, the Law Students Civil Rights Research Council, assemble law students to participate in a summer research project. Chosen on the basis of academic performance and interest in civil rights, each student would be paid a modest salary by the Fund to gather facts on rape case sentencing in eleven Southern states. In June the students were brought to the Philadelphia campus of the University of Pennsylvania, instructed

how to record data for each case on a lengthy questionnaire, and given tips to help find useful information in
cryptic court records. If court records were incomplete, the
students were to consult newspaper accounts, lawyers' files,
or actual participants. Sources of information had to be
shown on the questionnaires.

They were also cautioned to conduct themselves deferen-
tially when interviewing and seeking access to official records. If questioned about their intentions, they were to
identify themselves as student researchers. Each received a
geographic assignment and a list of friendly local contacts.
"I feel," quipped one student, "as if we're parachuting
behind enemy lines."

After the briefing, the students dispersed. Heffron in New
York, and Amsterdam and Wolfgang in Philadelphia
waited for an explosion from the courthouses of the South.
Court clerks—North and South—are notoriously inhospi-
table to outsiders who have come to rummage through their
filing cabinets. No one was sure that they would render the
assistance that was essential for fact gathering, and without
the raw data, a serious court challenge to racial discrimination in sentencing rapists was unthinkable.

As the summer wore on, it became apparent that the
open and honest appearance of the students had succeeded
in opening the files. In those days before the full flower of
student rebellion, earnest student researchers could make
"public records" really public by trading on the respectabil-
ity of their demeanor. As the bulky questionnaires describing all rape convictions in sample counties from 1945 to
1965 slowly arrived at the Fund's New York office, it
became clear that, though the outcome was much in doubt,
the facts with which to build a legal argument were at least
accessible. As the student teams—white-collar guerrilla
bands—moved across the South, Heffron reported that data
gathering had gone so well that they would visit virtually all
of the sample counties during the summer.

In September 1965 Wolfgang began the laborious and

expensive process of transferring the collected data from the questionnaires to computerized cards, and analyzing and evaluating the results. Because of the cost involved, his hurriedly assembled staff of University of Pennsylvania graduate students processed questionnaires from a state only when Heffron or Norman Amaker, a senior Fund lawyer, learned that a death-row inmate faced critical court proceedings. As Wolfgang fed the computer, Fund lawyers moved in Southern courtrooms to ensure enough time to enable completion of the statistical analysis for the particular state.

Postponement was sometimes accomplished merely by a letter to the trial judge requesting delay, but often it took complicated procedural maneuvering. In one case, Heffron flew to Columbia, South Carolina, where a black, Louis Moorer, Jr., had challenged his rape conviction and death sentence. Heffron asked federal district judge Robert W. Hemphill for a sixty-day postponement in order to process the study results for the 355 South Carolina rape cases investigated. After an acrimonious hearing, at which he expressed disbelief as well as disapproval of the study, Hemphill impounded the original questionnaires and refused to permit Heffron to duplicate them so that statistical analysis could proceed. With only a few days left before Moorer's execution, the Fund took an emergency appeal to the United States Court of Appeals in Richmond, where Matthew Perry, Moorer's South Carolina lawyer, obtained an eleventh-hour stay of execution from Chief Judge Clement Haynsworth. A three-judge panel of the court subsequently rebuked Hemphill and ordered release of the records.[12]

When Fund lawyers took on a death case, they raised all available legal claims. As a result, many of the men whose cases the Fund entered in order to challenge capital punishment won their appeals on grounds that had nothing to do with the death penalty. The courts prudently avoided the capital punishment issue when another ground clearly entitled the defendant to a new trial. In Moorer's case, the trial jury had improperly learned of the existence of an illegally obtained confession. Enough appeals by men under sentence of death were won in this manner to make Fund lawyers speculate that there might be legal errors lurking in every capital case.

In Alabama, a state he knew as well as any native, Amaker employed a different method to persuade trial judges to permit extended delay. A great bear of a man, with a mellifluous voice that seemed made for the pulpit, Amaker simply jawboned the opposition into submission. At pretrial conferences with judges and prosecuting attorneys, he insisted that if the state forced him to trial prematurely, he would subpoena every court clerk in the state and demand that they bring their files to court so that he could place directly into evidence the facts collected in the questionnaires. If the subpoenas were quashed, he would appeal. Faced with the possibility of either a massive disruption of court business or reversal on appeal because they had blocked a death-row inmate's attempt to prove discrimination, the judges relented. They would wait until Wolfgang's report on Alabama rape cases was completed.

During 1965 and 1966 there were similar skirmishes in a dozen or so rape cases, but the first direct confrontation came in Arkansas. In 1962 William L. Maxwell, a twenty-two-year-old black Hot Springs youth, had been convicted in Garland County for the 1961 rape of a thirty-five-year-old unmarried white woman. The evidence against Maxwell suggested that he had been surprised breaking into the woman's house. She lived with her invalid father and was awakened one autumn night to find an intruder with a nylon stocking over his head cutting his way through a screen into her living room. Despite a warning that she would call the police if he did not leave, the intruder entered the living room and grabbed her. The telephone receiver fell to the floor, but her screams were heard by the operator, who called the police. Before the source of the call was located, the woman was dragged some two blocks from her home and raped. Although she had failed to identify Maxwell from a hospital bed shortly after the crime, at the trial she named him as the rapist. As the jury which convicted Maxwell did not vote to extend mercy, he was sentenced to death.

Christopher Mercer, the black Little Rock lawyer hired by a group of Hot Springs citizens to defend Maxwell, appealed to the Supreme Court of Arkansas. One of the errors he claimed was the local circuit court's rejection of his assertion that Arkansas juries followed a pattern of racial discrimination in the application of the death penalty for rape. Predictably, the Supreme Court of Arkansas took the view that Maxwell's then-available evidence of racial discrimination—statistics showing nineteen executions of blacks for rape and one execution of a white for rape between 1930 and 1960—did not prove that Arkansas juries were acting discriminatorily, at least in the absence of "evidence . . . even remotely suggesting that the ratio of violent crimes by Negroes and whites was different from the ratio of the executions."[13]

After trial and conviction, a serious criminal case can generally be appealed to the highest court of the state. Usually the evidence of guilt on the record is strong. As appellate judges are not present when witnesses testify, they are almost compelled to accept the trial transcript at face value and find that the guilty verdict is not so much against the weight of the evidence as to warrant reversal. Nor does the law of most states permit a convicted defendant to appeal on the ground that a sentence, even the sentence of death, should be reduced. Even in those few states which permit the practice, appellate judges use very sparingly their power to reduce sentences set by trial courts. In capital cases, modification of penalty, even when authorized, is all the more difficult because it generally involves tampering with the mystical sentencing decision of "the conscience of the community," the jury.

Appellate judges, therefore, had a restricted capacity to review the results of capital trials. Whether willing or unwilling, they were prisoners of the absolute discretion in sentencing conferred on the jury. The judges were left with the rules of the game: was evidence improperly excluded? did the trial judge correctly instruct jurors about their role in weighing the evidence? did he hamper defense lawyers? To the extent that appellate courts were attuned to the danger of abuse in capital cases, they could only fight it by fashioning fairer procedure, rules which primarily applied to the determination of guilt. As a result, judges agonized over nice questions of procedure, when what really concerned them was the appropriateness of the death sentence.

Once an appeal like Maxwell's is lost in a state supreme court, a defendant is permitted to petition the United States Supreme Court to review his case, usually by filing a legal document called a petition for a writ of certiorari—technically, a request that the Supreme Court order the lower court to transmit the case record to the high Court. Whether the Supreme Court agrees to hear oral arguments, receive briefs, and decide the legal issues depends on whether a minimum of four Justices vote to review a case after reading the petition for a writ of certiorari and the state's reply brief. While the grant or denial of a petition for a writ of certiorari is often based on intangibles, the Justices generally can only consider legal claims involving some provision of federal law—the Constitution, federal statutes, administrative regulations, or treaties. A claim that a guilty verdict, for example, is not justified by the evidence qualifies as a question of federal law only in the extraordinary circumstance where there is absolutely no evidence of guilt present—almost never the situation in a capital case. Supreme Court Justices, moreover, find issues of federal law that require high Court resolution only in a small proportion of the cases which they are asked to review. Thus, while many seek, few are chosen.

After the Supreme Court denies a petition for a writ of certiorari, the jockeying begins. A defendant may have a claim which rests on a provision of the federal Constitution—say that his right to counsel has been denied or his privilege against self-incrimination has been breached. If the Supreme Court declines to review the claim—or even if Supreme Court review has not been sought—the defendant may present his contention to a lower federal court by bringing what is called a "post-conviction" proceeding. A state prisoner does this by petitioning for a writ of habeas corpus. A series of Warren Court decisions authorized—and in some cases required—the federal courts to decide the constitutional questions involved and to consider new evidence. If a federal district court rejects the defendant's petition for a writ of habeas corpus, he may take an appeal to a court of appeals, and thereafter, if he loses in the court of appeals, again seek a Supreme Court hearing.

The states also permit defendants to apply for post-conviction relief in the state courts. Once a state trial court denies such a petition, a defendant may appeal this rejection to higher state courts. If he loses this second round in the state courts, the defendant may also seek review in the United States Supreme Court of the state court denial of any federal claims he has raised.

There are, therefore, three separate paths of judicial review to explore—appeal from a state court conviction, a state court post-conviction proceeding, and a federal habeas corpus proceeding—each route potentially ending at the Supreme Court. Not every defendant may end up in federal court because not every defendant has a claim based on federal law. But in other cases, like Maxwell's, in which new legal issues and evidence emerge, federal law permits the filing of successive habeas corpus petitions. As a result, a defendant whose federal claims have enough substance to require serious consideration—especially if he is able to obtain the services of an attorney—usually is able to litigate for years.

Only the legal mind—and barely that—can contemplate with equanimity a set of procedures that, on the surface at least, seem so needlessly expensive, complicating, and dilatory. They certainly are costly, complex, and time-consuming, but many lawyers feel that they are far from needless. They have developed because appellate court judges often believe that criminal defendants do not get a fair shake from state trial courts the first time around. Not only are most defendants poor and seriously disadvantaged in defending themselves against criminal charges but, as Amsterdam had told an Airlie House meeting: "They have relatively little access to the facts. The prosecutor has superior resources for investigation, and the cooperation of the police. He controls the timing of the litigation and the jury is usually friendly. The indigent's attorney enters the case late, his witnesses are likely to be marginal types difficult to find and unappealing as witnesses. The defendant is frequently jailed in default of bail and cannot assist in defense investigation. The processes of state court justices are often hurried and inexcusably lax in guaranteeing the constitutional prerequisites of fair trial." In short, because the reliability and fairness of the initial encounter between the defendant and government are both mistrusted and left unreformed, additional layers of judicial proceedings are made available.

To many, ready availability to convicts of the writ of habeas corpus suggests the capacity of the law to correct injustice and to restrict the excessive zeal of public officials. To others, this use of what the English called the Great Writ is a source of unending mischief, a burden on judges, policemen, and state officials imposed by recalcitrant criminals who refuse to accept their guilt and its consequences. Another view is that the availability of habeas corpus provides only the appearance of justice—a clean bandage for an infected wound—a too-long-after-the-fact investigation of legal rights which should be accorded in the first court in which the defendant appears.

Powerful arguments have been marshaled to support these differing positions, and each has its attraction. It is indisputable, however, that the federal habeas corpus jurisdiction as it exists at present is proof of a profound skepticism toward criminal adjudication. And while it cannot be justified in the name of efficiency, it has over the years righted many an injustice.

When, in 1963, the Supreme Court finally settled[14] that a defendant could freely raise alleged denials of federal rights by means of habeas corpus, the impact on death-row inmates was enormous. Any criminal sentenced to a prison term could litigate his claims after conviction, but most would remain in jail while they did so. The delay inherent in the judicial process, even slower than usual in post-conviction cases, generally worked against their interests. But to the condemned man, the opportunity to raise legal claims anew, to relitigate old ones with supplementary evidence, and to take advantage of changes in constitutional law was a chance to live. His prospects for success were still slight—federal judges granted the writ in only a fraction of the cases they heard—but at least he had access to the courts for such claims as he or his lawyers could devise.

In 1964, before the rape survey was undertaken, Heffron had helped George Howard, a black attorney from Pine Bluff, Arkansas, and a leader of the state's NAACP, apply for a writ of habeas corpus in federal court on Maxwell's behalf. Along with several other claims, Heffron and Howard again argued that the Equal Protection Clause of the Fourteenth Amendment had been violated because Arkansas juries systematically discriminated against Negroes in rape case sentencing. Heffron made a modest attempt to offer additional proof of racial discrimination by interrogating three court clerks about rape cases in Garland, Jefferson, and Pulaski counties. In Garland County, seven whites had been charged with rape in the previous decade: four were not prosecuted and three were sentenced on reduced charges. Of the three blacks charged with rape, one was not prosecuted, another received a jail term, and the third, Maxwell, received a death sentence. The results in Jefferson and Pulaski counties were no more helpful, and federal Judge Gordon E. Young was not impressed. Like the Supreme Court of Arkansas, he ruled that the showing of racial discrimination was insufficient.[15]

The following year the Court of Appeals for the Eighth Circuit in St. Louis, the federal appellate court with jurisdiction over Arkansas, rejected Maxwell's appeal[16] and the United States Supreme Court refused to review the case.[17] Unless extraordinary action was taken, William Maxwell would die as scheduled on September 2, 1966.

In July 1966, Arkansas Governor Orval Faubus, who had not signed a death warrant in several years, signed six of them and then left the state to attend a governors' conference. At this time, Maxwell was represented by Howard, and Luther Bailey, another death-row inmate was represented by Christopher Mercer. The other men whose warrants were signed were unrepresented. Howard and Mercer called New York, where a Legal Defense Fund planning session was in progress. Amaker and Amsterdam hurriedly left a workshop when the call came through. During a period of several hours, they dictated habeas corpus petitions to Howard's secretary, and these were filed the next day. After the Maxwell and Bailey petitions were filed, the lieutenant governor of Arkansas, acting in Faubus' absence, agreed to stay the other four scheduled executions and to abide by the results in the two cases. Subsequently, the Bailey case was shelved pending a ruling in Maxwell's case.

Decisions of the United States Supreme Court permitted LDF to file a second habeas corpus petition on Maxwell's behalf. They could not, however, ensure that the judge to whom it was presented—J. Smith Henley—would remain uninfluenced by Maxwell's earlier habeas corpus defeat. It was more likely that Henley would summarily deny the second petition unless something new caught his eye. Thus, in order to get serious consideration, and thereby a stay of Maxwell's scheduled execution, Amsterdam and Amaker included in the petition every legal ground they could relate to events subsequent to Judge Young's 1964 denial of Maxwell's first habeas petition. They raised the sentencing discrimination issue, emphasizing that new facts (the rape study) had become available. They tied the single-verdict issue to a 1964 Supreme Court decision, *Jackson v. Denno*,[18] which questioned the capacity of jurors to disregard evidence derived from an illegal confession when deciding whether or not to convict. They related the standards issue to a 1966 decision, *Giaccio v. Pennsylvania*,[19] which had thrown out a Pennsylvania law authorizing the jury to impose court costs on a defendant whose conduct the jury disliked even though it had decided to acquit him of all criminal charges. The Supreme Court had said that the statute was unconstitutional because it did not specify standards fixing the conduct that would warrant such treatment.

Amsterdam and Amaker also renewed Maxwell's claim that black jurors had been unconstitutionally excluded at his trial on the basis of a June 1966 Supreme Court decision to review a Georgia discrimination case, *Sims v. Georgia*.[20] Lastly, the petition asserted that the principle of another 1966 Supreme Court decision, *Pate v. Robinson*,[21] had been violated because Maxwell had been mentally incompetent to stand trial in 1962.

Conversely, Amsterdam and Amaker did not include issues in the petition where the law had remained unchanged since 1964 (except the discrimination claim, where new *facts* were claimed). Such issues would not hold Henley's attention and they might fatally detract from the force of the new issues by making the petition look too much like leftovers cooked up at the last minute to save Maxwell's life. For these reasons no mention was made of the arguments that the death penalty was cruel and unusual punishment or that scrupled jurors had been wrongly eliminated from the jury panel.

Fund lawyers thought that the claim of racial discrimination was the strongest issue, but wondered whether a federal court would ever write a decision that characterized hundreds of past executions as the product of racial discrimination. If not, it was hoped that suspicion of discrimination would at least influence the court to tighten capital case procedures and, in the process, restrict use of the death penalty.

On August 5, 1966, Judge Henley called the lawyers to a pretrial conference to discuss the case. He refused to sign an order postponing Maxwell's execution—still set for September 2—but promised a speedy hearing. Amsterdam and Amaker described the evidence they would present, and urged that Henley adopt the following procedure: they would file all the Arkansas questionnaires with the court and serve copies on Fletcher Jackson, the assistant attorney general who was handling the case for the State; if Jackson wanted to contest any of the facts recited in the questionnaires, he would notify Amsterdam and Amaker; failing such notification, the facts in the questionnaires would stand as admitted.

Judge Henley bought the suggestion because it would expedite the hearing by avoiding courtroom hassles over the admissibility of evidence. Amsterdam and Amaker did not want the hearing to get bogged down in evidentiary questions either, but their motives in suggesting the procedure to Henley were more complex. It placed the burden on Jackson to specify his objections to the facts contained in the mass of paper served on him, or to waive them. Lawyers often fight hard for such tactical advantages, knowing that their adversary may be too overwhelmed by bulky documents, or simply too lazy to dispute the facts.

Whatever Jackson's reasons, he filed no notice objecting to the questionnaires. This concession removed a major obstacle to success, for it meant that the data would be treated as authentic and Wolfgang's testimony would be considered as an expert's evaluation of conceded facts. Thus, the state—rather cavalierly, some observers felt—would only dispute the soundness of the Fund's legal theory and whether the facts assembled supported it, not whether the evidence was true and legally admissible.

On this understanding, Maxwell's habeas corpus hearing began on August 22 in a courtroom at the Little Rock Post Office Building. Wolfgang, the chief witness, is a towering intellect. A scholar of international repute, his curriculum vitae fills many pages, but he had no experience in testifying about sociological matters in court. Indeed, this was one of the many reasons that the lawyers thought he would be an extremely effective witness—here was no "expert" witness for hire.

Although his testimony should not appear canned, Wolfgang did have to know precisely how the lawyer questioning him intended to bring out the purpose and results of the rape study. He also had to learn what he might expect on cross-examination.

Long before Maxwell's second habeas petition was filed, Wolfgang's schooling as a witness had been attended to, for Amaker and I had traveled to Philadelphia to help him prepare. We wrote out long lists of questions, and posed them to Wolfgang. After he responded, we discussed his answer—had a word of jargon crept in? would the judge understand a particular scientific concept?—and then moved on. It was tedious work for all concerned, but we knew that the best stories told in court had generally been told in lawyers' offices first.

Wolfgang began his testimony in Maxwell's case by describing the study's objective: to collect empirical data either in support or in rejection of the underlying assumption—that there is racially differential imposition of the death penalty for rape in the states studied—and to give the empirical data the appropriate kind of statistical analysis that would satisfy scientific requirements. Then he told Judge Henley of the students' efforts to gather the facts of every conviction for rape, fifty-five in all, during the twenty-year period in the sample of nineteen Arkansas counties. The study, he explained, began with all cases of conviction for rape regardless of sentence in order to address itself to the possibility, suggested many years earlier in Maxwell's case by the Supreme Court of Arkansas, that any showing that blacks were more frequently sentenced to death for rape than whites might be accounted for by proof that they committed rape, or were convicted of rape, more frequently than whites. Arrests, charges, and trials for rape all could have been compared with sentencing patterns, but a variety of elusive factors might have intervened to alter the proportion of one racial group actually convicted. To avoid the Herculean task of finding out why some people who were arrested were not charged, why some who were charged were not tried, and why others who were tried were not convicted, only those who had actually been convicted of rape were studied to compare capital sentencing of black and white defendants.

Fortune had chosen a capable and interested judge for this critical round in Maxwell's case. As Wolfgang continued, Henley, a former Justice Department lawyer appointed to the bench by President Eisenhower in 1958, asked questions which showed that he had examined carefully the detailed twenty-eight-page questionnaire which the students had completed for each Arkansas rape case in the sample counties.

Crammed with information, the completed forms represented an exhaustive attempt to investigate whatever factors, for which data was available, might be thought to affect sentence. Answers traced the defendant (age; family status; occupation; prior criminal record, etc.), the victim (age; family status; occupation; husband's occupation if married; reputation for chastity, etc.), defendant-victim relationship (prior acquaintance, if any; prior sexual relations, if any), circumstances of the offense (number of offenders and victims; place of the offense; degree of violence or threat employed; degree of injury inflicted on victim, if any; housebreaking or other contemporaneous offenses committed by defendant; nature of intercourse; involvement of alcohol or drugs, etc.), circumstances of the trial (were there defenses of consent or insanity, etc.), joinder of the rape trial with a trial on other charges, or trial of other defendants, and defendant's representation by counsel (retained or appointed) at various stages (trial and sentencing, etc.).

According to Wolfgang, these were "variables . . . which reasonably might be supposed to either aggravate or mitigate a given rape," and which might "rather than race . . . play a more important role in the disproportionate sentencing to death of Negro defendants convicted of raping white victims." Prodded by Amsterdam's questions, defining statistical terminology whenever possible, Wolfgang patiently explained that the students had gathered sufficient data to permit study of some twenty-two variables. Wolfgang had run a computer analysis; the results showed that none of the variables were sufficiently associated with both sentence and race to account for the disproportionate frequency of death sentences meted out to black rapists of white women. Other variables (like the degree of force employed by the rapist and his record of prior convictions) occurred so frequently (or rarely) in the cases studied that they could not explain the racial disproportion.

Wolfgang found that the disparity between the number of death sentences imposed on Negroes with white victims and all other racial combinations of convicted defendants and victims was such that it could have occurred less than twice in one hundred times by chance. Put another way, if race were not related to capital sentencing in Arkansas, the results observed in the twenty-year period studied could have occurred fortuitously in two (or less) twenty-year periods since the birth of Christ. He believed that the study documented racial discrimination that previously available data—not collected systematically or in a form permitting rigorous analysis—could only suggest. With the qualification that "information is always limited," Wolfgang concluded that the study had made definite what before had been merely suspected.

After John Monroe, a Philadelphia statistician, gave Henley a description of the manner in which the sample counties had been selected, the hearing abruptly terminated. Arkansas presented no evidence of any sort in rebuttal, and argued to Judge Henley that racial discrimination had not been proven.

Just as abruptly, on August 26, Henley decided that the state was right.[22] His written opinion, however, contained some surprises. He accepted Wolfgang's conclusion that sentencing patterns of Arkansas Negroes convicted of raping white victims "could not be due to the operation of the laws of chance." A black convicted of raping a white woman had about a 50 percent chance of receiving a death sentence. Any man convicted of raping a woman of his own race stood only a 14 percent chance. But Henley thought the difference explainable on other than racial grounds. It might be due to some factor for which statistical analysis had not been possible. The students had not been able to answer every question about "the details of the cases." Some court records had been destroyed. The sample was too small: only seven blacks were sentenced to death for rape of white women.

Between the lines, Henley seemed to be saying that a federal court would not abolish capital punishment on the basis of statistics. The "variables which Dr. Wolfgang considered are objective . . . broad in instances . . . imprecise . . . Discrimination, moreover, is a highly subjective matter" and might not "be detected by a statistical analysis . . . Statistics are elusive things at best, and it is a truism that almost anything can be proven by them."

Henley also found it significant that the sample counties

—although randomly chosen—had turned out not to be evenly dispersed geographically, and did not include many counties of sparse Negro population. He could not agree that "the Garland County jury which tried [Maxwell] was motivated by racial discrimination" since it was not—as a result of the happenstance of the areal sampling technique used—included in the study. (The Fund's argument, however, had not been that the particular twelve men who had condemned Maxwell to death had acted discriminatorily— this was impossible to prove—but that analysis of a random sample of Arkansas rape cases showed that only race could explain sentencing patterns.)

Finally, Henley speculated that Arkansas rape case sentencing patterns were explicable by a variable the study had not considered. Consent was often raised as a defense to a rape charge in intraracial cases, but rarely in interracial cases. A black who claimed to a Southern jury that a white woman had agreed to intercourse—even if it was true— was asking for trouble. Perhaps, the judge suggested, Arkansas jurors often gave weight to the consent defense in lightly sentencing men charged with intraracial rapes.

For all these reasons Henley dismissed Maxwell's petition and refused to issue the "certificate of probable cause" necessary for appeal in this type of case—finding, in effect, that any issues appealed would be frivolous. To Amsterdam's and Amaker's dismay, he declined to stay Maxwell's September 2 execution, now seven days away, until the Court of Appeals for the Eighth Circuit could be asked to permit an appeal.

On August 27, 1966, while many an American drove to the beach, Amsterdam, Amaker, and Jim Nabrit converged on the Fund's New York office to prepare the new legal papers that would be needed to try to save Maxwell's life. They worked through the hot summer weekend, and on Monday, August 29, Amaker flew first to Little Rock, where he gathered necessary documents, and then on to St. Louis, where he presented applications to a judge of the court of appeals for a stay of execution and a "certificate of probable cause."

After filing the motions with Robert Tucker, the Eighth Circuit's clerk, he returned to his hotel room and waited by the phone. A few hours later Tucker called to tell Amaker that Circuit Judge M. C. Matthes had refused to issue a stay or to permit an appeal—ruling, as had Henley, that Maxwell's arguments had so little merit that there was no reason to postpone his execution while he appealed to a higher court. A weary Amaker phoned the disappointing news East.

Aside from the mercy of Governor Faubus, the only opportunity left to save Maxwell's life was to seek a stay of execution from a Justice of the Supreme Court of the United States. For Maxwell to prevail, a Supreme Court Justice would have to conclude that the issues raised by Maxwell's appeal were at least worthy of consideration by the court of appeals. Amsterdam, Amaker, and Nabrit flew to Washington and filed a stay application with Edward Cullinan, the Supreme Court's deputy clerk. Cullinan in turn presented it to the Justice assigned to hear such motions in cases arising in the Arkansas federal courts—Byron White.

The three lawyers checked into a Washington hotel to sweat out White's decision. Unwashed and unshaven after two all-night stints preparing the stay papers, they showered and shaved in case Justice White requested oral argument of the application. Just as the last of the three had finished, White made unnecessary the showers and the shaves, as well as resort to Governor Faubus, by granting the application on the papers. He ordered the execution postponed solely to permit Maxwell to present to the entire Supreme Court his claim that Judge Matthes had erred in denying him an appeal.

Several months later, after it returned from summer recess, the Court unanimously ruled that Matthes had misapplied the law.[23] Maxwell might not win the appeal, but his arguments were not so trifling that he could be denied a hearing before the court of appeals.

As if to emphasize that it took Maxwell's appeal seriously, the court of appeals did not issue its decision[24] until June 11, 1968, well over a year after the Supreme Court had returned the case to the lower court. The court's long opinion, written by Judge Harry Blackmun of Minnesota, rejected every argument made on Maxwell's behalf. Blackmun conceded the general validity of Wolfgang's methodology and agreed that there were "recognizable indicators . . . [that] the death penalty for rape may have been discriminatorily applied over the decades in that large area of [Southern] states whose statutes provide for it." But " . . . improper state practice of the past does not automatically invalidate a procedure of the present."

Blackmun thought the statistics showing discrimination were irrelevant to the case at hand. They did "not show that the petit jury which tried and convicted Maxwell" sentenced him to death because of race: "Whatever it may disclose with respect to other localities, we feel that the statistical argument does nothing to destroy the integrity of Maxwell's trial." The Arkansas statistics did not even "relate specifically to Garland County where this particular offense was committed and where Maxwell was tried and convicted."

There had been only three death sentences in Garland County in the last thirty years, a number by far too small to permit statistical analysis. The Fund had argued that it was absurd to round up the jurors who had sat on Maxwell's case in 1962—assuming they could be found—and ask them if they had sentenced Maxwell to death because he was black. It was not Garland County but the state of Arkansas, LDF contended, which was made responsible by the Fourteenth Amendment to provide all persons equal protection of the laws. If the juries of a state systematically applied one standard to blacks and another to whites, then it must be unconstitutional for any jury of that state to sentence to death for rape. This had to follow because even a team of psychoanalysts could not discover whether Garland County juries, or Maxwell's particular jury, sentenced to death because of race.

But Blackmun disagreed. His message was the same as Henley's: "We are not certain that, for Maxwell, statistics will ever be his redemption."

Once again, only the Supreme Court of the United States stood between William Maxwell and the electric chair. To save him, four Justices would have to agree that at least one of Maxwell's three major constitutional claims—that racial discrimination infected jury sentencing for rape in Arkansas; that standardless jury sentencing was so arbitrary as to violate the Constitution; or that the single-verdict procedure should be prohibited in capital cases—was substantial enough to merit consideration by the full Court. It was now 1968, however, and several intervening developments had made it far more attractive for the Supreme Court to confront the constitutionality of capital case procedures. Prodded perhaps by a growing awareness that LDF had halted executions across the nation, the Court itself had contributed to legal developments which made decision of larger questions inevitable.

6

Moratorium

While Billy Maxwell's case took its roller-coaster ride through the federal courts, the Fund's war council of capital case lawyers made a decision which was to determine the path of their efforts for the next six years: henceforth they would attempt to block all executions. They would defend murderers as well as rapists, whites as well as blacks, Northerners as well as Southerners.

It is not easy to trace the evolution of this change in policy, for it came about only after a number of complex, interrelated, tactical and moral considerations coalesced, but of its importance there can be no doubt. One factor prompting the decision was the unpleasant lesson taught by the reaction of the courts to the rape study in Maxwell's case: notwithstanding that the evidence was as convincing as men with finite resources could produce, judges resisted an argument that on the basis of statistics asked them to brand hundreds of trial juries as prejudiced. Proof of racial discrimination in rape sentencing might ultimately influence judges to require standards, split verdicts, or different rules governing the exclusion of scrupled jurors. If the lawyers unearthed more facts, judges might even come to accept the statistical argument itself. But such results were unlikely for several years and they would never be possible unless the fact that a high proportion of blacks were subject to execution emerged as but one distasteful aspect of a far greater evil. For this to occur, the courts had to take a fresh look at the venerable institution of capital punishment. In turn, to catch the conscience of the courts, the death penalty had to be a "problem"—one that was discussed, attracted attention and, in a more immediate way than in the past, affected the work lives of the judges and prison officials who administered it. Abolition needed a symbol, a threat of crisis, to overcome inertia and to win favor from a reluctant judiciary.

One way to promote this end was to raise the entire range of capital punishment arguments in all cases where execution was imminent, thereby stopping the killing and eventually presenting any resumption of it as likely to lead to a blood bath. The politics of abolition boiled down to this: for each year the United States went without executions, the more hollow would ring claims that the American people could not do without them; the longer death-row inmates waited, the greater their numbers, the more difficult it would be for the courts to permit the first execution. A successful moratorium strategy would create a death-row logjam. Regardless of political stripe, there were very few governors who wished to preside over mass executions. Even if state legislatures did not act to abolish the death penalty despite the threat of numerous gassings and electrocutions, many chief executives might readily acquiesce in judicial action that would permit them to avoid making scores of clemency decisions.

But there were dangers, not to mention difficulties, in agreeing to represent every death-row inmate who sought LDF assistance. It was a close question whether a particular Fund client would be helped by tying his fate to a general campaign against the death penalty. Test cases have a way of scaring off judges because their implications are often so enormous. And the Fund was planning a campaign of test cases. If the strategy worked and capital punishment was abolished or severely restricted, the racially discriminatory sentences complained of by LDF clients would be eliminated. If the strategy failed, however, Southern black rapists as a class might actually be far worse off than before because, to cite one consideration that troubled the lawyers, a general challenge to capital punishment tended to lump together men who had killed with men who had not, creating a situation in which the fate of the nonkillers would be likely to hinge on the fate of the whole.

There were many such imponderables to weigh; some of the lawyers were given to making lists. We tried to read memoranda on the subject in a kind of mental deep-freeze. If anything proves the intolerable capriciousness of capital punishment, it is that life and death turn on such evaluations by lawyers for the condemned. These are matters better left to the gods.

If there had not been other forces at work, LDF lawyers might have stuck to representation of Southern black rapists and only taken on cases of blacks convicted of murder when they believed that justice had miscarried or that racial discrimination was involved. But once the lawyers knew the legal theories that could win stays of execution, they felt morally obliged to use them. "We could no more let men die that we had the power to save," Amsterdam commented, "than we could have passed by a dying accident victim sprawled bloody and writhing on the road without stopping to render such aid as we could." Indeed, the lawyers confronted a choice as immediate as if they had stumbled upon a highway smash-up. Calls for help were coming in from all parts of the nation: the governors of California, Florida, Louisiana, and Texas had signed death warrants.

For the moratorium strategy to work, Fund lawyers would have to intervene directly in hundreds of cases in over thirty of the forty-two jurisdictions whose law still provided the death penalty. Even if LDF declined to enter a case until after a defendant lost at trial and completed his

first state court appeal, the undertaking was massive, and
without precedent. Legal papers that could be used in each
capital punishment state were a necessity. The Fund required men and money which it simply did not have. It was
essential to develop relationships of confidence and trust
with scores of lawyers and other professionals.

Amsterdam began to forge a strategy by circulating
elaborately documented drafts of legal arguments designed
to show that standardless jury sentencing, the single-verdict
procedure (only California, Connecticut, New York, Pennsylvania, and Texas had split trials), and the exclusion of
scrupled jurors violated notions of fairness embodied in the
Fourteenth Amendment's vague and open-ended promise
of due process of law.

The money became available in 1967 when the Ford
Foundation granted the Fund a million dollars to create a
National Office for the Rights of the Indigent (NORI),
a project—brilliantly conceived by Leroy Clark—to bring
test cases to improve treatment of the poor by the legal
system. Although the Ford Foundation probably did not
have capital punishment in mind when it made the grant, it
had authorized NORI to go to court to upgrade the quality
of criminal justice. The elaborate trials and numerous appeals involved in capital cases swallowed up large amounts
of money which the states could have used to supply desperately needed services for indigent defendants; many
thought discrimination against the poor in the application
of capital punishment more blatant than discrimination
against blacks. For these reasons, Jack Greenberg decided
to use the Ford money to finance abolition cases.

Soon after the moratorium strategy was announced,
criminal lawyers invited the Fund to defend murder cases,
involving both blacks and whites in California, New Jersey and Colorado—states where LDF activity had been
slight. Overburdened public defender agencies and death-
row inmates themselves sought LDF assistance. By March
1967, the Fund was responsible for over fifty men subject

to execution, and the number climbed each month. With no shortage of potential clients, it soon was apparent that a staff lawyer had to be given full responsibility to manage the growing docket of death cases and to coordinate the efforts of those attorneys who sought LDF assistance. A national moratorium strategy demanded that each cooperating lawyer quickly learn the latest developments and, when necessary, receive fresh pleadings and briefs.

The small group of staff attorneys who had worked on capital cases (Nabrit, Amaker, Clark and myself; by this time Heffron had joined a Boston law firm) was familiar with the pressures of applying for last-minute stays of execution and gerry building legal arguments overnight. Now there was need for a theoretician and planner—a managing attorney who would collect evidence demonstrating the barbarity of death-row incarceration, and the character of death case juries; engage psychiatrists to study the deterioration of men awaiting execution; induce pollsters and statisticians to measure the bias of the jurors who remained after those with scruples against capital punishment had been removed; and find churchmen, wardens, and correctional officials to lend their prestige.

Further, the managing attorney had to interest law professors in generating imaginative constitutional theories based on evolving doctrine, and interest law students in documenting the varied forms taken by capital case procedure in different states. He had to cultivate journalists in order to persuade them that something newsworthy was happening in a field in which they had rarely shown sustained interest. Most important, he had to stand a death watch: upon learning of an imminent execution, he had to find a lawyer willing to take the case and place the proper papers in his hands.

I recommended that Greenberg offer the job to Jack Himmelstein, a twenty-six-year-old Harvard Law School graduate, who some years earlier when he was still a law student had held a summer research job with the Fund. He was unmistakably bright, but that was not rare in the shiny minds from the best law schools who graced our office library—filled with so many future professors, senatorial aides, and Supreme Court clerks that my colleagues saved their most demanding research projects for the summer months. But maturity and balance marked Himmelstein as one who could, despite his youth, keep in mind a hundred execution dates without cracking under the pressure. Born in Philadelphia, he had graduated with honors in philosophy from Cornell in 1962 and cum laude from Harvard Law School in 1965. Himmelstein had done poorly only once in his academic career—in a debate on capital punishment for a college speech class. "I did not take the issue very seriously," he told me years later.

During law school, Himmelstein attended several Harvard Medical School classes to obtain clinical experience in psychiatry, but only after winning a battle with a fussy law school administrator who thought he should register for more commercial law courses. One of his professors warned him that by not signing up for more "bread and butter" offerings he was in danger of failing the bar examination and making himself unhireable. After graduation, with a Knox Fellowship in psychiatry and law, he went to England to study civil commitment of the mentally ill. In London, he spent most of his time at the Anna Freud Clinic at Hampstead, an experience which later helped him see beyond the legalisms to the tortured psychic reality of each death case.

Returning to the United States in 1967, Himmelstein eagerly accepted the offer to work at the Fund because at the time there were few nongovernmental opportunities to practice law in the public interest rather than for private profit. When he arrived, he had no idea of his assignment. Jack Greenberg welcomed him to LDF, saying, "I want you to work on the capital project." For a moment, Himmelstein was crushed, thinking that "capital" referred to finance. "I thought," he said, "that all my efforts to reach the good, true, and beautiful had come to naught." But he learned soon enough what was to be the stuff of his life for the next several years.

Shortly after Himmelstein officially started work, Amsterdam drove him back to Philadelphia from an Airlie Conference. In the four-hour trip, he learned, issue by issue and step by step, the nature of the legal challenge to capital punishment and where it might lead. For the next five years hardly a week passed, and for long periods not a day, when these two men did not speak together. When Amsterdam, who had joined the Stanford University Law School faculty in 1969, was involved in important California litigation—such as the defense of black militant Angela Davis or the attempt to quash the grand jury subpoena of *New York Times* reporter Earl Caldwell—they talked late at night. Every few months they met in Washington, New York, or San Francisco. Himmelstein might go camping for a few days to get away from it all, but he was never far from a phone.

Their first joint project was to draft a set of petitions for habeas corpus, applications for stays of execution, and legal briefs that put forth every significant constitutional argument against the death penalty. The collection was bound, distributed to hundreds of lawyers, and dubbed the "Last Aid Kit." The papers in the "Kit" were arranged so that even an attorney totally unfamiliar with the Fund's legal strategy found himself able, upon minimum inspection, to present a court with substantial legal reasons for postponing an execution.

With circulation of the "Last Aid Kit," requests for LDF intervention in capital cases grew steadily; Himmelstein and Audrey Fleher, his skilled secretary, opened a file for every man on death row. He prepared a list of lawyers in every capital punishment state willing to participate in capital cases and coaxed several of the attorneys into serving as state reporters, committed to keeping him informed of scheduled executions and changes in local law.

Next, Himmelstein and Amsterdam expanded the latter's

already prodigious correspondence with interested lawyers to include scholars such as Hugo Bedau, Leslie Wilkins, Hans Mattick, Hans Ziesel and Harry Kalven, and psychiatrists Dr. Bernard Diamond and Dr. Louis J. West. They talked to prison wardens and psychologists who had studied the deleterious effects of long-term incarceration on death-row inmates; abolitionists like Ruth Kitchen of the New York Committee to Abolish Capital Punishment, Sol Rubin of the National Council on Crime and Delinquency, Donald E. J. MacNamara of the American League to Abolish Capital Punishment, and twenty-two-year-old Douglas Lyons, who as a college student had formed Citizens Against Legalized Murder (CALM).

Lyons was a one-man band, the 1960's most active and effective abolitionist. Because he was the son of a famous newspaper columnist, Leonard Lyons, CALM's letterhead boasted of the support of celebrities like Burt Lancaster, Truman Capote, and Steve Allen. But Douglas was actually the organization's sole staff member and often its only source of money.

In 1967 Lyons held a vigil at San Quentin to protest the execution of Aaron Mitchell; in 1968, he helped arrange hearings on a federal abolition bill for a United States Senate Judiciary Committee Subcommittee chaired by Senator Philip Hart. Later, while a law student, and a part-time Fund staff member, he continually checked with prison wardens, governors' offices, and interested lawyers to learn whether there were executions scheduled. Most of the time he was told "None this month." Every so often, however, Lyons learned of a previously unknown execution date. Working in this manner, he provided Himmelstein with information which led to last-minute stays of execution for over thirty men.

By May of 1968, almost twelve months had elapsed without a legal killing. Luis Jose Monge had been the last man to die, asphyxiated on June 2, 1967, in Colorado. Monge, a deranged man who had murdered his pregnant wife and three of his seven children, displayed a trait psy-chiatrists have noted in some killers—he could not wait to die. Monge called the police, pled guilty, and refused to appeal. At a four-hour "Last Supper" with relatives he told them, "I am ready to die, and I don't want any of you to claim my body."

Due largely to Himmelstein's spadework, LDF felt con-fident enough to assemble over a hundred lawyers and abolitionists for a National Conference on Capital Punish-ment at a New York hotel. At the opening of the meeting, Jack Greenberg gave a moving speech which alluded to the years not so long before when every Southern capital trial was a potential lynching, and described the background of the Fund's involvement. In staccato style, Amsterdam gave an overview of the legal strategy. Then each of the major constitutional claims was analyzed in some detail by speakers from various law schools: Caleb Foote, by then teaching at the University of California at Berkeley; Donald MacDonald of the University of Colorado; John Griffiths and Stephen B. Duke of Yale.

The purpose of the 1968 conference, however, was not technical; its aim was to bring the participants together for a face-to-face encounter, and at this it succeeded hand-somely. This first confrontation of numerous professionals who usually worked alone, ignorant of the efforts of others like themselves, gave the movement for legal abolition a cohesion that it had lacked. Largely because of this confer-ence, those who were present came to accept the Fund's role as overseer and clearinghouse. As a result, in the years that followed, no execution date went unchallenged.

In 1968 Dr. Martin Luther King, Jr., and Senator Robert F. Kennedy, two men who carried the hopes of many for a reconstructed America, were assassinated. Both murders took place in death penalty states, committed by men who were obviously undeterred. For many of those who attended the 1968 conference, especially Fund lawyers who had worked closely with Dr. King for years, his assassination dramatized as could nothing else the senselessness of killing, unofficial or official. If some dreamed of revenge, the impotence of such feelings to bring back men who were loved for their presence, or the hopes they evoked, reinforced the disgust with which the lawyers contemplated the prospect of more legal death. Ironically, this most miserable year in that "slum of a decade," to use John Updike's oft-quoted phrase, strengthened abolitionist resolve; it was also the year that brought the first two Supreme Court decisions which significantly limited state power to impose the death penalty. In both cases, the Court acted in a way which opened up the prospect of endless litigation, if not ultimate success.

In 1932 an increasing number of professional kidnapings (the most notorious being that of Charles Lindbergh's child) and the limited ability of local authorities to cope with interstate flight had led Congress to enact a federal kidnaping statute—better known as the Lindbergh law. Congress made kidnaping punishable by death in 1934, after the rampaging criminals of the thirties had had an even more pronounced effect on public opinion. The Lindbergh law made the crime punishable by death *only* if the defendant charged with harming the kidnaped person chose to plead not guilty *and* to go to trial before a jury rather than a judge. In other words, if a defendant pled guilty, or waived his right to trial by jury, a judge could sentence him to a maximum of life imprisonment.

In 1966 a Connecticut federal grand jury had charged three men, Charles "Batman" Jackson, Glenn LaMotte and John Albert Walsh, Jr., with the kidnaping of John Joseph Grant III, a truck driver whose load of razor blades had been hijacked and taken from Connecticut to New Jersey. Because Grant had suffered rope burns while freeing himself, he had been harmed sufficiently to invoke the death penalty provisions of the law.

Before Jackson and his codefendants pleaded to the indictment, the federal district court in New Haven appointed an especially able advocate, Stephen B. Duke, to serve as one of his lawyers. Professor Duke, a former clerk to Supreme Court Justice William O. Douglas, had joined the faculty of the Yale Law School in 1961 as a tax law teacher but soon became interested in criminal law. After receiving word of his court appointment, Duke quickly examined the Lindbergh law and noticed a potential defect in the statute which apparently had never been challenged in the more than thirty years that it had been on the books. Duke thought that the statute was unconstitutional because it coerced defendants to plead guilty and to waive trial by jury by making them risk their lives only if they contested their guilt before a jury. On this basis, he filed a motion to dismiss Jackson's indictment.

The government urged United States District Judge William H. Timbers to turn back the challenge. Before a defendant could plead guilty or waive a jury trial, the United States argued, both prosecuting attorney and trial judge had to consent. They could be relied upon to protect a defendant from actually being coerced to avoid trial or to waive a jury.

Timbers, however, agreed with the thrust of Duke's argument and dismissed the kidnaping charge. He thought the entire kidnaping statute unconstitutional because it had an inherent tendency to impair the right to trial by jury, guaranteed by the Sixth Amendment.[1] The United States appealed this ruling directly to the Supreme Court, but in 1968 the Court upheld Duke's contention that the kidnaping statute wrongly encouraged an accused to plead guilty and to waive his right to a jury trial.[2]

The fact that trial judges and United States attorneys monitor pleas of guilty and waivers of jury trials is no answer to the statute's invitation to avoid death only at the price of waiving rights, wrote Justice Potter Stewart for a majority of the Justices. "The evil" of the Lindbergh law is not that it "necessarily *coerces* guilty pleas and jury waivers," but "that it needlessly *encourages* them." The statute sets up a system which discourages and deters defendants from "insisting upon their innocence and demanding trial by jury" because death is threatened only when they do so.

Justice Stewart, however, did not agree with Judge Timbers that the entire kidnaping statute was void. Instead, the Supreme Court decided to excise merely that portion of the law which authorized the death penalty. Capital punishment, Stewart reasoned, was added in 1934 simply to increase the penalty for kidnaping, rather than to change the nature of the offense. As the Court read the legislative record of the statute's enactment, it was clear that, with or without the death penalty, Congress wished to make kidnaping a federal crime.

The government had also defended the statute's authorization of the death penalty *only* after trial by jury on the ground that it benefited defendants by permitting them to avoid totally the risk of capital punishment. Stewart replied that the Constitution plainly empowered Congress to mitigate the severity of the death penalty, but that Congress could not accomplish this end by penalizing defendants who wished to plead not guilty and demand trial before a jury rather than a judge. The Court recognized, therefore, that the risk of a death sentence created a unique stress on an accused to waive his rights in the hope of escaping death, and concluded that to impose upon a defendant an appreciably greater risk of incurring the death sentence if he did not waive his procedural rights was a denial of those rights.

Seven of the sixteen federal death penalty statutes arguably contained the same defect as the Lindbergh law. Additionally, ten states had adopted one form or another of the Lindbergh procedure as a device both to limit application of the death penalty and to induce guilty pleas from recalcitrant defendants. New Jersey law, for example, simply provided that a plea of guilty (called *non vult* or "no defense") assured a defendant's escape from a death sen-

tence. LDF prepared to argue that all such laws illegally
induced pleas of guilty motivated by a desire to avoid capital punishment.

As Himmelstein revised the "Last Aid Kit" to reflect the
Supreme Court's decision in this case, known as *United
States v. Jackson,* Fund lawyers felt that they had turned a
corner. The Supreme Court had not merely demonstrated a
willingness to tackle a murky question of capital case procedure, but had answered the question in a way which permitted abolitionists to challenge the practices of states with
similar defects in their laws. Additionally, the Court had
acted shrewdly by striking down the death penalty provision, but saving the kidnaping statute. No one could claim
that the *Jackson* decision freed dangerous criminals.

The second and even more significant 1968 Supreme
Court decision raised further hopes. This one involved
William Witherspoon, a man who had spent eight years on
death row in Illinois after conviction for the murder of a
Chicago police officer. Witherspoon had fifteen dates with
the executioner postponed. While fellow convicts took their
last steps past his cell, he had written two successful books.
At the time of his 1960 trial, an Illinois law, similar to
statutes in almost every other capital punishment state, provided that "in trials of murder it shall be a cause for challenging of any juror who shall on being examined, state that
he has conscientious scruples against capital punishment, or
that he is opposed to same."[3]

To understand how such laws operated, it is necessary to
describe a typical pattern of jury selection. Fifty to a hundred people are summoned to serve on a jury and seated in
the courtroom. Twelve are randomly chosen to constitute a
panel and asked to take places in the jury box. The prosecuting and defense attorneys then question the panel, collectively and individually, with a view to discovering bias
that will make it difficult for a juror to be impartial. Natu-

rally, the lawyers also look for signs that a juror might favor their side. The prosecution and the defense appeal to the judge to remove "for cause" any juror whose replies indicate attitudes, employment, or family relationship that might make him hostile to their side. Because of the jury's critical role in the trial process, the right to exclude any particular juror is hotly disputed.

Lawyers for each side are also given the right to exclude a limited number of jurors by exercising peremptory challenges which do not require the judge's approval. After a juror is excused "for cause" or peremptorily challenged, a new one takes his place. This process continues until the jury panel is chosen. Scrupled juror statutes work to give the prosecution a right to have the jury "death qualified," to exclude "for cause" any juror who reveals that he disfavors the death penalty.

At Witherspoon's trial, the rule had been invoked to eliminate nearly half the list of prospective jurors. The trial judge announced: "Let's get these conscientious objectors out of the way, without wasting any time on them."[4] In rapid succession, the prosecution successfully challenged "for cause" forty-seven jurors on the basis of their attitudes toward the death penalty. Only five of the forty-seven explicitly stated that under no circumstances could they vote to impose capital punishment. Six said they "did not believe in the death penalty" and were excused without any attempt to determine whether their scruples would invariably compel them to vote against capital punishment. One juror admitted that she disliked "to be responsible [for] deciding somebody should be put to death." Without more ado she was excused. Thus the state had been able indiscriminately to exclude persons with a range of potential objections to capital punishment from total rejection of the penalty to mild opposition. It was the constitutionality of this practice which the Supreme Court agreed to consider in *Witherspoon v. Illinois*.

The circumstances leading up to presentation of the

Witherspoon case to the Court illustrate the kind of complicated intellectual jockeying that makes the practice of constitutional law adventurous. Witherspoon, represented by
Albert E. Jenner, Jr., a prominent Chicago attorney with a
national reputation, wanted the Court to decide his appeal
on the question of bias—i.e., that a jury left without persons who have scruples against the death penalty is likely to
be more "prosecution prone" or biased against a defendant
than a jury from which such persons are not excluded.
Jenner relied primarily upon two unpublished opinion surveys, by psychologists Faye Goldberg and W. Cody Wilson.
The studies measured the attitudes of college students,
rather than potential jurors, and had not been prepared
with a view to use in legal proceedings, but both surveys
had tentatively concluded that jurors without scruples
against capital punishment were more likely to vote for
guilt than jurors with such misgivings.

LDF lawyers feared that this evidence was too slender to
hold up the weight of a major constitutional ruling. The
danger was that in the absence of more reliable research
demonstrating that, as a group, persons in favor of capital
punishment were more likely to accept the prosecution's
version of the facts and less likely to credit the accused's
defense, the Supreme Court might well reach an adverse
decision. Such a defeat would knock out a chief prop of the
moratorium strategy. As Witherspoon's counsel, Jenner was
obliged to raise every legal claim which might possibly win
a new trial. If the Fund intervened in the case as amicus
curiae, it might represent the interests of other death-row
inmates and urge the Court to avoid the bias question.

Amsterdam's response to the threat posed by the bias
issue was to write a ninety-four page amicus curiae brief for
the Fund urging that the sort of factual information necessary for a wise decision of the question was not yet available. Witherspoon's conviction could be reversed on other
grounds: for example, that the jury which convicted and
sentenced after exclusion of scrupled jurors did not reflect a

cross-section of the community, for several years earlier roughly half of the adult population questioned had told the Gallup Poll that they entertained some doubts about capital punishment. Under no circumstances, the brief argued, should the prosecution-proneness issue be decided on such scanty evidence as was available. Rather than do this, the case should be sent back to the lower courts for an evidentiary hearing. This would allow time for facts showing bias to be brought to light.

The Fund, the brief announced, had commissioned the Louis Harris polling organization to conduct a study of a random sample of potential capital case jurors. People with the legal qualifications to serve on capital case juries were to be questioned by simulation of the attitudinal examination employed in actual death cases. Inquiries would probe whether or not each respondent had a particularized objection to capital punishment.

Other questions measured demographic factors and the attitudes of potential jurors toward "punitiveness, alienation, prejudice, authoritarianism," in order to determine whether scrupled and nonscrupled jurors represented different subgroups and personality types. The study also would test the "respondents' perception of the role and reliability of . . . the judge, prosecutor, defense counsel, jury and witnesses"[5] and their reaction to common defense and prosecution trial tactics. Ability to decide a criminal case on the basis of the evidence would be measured by questions based on simulated trial records. Respondents would also be asked to rate the difficulty they encountered in reaching a decision about the defendant's guilt.

LDF told the Supreme Court in *Witherspoon* that it was necessary to wait for the results of the study, which would serve as a basis for an informed consideration of the prosecution-proneness issue. Advocacy of this position was dictated by a wretched fear that someone would be killed by a premature decision on the bias question: if the Supreme Court were to decide the issue before a fuller development of the evidence, its decision would most likely be adverse. But this strategy placed LDF lawyers in the awkward position of arguing that Witherspoon might not be entitled to an entire new trial of his guilt, but only to a new hearing on sentence. Witherspoon's lawyers, however, believed that they had a winning issue which not only affected their client's death sentence, but entitled him to a new trial (because "prosecution proneness," if proved, was an error affecting the determination of guilt as well as punishment). Several of Jenner's younger associates were furious and dashed off angry letters after they read the Fund's brief, for they had expected an argument in total agreement with their own. From Witherspoon's personal point of view, they may have been justifiably upset, but concern for the five hundred other men on death row forced the Fund to take a contrary position.

Ultimately the Supreme Court declined to consider the bias question: it agreed with the LDF that the available evidence was too "tentative and fragmentary." In deciding the case, however, Justice Stewart, writing for a majority of the Court as he had in *Jackson,* took a route treated only summarily by both Jenner and the Fund and narrowly defined the issue that the Court would decide. It did not involve whether Witherspoon's jury was lawfully chosen from a random cross-section of the community, or deal with the bias question; these issues the Court reserved for decision in the future. In this case, Stewart wrote, the Court treated the question of whether a jury chosen by excluding scrupled jurors could be impartial in determining *punishment,* not guilt. Stewart ruled that Witherspoon's jury had not been impartial because everyone with any manner of objection to the death penalty—no matter how loose—had been excluded. The Constitution did not permit the process of challenging jurors with conscientious or religious scruples against the death penalty to produce a "hanging jury." He concluded that judges might exclude jurors who would "automatically vote against the imposition of capital punishment no matter what the trial might reveal" or who made it "unmistakably clear" that their opposition to the death penalty would prevent them from even convicting a man who might later receive a death sentence. But more ambiguous opposition to capital punishment would not be sufficient to disqualify. Consequently, a full inquiry into each juror's disposition was necessary before a valid exclusion. As this had not been done in Witherspoon's case, his death sentence was unlawful.

In much the same shrewd way that the Court had ruled in *Jackson* that the death penalty provision of a federal law had to be voided but not the entire kidnaping statute, the Justices acted in a manner which diminished the likelihood of an adverse public reaction. When a case ran afoul of what became known as the *Witherspoon* rule, the death penalty was unconstitutional and had to be vacated, but it was not necessary to set aside the *conviction*. (In another case, *Bumper v. North Carolina*,[6] announced later the same day, the Court qualified the *Witherspoon* decision by making it clear that persons who had received non-capital sentences at the hands of "death-qualified" juries could not complain of a violation of the *Witherspoon* rule.)

Initially, *Witherspoon* gave abolitionist lawyers cause to believe that no one would ever be executed again, for the decision plainly added many opponents of capital punishment to the pool of eligible jurors. Because the rule laid down was retroactive, it applied to anyone on death row tried by a jury not selected in accordance with its terms. Most death-row inmates, LDF lawyers thought, had winning claims that their juries had been wrongly constituted, and thus would be entitled to a fresh determination of penalty. Some men had been sentenced to die by judges, but it might be possible to argue successfully that these men had waived their rights to jury trials because they feared trial by the sort of "hanging jury" the Supreme Court had disapproved. In cases in which the court reporter's stenographic notes reflecting the manner in which jurors were chosen had been destroyed, *Witherspoon* seemed to place the burden on the state to prove that the jury selection process had worked properly. If the state could not do so, the death sentence must be quashed.

At the least, then, LDF lawyers expected that there would be hundreds of resentencings before juries which might decline to reimpose the death penalty. Even defendants who had been condemned by fairly chosen juries might be saved in the wake of a widespread movement to reduce death sentences. If these predictions were overly sanguine, there still remained other capital punishment issues to present to the Court.

The Fund's impression of the significance of the decision was shared by many. United Press International assigned a reporter to record some of the first reactions. Witherspoon heard the news on the prison radio and was naturally "overjoyed." But Stanley Kirk, the district attorney of Wichita Falls, Texas, told a reporter, "I'm so mad, I'm speechless. We don't know what to do." Jack Gremillion, Louisiana's attorney general, merely said, "ridiculous." Almost everyone questioned believed the decision meant the end of capital punishment in the United States. The attorney general of Texas said that "It would be a very, very remote case where anyone would get the death penalty." Henry Wade, the Dallas district attorney in whose courthouse Lee Harvey Oswald was murdered and Jack Ruby convicted of the crime, agreed that the decision "would have the effect of abolishing capital punishment." Melvin Belli, who defended Ruby, concurred. William Saxbe, Ohio's attorney general and later United States Senator, commented, "This is another nail in the coffin which is finally going to do away with capital punishment." Arthur Bolton, attorney general of Georgia, thought that *Witherspoon* "will definitely end capital punishment in Georgia." Joe Patterson, Mississippi's attorney general, probably expressed the consensus best when he said, "It looks like the Supreme Court has set about to repeal the various death penalty statutes in the States."

It is doubtful that anyone, friend or foe, accurately estimated the extent of the reaction to this first hard evidence that abolition was on the Supreme Court's agenda. To be sure, there was no public outcry similar to the outraged criticism which often greeted Warren Court decisions restricting the police. Numerous death sentences were vacated by state and federal courts because of violations of the *Witherspoon* rule, though many were quickly reinstated after new penalty hearings. But the general response of courts that were asked to apply *Witherspoon* to other cases, especially state courts, was hostility all out of proportion to the narrowness of the *Witherspoon* rule and the precision of the Supreme Court's opinion.

The lower courts did not, of course, openly defy the Supreme Court. That is not the way the system works. *Witherspoon v. Illinois* was, in Amsterdam's phrase, "cut to ribbons" in the name of assorted legal and factual differences said by lower courts to distinguish it from other cases. Some of these distinctions were obvious makeweights; others were contorted readings of Stewart's opinion. Nevertheless, men could die on the basis of them. One federal court decided that *Witherspoon* applied to systematic exclusion of scrupled jurors; wrongful removal of a small number of jurors did not count heavily enough to vacate a death sentence.[7] The Supreme Court of New Jersey stood Stewart's opinion on its head by ruling that there was no violation where an excluded juror's attitude toward capital punishment was ambiguous.[8] Illinois even enacted a law which proponents thought would totally avoid the impact of *Witherspoon* by providing that any man whose death sentence had been vacated by reason of the Supreme Court decision would be resentenced by a judge rather than by a jury.[9] One purpose of the legislation was to ensure that Richard Speck, the notorious killer of eight Chicago nursing students, would be resentenced to death even if his lawyers successfully argued that he had been condemned in violation of the *Witherspoon* decision.

7

Simon's Frolic

The *Jackson* and *Witherspoon* decisions did not directly threaten government's right to kill; once the states adjusted their criminal procedure to conform to the new rules, they could continue to impose the death penalty. But the two decisions did prove that at least some Supreme Court Justices were prepared to take a hard look at the way men were condemned. As a result, it became somewhat easier to win postponements of impending executions.

Nevertheless, obtaining a stay of execution was still a tense, uncertain business. Lawyers were required to demonstrate ingenuity and persistence in finding a judge or a governor did not act, the judge would be forced to make a prieves. Trial judges had the habit of holding stay applications in abeyance until shortly before a scheduled execution in the hope that the governor would postpone it. If the governor did not act, the judge would be forced to make a decision himself. This might mean that he would deny the application with only days, or even hours, remaining. The result was a series of almost monthly mad cross-country scrambles, with secretaries typing legal papers long into the night and lawyers hurrying them to faraway appellate judges.

Until the two 1968 decisions increased LDF's leverage,

obtaining a stay of execution demanded a great deal of coolness under stress. Although the pressures were great, they were manageable (especially after the "Last Aid Kit" had been distributed to cooperating attorneys) in states where scheduled executions were infrequent. But a year before *Jackson* and *Witherspoon* a more certain method had to be found if executions were to be stopped in California and Florida, the states with by far the largest death-row populations (roughly fifty in Florida, seventy in California). Each had elected new governors in 1965, and both Ronald Reagan in California and Claude Kirk, Jr., in Florida, had campaigned on "law and order" platforms, making a minor campaign issue out of the failure of their predecessors to use the death penalty as a deterrent to crime.

During his election campaign, Kirk made his intentions known dramatically by visiting the Florida State Penitentiary at Raiford. He shook hands with the inmates of death row, and with a courteous smile told them, "If I'm elected, I may have to sign your death warrant." After the election he made his campaign promise good by signing a handful of death warrants which had gathered dust on the desk of the previous governor, Farris Bryant.

For many years, the opponents of capital punishment in Florida had been led by Tobias Simon, a puckish, free-wheeling Miami lawyer who was both an LDF cooperating attorney and chairman of the state chapter of the American Civil Liberties Union. While ostensibly in the private practice of law, Simon was a maverick, temperamentally unable to accept the quiet life of a commercial lawyer. Whenever there was a civil rights skirmish, a teacher strike, or an antiwar protest in Florida, Simon surfaced on the side of the insurgents. He had the reputation of being a man who would try anything once—and sometimes twice.

When Kirk threatened to resume executions, Simon and Alfred Feinberg, his young associate and a former Legal Defense Fund staff member, devised a novel lawsuit to stop him. After the smoke had cleared, it was apparent that they had tapped a new willingness on the part of the judiciary to hear out the arguments against capital punishment.

Simon and his ACLU colleagues represented several of the men in grave danger of electrocution. Hence, they were able to initiate individual lawsuits asserting that each man's death sentence was unconstitutional because of the deficiencies in capital case procedure which Fund legal papers had identified, as well as raising issues particular to each inmate's case. They did this in several Florida cases, including the notorious convictions of Freddie Lee Pitts and Wilbert "Sling Shot" Lee.

In late July 1963, Pitts, Lee, and a group of blacks, including Lee's wife, had stopped at a gas station in Port St. Joe, Florida. Mrs. Lee attempted to use the ladies' room, but two white gas station attendants turned her away; toilet facilities were for "whites only." Several days later the gas station attendants were murdered.

Pitts and Lee pleaded guilty to the crime and were sentenced to death. Later both men claimed that they had been brutally beaten by the police and threatened with death if they did not confess. So far the case was commonplace; men faced with execution often deny their guilt in spite of overwhelming evidence. But in 1968 a white convict named Curtis "Boo" Adams, Jr., confessed that he had committed the murders (he later recanted). It also became known that the state prosecuting attorney had not told defense counsel that the state's chief witness had first falsely accused another man instead of Lee. After this disclosure, brought to public attention by Gene Miller of the Miami *Herald* and lawyers Maurice Rosen and Philip Hubbart, Florida Attorney General Robert L. Shevin eventually asked the state courts to grant Pitts and Lee a new trial.[1] At this trial, held in spring 1972, the judge would not let the jury hear Adams' tape-recorded confession, and Pitts and Lee were again sentenced to death.

Apparent miscarriages of justice like the Pitts and Lee

convictions could not go unchallenged, but at this point Simon and Feinberg felt that the most pressing concern was the death-row inmates who were not represented by law-yers. Angered by Kirk's posturing, they feared that he would execute one of the many men on death row who had no lawyer, no concerned friends, and no pending lawsuit. There were men on the row who risked execution simply because they did not know how to file a suit to block it. The lawyers' anxiety grew after state officials refused to divulge the name and status of every death-row inmate.

If there was anything unconstitutional in the state's administration of the death penalty, Simon and Feinberg reasoned, all Florida death penalties suffered from identical defects of unconstitutional procedure. On this premise, Simon decided that death-row inmates represented a class of persons whose constitutional objections to death case procedures and execution itself could be joined and resolved in one proceeding. Why not present a petition for a writ of habeas corpus to a federal judge in the name of the men Simon represented personally, and ask that it be treated as though it had been filed on behalf of all death-row prisoners? If such a suit was proper, the courts would have to postpone all executions until they finally decided whether the legal rights of the inmates had been infringed.

Resolving common legal claims in one suit, rather than in a score, might seem perfectly sensible to a layman, but to a lawyer such a use of habeas corpus (more precisely habeas corpi) was novel and startling. The writ of habeas corpus, as it took form in medieval England, was a device for determining whether a particular person was unlawfully held in jail. While the writ had undergone great change since the days of Blackstone (1765), use of it to simultane-ously overturn a large number of illegal convictions or sentences was unprecedented.

A class action, as such a suit is called—in which one or several named individuals ask a court to determine their rights, as well as the rights of persons who are legally similarly situated—is a child of modern commercial law. Class actions are often used to simplify dividing up a sum of money among a large number of claimants. When racial discrimination takes the form of a general rule or pattern of behavior against the racial group, civil rights cases are brought as class actions in order to obtain court orders which protect the rights of all Negroes who might suffer discrimination. The plaintiffs in *Brown v. Board of Education,* for example, were entitled to a decree which ordered the school board of Topeka, Kansas, to respect not only their individual rights to a nondiscriminatory school system but the rights of every black parent and schoolchild in the city. Stockholders and consumers have made much use of class actions to allow persons with small individual claims to band together in a single suit and recover damages.

Although the class action device is a common lawyer's tool in civil cases, it had never been used successfully to challenge the convictions or sentences of all the criminals who might benefit from a particular decision. Lawyers always assumed that each convicted criminal had to present a claim that he was entitled to release, a new trial, or a different sentence individually, in a separate proceeding.

It was with considerable skepticism that I heard Feinberg's hurried telephone description of the proposed lawsuit. I tried to be polite, but privately I thought, "Another Toby Simon frolic." At my suggestion, Feinberg added language to the draft petition asking the court to employ a device called a declaratory judgment, and to simply declare the constitutional rights of all death-row inmates to sentencing standards (split verdicts and the like) if it could not actually decide their cases together.

everal days later, on April 13, 1967, surprise replaced pticism when United States District Judge William A. :Rae, Jr., ruled that there was enough substance to the ass action idea to justify a temporary stay. McRae prohibited Florida from executing anyone until he had an opportunity to decide what to do with the unusual suit, and called for legal memoranda. Simon's daring had paid off.

Amsterdam, Greenberg, and Simon immediately flew to Boston to discuss the class action question with Harvard law professor Albert M. Sacks. As a consultant to the committee that revised federal civil procedure rules, Sacks knew a grat deal about class actions. He also had access to Benjamin Kaplan, the Harvard professor who had drafted the pertinent federal rule—known as Rule 23. Sacks thought the suit was a long shot, but said there was no solid doctrinal reason why an argument under Rule 23 could not be sustained.

Amsterdam agreed to try to put the argument on paper. After returning to New York, he worked out the theory that essentially habeas corpus was only a form of procedure for the protection of human liberty, but one which had greatly and consistently evolved into new forms to respond to new threats to liberty. Habeas corpus ought to be sufficiently flexible to meet the needs of this case if, as a matter of fact, it was the only vehicle by which the unrepresented man on death row could obtain access to a court.

This argument required a factual investigation of the legal situation, financial condition, and literacy of the men on death row before the propriety of the class action could be determined. This pleased Amsterdam, for it avoided forcing Judge McRae to decide a difficult procedural issue before he had seen the hard facts depicting the hopeless legal plight of the unrepresented men. It also postponed decision on the class action issue until a time when the initial adverse public reaction to McRae's April 13 order had subsided. Finally, if McRae refused to permit the investigation, Amsterdam could go to the Fifth Circuit Court of Appeals on a record showing that the district judge had refused to let the lawyers gather facts showing that the class action device was the only method of procedure whereby Raiford's unrepresented condemned men could be heard in court.

Four months later McRae concluded that a full factual inquiry was necessary before he could decide whether or not to entertain the class suit. The use of a class action, he agreed, depended on whether or not death-row inmates had effective access to the courts. Were they without lawyers? Were they poor, ignorant, or illiterate, and thereby unable to protect themselves by retaining an attorney or filing their own habeas corpus petition in court? If the answer to these questions was yes, a class suit might be the only way they could assert their legal claims.

In order to find out the answers, McRae accepted an ACLU-LDF offer to interview each consenting death-row inmate and to report back to the court. Amsterdam prepared a questionnaire, Simon scheduled the interviews, and they both put together a task force of ACLU volunteers, LDF cooperating lawyers, and law students who went to Raiford to inquire into the background, employment, education, prior criminal record, financial status, and legal representation of each inmate who agreed to talk to them.

When the job was done, Simon had a profile of forty of the fifty-two men on death row to present to Judge McRae. Of these, thirty-four inmates had already lost their appeals to the Florida Supreme Court and were subject to electrocution at Governor Kirk's whim unless new legal proceedings were brought on their behalf. As Simon had feared, half of these thirty-four had no lawyers or means to hire them; all but six of the other half were represented by the small group of ACLU-LDF lawyers. Fourteen of the men were unskilled laborers; seven were farm laborers; thirty-seven of the forty were entirely destitute; and the remaining three reported having less than a hundred dollars.

At the time of the interviews, death-row inmates were given the Beta test, a nonverbal IQ test commonly used to test prisoners, in order to measure their likely understanding of legal proceedings. If sufficient numbers were of subnormal intelligence, it would be strong evidence that they could not have taken even the initial steps necessary to bring their cases to court and that therefore a class action was necessary to protect their interests. Here again, Simon's position was vindicated. The mean IQ for the group of forty men was 88.35 (80 to 89 is considered "low average"), and the mean number of years of school attendance was 8.62. Further, when the inmates were divided into three groups, those with non-ACLU-LDF counsel had had the highest IQ—almost normal; those without counsel had lower IQ's—distinctly subnormal; and those with ACLU-LDF counsel had the lowest IQ's of all. The lawyers later argued that the results demonstrated that helpless men were without help—though the private joke was that any death-row inmate with any brains was too smart to want ACLU-LDF counsel.

The results of the interviews and tests were forwarded to Judge McRae and a court hearing scheduled. Amsterdam flew to Jacksonville to tell McRae why the facts adduced required treatment of death-row inmates as a class. He told the Judge that the unrepresented, ignorant, and indigent men of Raiford's death row must be heard in one case for want of the ability to institute and maintain individual legal proceedings designed to secure their rights. The punch line of his plea was: "They will be heard together or they will be electrocuted individually. There is no third possibility." One simply could expect no other result, Amsterdam insisted, given their level of intelligence, their poverty, and the fact that their communication with the outside world was totally dependent on the will of their keepers.

Months later McRae decided that the class action was proper.[2] He continued the prohibition on execution and told the lawyers that he would consider their arguments about Florida capital punishment laws.

As soon as Simon's unusual lawsuit and McRae's unexpected response had become generally known, civil rights lawyers in several other capital punishment states implored the Fund to assist them in bringing their own class actions. With the exception of California, where a class suit was brought, Amsterdam, Himmelstein, and I actively discouraged duplication of the Florida case. This was a difficult decision to communicate to the harassed lawyers, many of whom saw a single lawsuit directed from New York as relieving the endless rounds of litigation in scores of death cases. Although there were compelling reasons to avoid presenting the courts with a series of death-row class actions, it was only because judicial abolition had become a national movement, of which the Fund was acknowledged leader, that these reasons were generally accepted by the interested lawyers. Nevertheless, it took great powers of persuasion to restrain them. Take Amsterdam's 1967 letter to a Louisiana lawyer:

I have discussed the question of a Louisiana class action to invalidate the death penalty with [a Louisiana civil rights lawyer]. . . .

The short of the matter is that I have urged him strenuously not to begin any such suit. . . .

The Florida and California cases originated in intense necessity. The governors of those States had begun signing death warrants wholesale, and literally dozens of men were going to die if something was not done. The state and federal judges in the areas were not bold enough to keep stepping into the whirlwind and snatching out individual condemned men. A class action was necessary to save life, and we filed one in each state.

The legal problems with such class lawsuits are staggering. Quite apart from substantive problems, the procedural questions involved in class action habeas, exhaustion of state remedies, federal injunction of state court judgments, res judicata, etc. are limitless, vexing and extremely difficult. Take it from me. I have spent the past couple of months on virtually nothing else.

Now, in the Florida and California actions, we have just about gotten our toes on the beach. We have won the most limited, provisional and precarious kind of interlocutory victories. . . .

What we do *not* need—what would be a disaster in these two cases involving one hundred and ten human lives—is the backwash of some third lawsuit which, if it fortuitously lands before an unsympathetic district judge in a third State, could result in a decisive dismissal with an opinion saying we are all wet. We would then have to go prematurely and precipitously to some Court of Appeals which—on hastily prepared briefs and an inadequate record—could well make a ruling that kills not merely the third lawsuit, but the Florida and California ones as well.

I myself am involved in the representation of condemned men in at least eight States other than Florida and California. I would not for one moment consider a class action suit in any of those States . . . So long as individual habeas corpus petitions and like traditional remedies on traditional legal grounds will suffice to keep these men out of the chair, we are using them. It is in their best interest that we do so. It is in the best interest of one hundred and ten men in Florida and California. It is in the best interest of hundreds of other condemned men, in other States, whose fortunes ride on the outcome of the Florida and California suits.

In the last few weeks, I have spoken to a number of attorneys in a number of States who contacted me because they were interested in bringing suits of this character. I have explained to each why I thought they should not, and they have universally agreed. The plain fact is that death cases are not occasions for venturesomeness in litigation. They are not cases in which making litigation is desirable. Test litigation is well and good, but not with human life at stake. There are enough occasions when one has to go to court to save life that is in immediate jeopardy, and it is these cases . . . that must be made the test cases.

As I understand the Louisiana situation, it presents no such case. No death warrants have been signed for three years. There are no men who are in immediate jeopardy of dying; and, if one or two should come close, they have plenty of traditional remedies to hold the fort. Under these circumstances, I cannot see a class action as anything but a gratuitous gamble with many, many lives. . . .

While McRae pondered the legal issues involved in the Florida death-row case, Ronald Reagan began to make good on *his* election promises. California's first execution in four years took place on April 12, 1967, the day before

McRae stayed all Florida executions. Aaron Mitchell, the thirty-eight-year-old black killer of a white Sacramento policeman, went to his death in the San Quentin gas chamber. While he bled from an unsuccessful suicide attempt with a razor blade, Mitchell chanted to Byron E. Eshelman, the prison chaplain, "I am the second coming of Jesus Christ."[3] Hours after the execution the Judiciary Committee of the California State Senate voted down an abolition bill sponsored by San Francisco Senator George Moscone. After Mitchell died the California way—by suffocation from the fumes of a mixture of cyanide and sulphuric acid—with Reagan's men scheduling new death dates, a class suit similar to Simon's Florida case was desperately needed.

Leroy Clark and Charles Stephen Ralston, soon to be appointed director of the Fund's San Francisco office, were in California at the time. They set up a conference call with Jack Greenberg in New York and after discussion decided to find a group of California attorneys willing to put the case together. Ralston got in touch with Gerald Marcus, a San Francisco attorney who headed an organization called Californians Against Capital Punishment. The next day Marcus agreed to arrange a meeting of interested attorneys, most of whom were volunteer lawyers for the American Civil Liberties Union of Northern California (ACLUNC).

One of the members of the group was Paul Halvonik, who had joined the staff of ACLUNC in November of 1966. Since by that year both the national ACLU and the Southern California ACLU affiliate considered the death penalty a civil liberties issue, Halvonik had been under the mistaken impression that ACLUNC would support pending legislation to abolish the California death penalty. His mistake quickly turned into a source of acute embarrassment when he was forced to inform Senator Moscone, author of the principal California death penalty repeal bill, that ACLUNC would not formally support his legislation. Embarrassment turned to horror when Reagan let Mitchell die.

Before Mitchell's execution, Halvonik had decided to do what he could to change the Northern California affiliate's policy. He approached Marshall Krause, who was then ACLUNC's staff counsel, with the idea of gathering a few death-row inmates for the purpose of a class action death-row suit. Krause agreed to put the matter to the Board of Directors once Halvonik represented a death-row client. Halvonik immediately contacted several lawyers representing men on the row. Before they could agree how to proceed, Halvonik found himself staring at a headline story in the Berkeley *Gazette:* a Florida judge had issued a class action stay for that state's death row. "Imagine," he thought, "some hotshot lawyer has come up with *my* idea."

Spurred by McRae's action, Halvonik entered serious negotiation with Gary Berger, Roy Eisenhardt, Jerome Falk, and Harry Kreamer, all of whom represented death-row inmates. When Marcus invited the group to meet with Amsterdam, Clark, and Ralston, they accepted readily. After several meetings, there was general agreement that a California class action modeled on Simon's suit should be quickly filed in federal court and, if possible, timed so that it might be assigned to a sympathetic judge. The one problem that emerged was a Civil Liberties Union policy against joining with other organizations in bringing lawsuits. No one doubted that the ACLUNC Board would waive the noncooperation policy when it was brought to their attention, but the Board did not meet again for a month. The affiliate's executive director could waive the rule but he was not inclined to do so.

The individual volunteer lawyers, however, made it clear that they were ready to work with the Fund even if ACLUNC did not participate. Halvonik decided that if necessary he would moonlight. With their help, Clark adapted the papers from the Florida case to fit California's somewhat different laws governing capital trials and hurriedly presented them to a San Francisco federal court, where they were assigned to Judge Robert E. Peckham, a forty-seven-year-old ex-state judge whom Lyndon Johnson had appointed the previous year.

Jerome Falk explained the case to Peckham and argued for a class stay. The fledgling lawyer, who had clerked for Mr. Justice Douglas and graduated at the top of his class from the University of California Law School, was to become one of the most highly respected attorneys in the state, but in 1967 he had practiced law for less than a year. By the time the brief hearing was concluded, Falk's stomach was in knots.

"Whatever anyone else may remember in retrospect," Halvonik recalls, "I remember quite vividly that none of us were sanguine about our prospects for success. On the day prior to the filing of the suit, I took some papers over to Leroy Clark who was working in Marcus' office. I handed the research to Leroy, he looked at me, smiled painfully and said, 'If nothing else comes of this, you have to admire my sheer nerve in going down and filing this thing.' I did."

On the day the suit was filed, Clark felt compelled to tell the press that he was not "show boating" and that he was quite "serious" about the suit. So was Judge Peckham. On July 5, 1967, with McRae's example before him and a dozen California inmates scheduled for execution, he prohibited California from killing anyone until he decided whether a class action was proper.[4]

In Florida, lawyers from the state attorney general's office had accepted, although begrudgingly, Judge McRae's stay of all executions until he determined whether death-row inmates were permitted to maintain a class action. But the attorney general of California, Thomas Lynch, a Democrat, was not going to let Reagan, a Republican, stand alone as the defender of capital punishment. Two days after Peckham issued his order, on Friday, July 7, Lynch's office applied to the Court of Appeals for the Ninth Circuit for a writ that would set aside the stay.

A hearing was set for Monday, July 10. One of the lawyers immediately called a court of appeals judge to request additional time to prepare a brief, but the judge refused. "You fellows are always filing these things at the last moment," he commented. The judge obviously thought this was another case of a death-row inmate seeking a late-hour postponement. He remained unconvinced when the lawyer patiently explained that "he" had not filed "this thing" at all—the attorney general had—much less at the last minute. "After all," the judge added, "there's an execution set for Tuesday."

While attempts such as Attorney General Lynch's to persuade federal appellate courts to interfere with ongoing proceedings in trial courts are rarely successful, the Ninth Circuit did not have a favorable track record on the issues which made up the Fund's challenge to capital punishment and it might well have been tempted to overrule Peckham. If Lynch succeeded, several unrepresented men would die almost immediately, and the effect on Judge McRae's resolve might be literally fatal. With but three days to meet the attorney general's challenge, Amsterdam flew from Philadelphia to San Francisco. With the assistance of the volunteer lawyers, he produced a heavily documented seventy-two page brief in defense of Peckham's stay. Halvonik pitched in and helped. He had persuaded his superiors that the Board of Directors would be upset if the ACLUNC received no credit for the work that was being done. (Later, the Board approved participation in the case.)

On the tenth, Amsterdam told three judges of the court of appeals that while death-row inmates had a "vital" interest in remaining alive to assert any rights they might have, California had no such weighty interest in killing them before a final decision in their case. The hearing was short; the judges were anxious to be off for a judicial conference in Seattle. Within an hour after the argument, while an exhausted Amsterdam stood before television cameras that had been set up at the courthouse, the court turned down the attorney general's plea.

Peckham's authority to hear the case now had been established, but a month later he decided not to take Mc-Rae's route. Uncertain of his authority to do so, he would not consider the case as a class action. Nevertheless, he thought that he did have the power to give the lawyers access to San Quentin's death row and to require the state to notify them of scheduled executions so that individual federal habeas corpus petitions could be filed in court for every death-sentenced California prisoner. Once such petitions were filed, stays of execution would be granted automatically: "Justice requires that no condemned man who has standing to raise any federal constitutional issue . . . should be executed until such question is finally adjudicated."[5]

Leroy Clark was bitterly disappointed that Peckham had not agreed to hear the case as a class action, and correctly predicted that other California federal judges would not easily agree to grant automatic stays of execution. Halvonik and Falk would make many "last moment" runs to court to get them. But Judge Peckham had set in motion events which tied the hands of the California executioner. In the course of considering whether to entertain the class action, he had ruled that several of the constitutional questions raised in the case had never been presented to the California state courts, and that before a federal judge decided these questions, state judicial remedies had to be exhausted. This meant returning to the state courts for extended litigation.

The lawyers were delighted to comply. A set of habeas corpus petitions was soon presented to the California Supreme Court in the names of Robert Page Anderson and Frederick Saterfield, two murderers whose executions had been scheduled. The court was asked to refer the cases to an impartial fact-finder and to order him to hear testimony from expert witnesses regarding several of the constitutional claims, such as the physical and psychological cruelty of the death penalty. If given the opportunity to make a factual demonstration of the cruelty of execution, Amsterdam and Himmelstein were prepared to put on the witness stand the social and behavioral scientists, criminologists, and wardens whom they had cultivated over the months.

But a lengthy factual inquiry into capital punishment was not on the agenda of the Supreme Court of California. The judges would consider legal arguments against the death penalty but would not receive oral testimony. Nevertheless, on November 14, 1967, the day before a man named Robert Lee Massie was to be executed, the court on its own initiative entered a stay of all executions in the state. Six months later, after receiving thick legal briefs, the court convened in a crowded San Francisco courtroom to hear the arguments of counsel. Amsterdam represented Anderson and Saterfield; a veteran attorney, Albert W. Harris, Jr., represented the state, and civil libertarians Abraham Lincoln Wirin and Gerald Gottlieb appeared for the ACLU as amicus curiae. Several of the judges seemed interested and sympathetic to the abolitionist position, and as Amsterdam left the courtroom, after having fielded friendly questions from four of them—a majority of the court—he felt relieved. California seemed safe, at least until the court reached a decision.

It took almost eight months for the seven members of the Supreme Court of California to decide the case brought on behalf of Anderson and Saterfield. When the result was announced,[6] the abolitionist position had failed by an eyelash.

In a lengthy opinion written by Justice Louis H. Burke, the court held by a vote of 4 to 3 (with Justice Mathew O. Tobriner, Chief Justice Roger C. Traynor, and Justice Raymond Peters dissenting) that capital punishment as administered by California was not cruel and unusual punishment, and that the Constitution did not require legal standards for the guidance of the jury. The court brushed aside the cruel and unusual punishment issue, but dealt at length with the standards question. It did, however, order new penalty trials for Anderson and Saterfield, on the ground that several persons had been excluded from their juries in violation of the Supreme Court's *Witherspoon* decision. The broad view that the court took of *Witherspoon* would help some inmates, if followed in subsequent cases, but *Witherspoon* alone would only briefly change the status of most men on death row; many would be resentenced to death.

Of the seven justices on the court, four wrote opinions. As the losers, LDF lawyers were disappointed with Justice Burke's reasoning, but welcomed Justice Tobriner's dissent because it contributed an approach which could be used to advantage in other courts: the notion that *Witherspoon* required a total reexamination by lower courts of capital sentencing procedures. In a concurring opinion, Justice Marshall McComb added that he did not even agree that Anderson and Saterfield should have an opportunity to be resentenced (to death or to a possibly lighter sentence).

The lawyers were surprised that they had come within one vote of success, even though the California Supreme Court had been long reputed the most progressive state supreme court, because no court had ever come close to ruling that a jury could not sentence a man to death without some legal principles governing its decision. But if the margin of defeat was unexpectedly slim, the manner of defeat was totally unpredictable. The crucial vote that swung the court against Anderson and Saterfield was that of Justice Stanley Mosk, a former attorney general of California and an outspoken opponent of the death penalty for many years prior to his judicial appointment.

Mosk's brief explanation of his decisive vote could only harden the opposition to abolition of those judges who disliked the death penalty but lacked confidence in their authority to end it. He wrote:

In my years as Attorney General of California (1959–1964), I frequently repeated a personal belief in the social invalidity of the death penalty, notably in testimony before California legislative committees in March 1959, July 1960 and April 1963.

Naturally, therefore, I am tempted by the invitation of petitioners to join in judicially terminating this anachronistic penalty. However, to yield to my predilections would be to act wilfully "in the sense of enforcing individual views instead of speaking humbly as the voice of law by which society presumably consents to be ruled . . ." (Frankfurter, *The Supreme Court in the Mirror of the Justices* (1957), 105 U. Pa. L. Rev. 781, 794).

As a judge, I am bound to the law as I find it to be and not as I might fervently wish it to be. I conclude that Justice Burke has properly stated the current law of California and of every other American jurisdiction that has considered the problem.

In short, restriction of capital punishment was a matter for the legislature; judicial abolition would be to write the prejudices of the judges into the Constitution.

Coming from a known abolitionist like Mosk, such reasoning struck like a blow to the midsection. LDF lawyers thought the death penalty was irrational as well as inhumane, but unwise and immoral laws are not necessarily unconstitutional. Because judges are constantly tempted to equate their own moral principles with the meaning of the law, they are particularly self-defensive the more obviously a legal question mingles with a political or ethical one. By invoking Felix Frankfurter's philosophy that they must exercise enormous restraint in construing constitutional provisions to invalidate legislation, Mosk stood on what many judges regarded as hallowed ground.

In the months that followed the decision, Anderson, Saterfield, and other California death-row inmates joined a parade of appeals to the Supreme Court of the United States, totally disarranging Jerome Falk's previously untroubled practice of real estate and tax law. Falk, along with Amsterdam, Himmelstein, Halvonik, and Ralston, spent hundreds of hours either preparing the necessary petitions or finding volunteers to do the job. Many were written half in New York and half in California and put together by cross-country phone.

One of these cases illustrates the care and tact they brought to this work and, not incidentally, the range of problems that had been taken on when the Fund decided that death row was part of its constituency.

In 1965, Robert Lee Massie had been convicted of robbery, assault with intent to commit murder, and murder, and sentenced to death.[7] An appeal to the Supreme Court of California proved unsuccessful. An execution date was set for October 10, 1967, and later postponed first to November 2 and then to November 15. Massie wrote to his attorney, Roger S. Hanson, requesting that Hanson take no further action in his behalf: he wished to die. Massie also wrote to Justice Douglas, Chief Justice Traynor, and Judge Peckham, informing them that he desired no interference with his execution.

Thirty-six hours before Massie was due to die in the gas chamber, Peckham asked Hanson and Falk to find out if he might change his mind. By the time the two lawyers drove across the Golden Gate Bridge to San Quentin, normal visitor facilities were closed for the night. Hanson and Falk were escorted through the darkened prison onto death row, admitted to a cell, and permitted to speak to the condemned man. A guard stood by the door with a shotgun. Massie was adamant about his wish to be executed and he treated Falk as an interloper. Falk suddenly realized that he was in a tiny room with a man who said he wanted to die, and that all that Massie need do to have his wish would be to force the guard to shoot. "I continued to listen to Massie," Falk reported, "but his words kept mingling with thoughts of ricocheting shotgun pellets."

The next morning, despite Massie's stubborn wish to die, Falk pressed Peckham to halt the execution until he could determine whether Massie was sane. Falk pointed to an affidavit obtained from Dr. Bernard Diamond, an experienced psychiatrist on the faculty of the University of California at Berkeley. Although Diamond had not examined Massie, he had concluded on the basis of Massie's background and public statements that there was a reasonable probability that he was suffering from serious mental illness and was therefore incapable of exercising normal judgment as to what was in his best interest.

While the lawyers waited for Judge Peckham to decide whether to stay the execution, a reporter burst through the courtroom door and announced that the Supreme Court of California had stayed all executions in the state. Hanson and Falk subsequently filed a petition for a writ of habeas corpus in the California Supreme Court asking for a determination of Massie's sanity. After its November 1968 decision in the *Anderson* and *Saterfield* cases, the California court denied the petition and an appeal was taken on Massie's behalf to the United States Supreme Court. But Massie again attempted to thwart efforts to save him by filing his own motion to dismiss the petition for review, arguing that as a party to the petition he no longer had any interest in the issue being litigated—i.e., his own life. Under the Supreme Court rules, dismissal appeared to be his right.

Massie was not unusual in employing the death penalty to realize a death wish. An amicus curiae brief filed by the American Psychiatric Association in Maxwell's case had identified three groups for whom capital punishment served as an incitement to kill rather than a deterrent: those who felt that the death penalty was a just punishment for their wrongdoing, and so might murder to bring it about; those to whom the risk of danger had an attraction; and those lured by the prospect of a spectacular trial and public attention.

In 1966 Dr. Louis J. West had delivered a paper before the annual meeting of the American Psychiatric Association in which he argued that capital punishment often becomes "a promise, a contract, a covenant between the society and certain warped mentalities who are moved to kill."[8] West illustrated his point with case histories, includ-

ing one of a man who had committed an impulsive, senseless killing because "I was just tired of living." In another,
an Oklahoma convict had formally petitioned a state court
to impose the death penalty and complained that though he
had pled guilty in an earlier case he had only received a life
sentence. Another Oklahoman, James French, asked for
the death penalty after he had been convicted of murder.
When he was sentenced to life, he attempted suicide. When
this failed, he strangled a cell mate in order to force the
state to do the killing that he felt he deserved. French was
the only man executed in the United States in 1966.

Massie's request that the Supreme Court dismiss his case
squarely presented the question of whether he had the right
to be executed by the state notwithstanding that litigation
might eliminate his death sentence. On December 2, 1969,
Falk and Amsterdam took the only route consistent with
legal ethics that might thwart Massie's wish to die. They
drafted a letter informing the United States Supreme Court
of the case and urged that "if Massie is to be the first man to
be executed in California in thirty-one months, and the first
man in the nation since June 1967," surely that should only
happen after "a fair determination . . . that his conviction
and death sentence are constitutionally valid" or that he is
legally competent to waive any constitutional claims that he
might have.

Massie's case also raised questions which went to the
heart of the lawyer-client relationship. The canons of professional ethics provide that a lawyer owes total devotion to
the interests of his client. It is generally the client who
defines these interests, while the advocate serves only to
accomplish them. But does a man have a right to demand
that the state kill him—if killing by the state is unconstitutional—by dismissing his attorney, by the mere failure to
pursue legal proceedings? If there is any truth to the assertion of the Joint Conference on Professional Responsibility
that the lawyer's "highest loyalty" is to "those fundamental
processes of government and self-government upon which

the successful functioning of our society depends,"[9] then the attorney's course is *not* dictated solely by his client's death wish.

For Amsterdam and Falk, the matter was complicated by the fact that Massie's death would have affected every other death-row inmate by breaking the moratorium, which was then over two years old. They took grateful refuge from the agonizing dilemma of his case in the possibility of Massie's insanity, which, if established, would destroy his capacity, legal as well as moral, to choose between life and death.

In the April 1971 issue of *Esquire* magazine, Massie publicly aired his position by publishing a blistering condemnation of "NAACP lawyers" who alleged in numerous courts without "supporting evidence" that he was insane. He could sympathize with men on death row who claimed that they had been convicted without sentencing standards, but he could not see how their cases applied to him. "I pled guilty to first degree murder and was tried by a judge, not a jury." Massie did not advocate capital punishment; indeed, he thought it the utmost hypocrisy in a Christian. But now that he was sentenced to death, he found that death was far preferable to life imprisonment, "a fate worse than death." His plea for a speedy end is worth quoting at length:

. . . it is only fitting that my life should culminate in the gas chamber. From the time I was seven years old I have been a ward of the State. From the years of seven to ten I was placed in a number of foster homes; from eleven to fourteen I lived in the state reformatory (euphemistically called a "Training School for Boys"); and from fifteen to twenty-three, I was in jails and penitentiaries. Finally, at the age of twenty-three I was delivered to the Warden at San Quentin, where it is hoped that I will shortly graduate to the merciful oblivion called *death*. It is readily apparent that my years of penal servitude have not helped me, nor has it helped society. Therefore, what would be gained by spending the rest of my natural life in prison? I have never contributed anything worthwhile to society and never will.

For what reason should I strive to have my judgment of death reduced to life in prison? Is life on earth such a blessing or so precious that I should be desirous of spending it in a dehumanized hellhole of steel and concrete where the law of the jungle and degeneracy reign supreme, where all human and moral values are considered a weakness? . . . Rotting away in prison for the rest of my days and deteriorating mentally, perhaps even going completely insane is not a very pleasing incentive for continuing to cling to this life.[10]

Brave, moving words, and certainly not written by a madman. Several years later, however, when his legal situation had changed, Massie had mellowed enough to ask Jerry Falk to be his lawyer.

The Supreme Court of the United States held all death cases, including Massie's, in abeyance while it pondered William Maxwell's. In 1968, after the Court of Appeals for the Eighth Circuit had finally upheld Judge Henley, the high Court granted review in his case, then called *Maxwell v. Bishop*.[11] But the Court limited its grant of review to the standards and single-verdict questions. Apparently it was unwilling to decide whether the rape study had proved racial discrimination. Perhaps, it was speculated, the Court wished to deal with capital punishment on a national basis, rather than strike at a sentencing pattern which only could be shown in the South. Fund lawyers hoped to learn more on March 4, 1969, the day Maxwell's case would be argued to the Court.

8

Maxwell

The image of the Anglo-American lawyer was once insepa-
rable from his identity as a master of oral advocacy. Bacon,
Webster, Erskine, and Darrow, to name several famous
lawyers of the past, were part of a great tradition of presenting ideas lucidly, and moving men by speech in ways often
unpredictable and against the weight of prejudice and fashion. Buttressed by the theatricality of the adversary system,
a form which sharpens moral alternatives by locking opposing forces in conflict, lawyers captured the public imagination through the beauty and pith of their words. Their
speech seemed all the more powerful because they periodi-
cally stood against the state as defenders of the small, the
unpopular, the rebellious, and the presumed guilty.

In England, judges still consider questions of law presented orally by lawyers without the benefit of written
briefs, but in this country the tradition of the eloquent
pleaders is in decline. Many of the most skilled and influential attorneys in the United States never appear before a
jury and rarely even go to court. The few lawyers that the
public knows best—Edward Bennett Williams, F. Lee
Bailey, Percy Foreman, William Kunstler—remain those
who have fired the trial courts with emotion, but most

lawyering is matter-of-fact, businesslike, and takes place outside the courtroom.

Appellate court judges can be moved by passionate advocacy of the sort which still occasionally stirs both juries and public opinion, but their attention is directed to considerations required by their professional role as rulemakers for future cases. Effective oral argument is conversational, not oratorical. Lawyers persuade appellate judges by their ability to reinterpret earlier rules of law in terms of contemporary social necessity, to suggest practical accommodations, and to expose unforeseen dangers in a particular course of action. Legal briefs filed with these judges marshal facts and analyze earlier court decisions, but the successful advocate must also demonstrate the rights of his clients by words spoken in open court.

The art of persuasion is particularly demanding for the law reformer. For his client to win, he must press social realities and expediency, as well as principle, on the judges; otherwise they will have no reason to alter the law as it stands. To do this effectively, he clothes factors such as poverty, discrimination, caprice and incapacity in the murky language of the law—which, until recently, rarely exposed the practical considerations that guided the judicial hand, and usually contributed to a pretense that a particular decision was as inevitable as the sunrise.

The Supreme Court of the United States is the law reformers' target. Most lawyers are happy to win their case in the local police court; attorneys with national policy objectives aim for Washington.

On the first Monday in October, the Court formally convenes in its tomblike Capitol Hill courthouse, and the following week it begins to hear oral arguments in the cases that it has agreed to review. During its 1971 term, the Court received some 3,200 applications for review and denied over 3,000; approximately 150 received full consideration requiring oral argument.[1] Depending on the complexity and importance of the few cases chosen for argument, the nine Justices listen to lawyers for each side for an hour or half-hour. This process continues for two weeks; the Court then recesses to decide the cases it has heard, write opinions, and pass on the stream of new applications for review, before it again picks up the schedule of cases awaiting argument.

In 1949 the Supreme Court decided that oral argument of questions of law before a federal court of review was not so essential to a fair hearing as to be required by the Constitution in every case. But over the years the Justices have been almost unanimous in regarding this deceptively simple process—in which a lawyer stands before the Court, describes the facts of the case, presents a legal argument, and is questioned—as of great consequence. Justice William J. Brennan probably summarized the published views of the Justices when he described oral argument as an "absolutely indispensable ingredient of appellate advocacy . . . often my whole notion of what a case is about crystallizes at oral argument." Brennan continued:

Oral argument with us is a Socratic dialogue between Justices and counsel. Woe the poor lawyer who comes there with a prepared argument. He doesn't get beyond, "Mr. Chief Justice, if the Court please," and bing, a question from the bench throws him off the track. That is as it should be, because oral argument is the way we get answers to things that are bothering us about the case.[2]

As Brennan suggests, oral argument breathes life into the deadly paper which is the material of the Justices' professional lives. It enables them to air publicly the doubts that they must resolve privately before deciding where to balance the competing claims which go into national resolution of an important legal issue. In the dialogue of argument, they openly test the limits of a proposed legal rule, learn more about the concrete circumstances from which a case arose, and attempt to cut through the ambiguities and evasions of the printed word.

But a good deal of the virtue claimed for this process in the writings of the Justices is wishful thinking. Too many lawyers appearing before the Court are untutored in its concerns and are not likely to be educated in the thirty minutes most are allotted to present the facts and law of their case. Just as visits to a trial court rarely approach the drama of the stage trial, with its stereotyped but exciting clash of stern judge, tough prosecutor, and wily defense counsel, so fresh ideas rarely emerge from the more aristocratic, cerebral, and calculated confrontation between intellectuals attempting to hammer out general principles of law from a particular lawsuit.

To be sure, the lawyers who argue before the Court are often the leaders of the profession and can be expected to have prepared their cases thoroughly. The informed viewer —as opposed to the befuddled tourists, who take in the Court between visits to the Washington Monument and the Pan American Union—often finds oral argument informative and factual. Nevertheless, many advocates doubt that what they say or do not say makes a difference. Perhaps this is because oral argument is rarely vivid or moving and because the time available for argument is often too short to do more than skim the surface. The sense that the principles governing a nation are evolved from the process, that the relevant considerations are being fully articulated and intensely felt, simply does not predominate.

Those interested in law reform must face another disappointment. The view that the Justices take of the "real" world is partially the product of the portrait rendered at oral argument by the lawyers, but the reality of the poor, the criminal, and the dissenter tends to be as remote from the lawyers as from the judges. Too often the hidden assumptions of the middle-class view of life color the character of the Court's public deliberations.

Relatively few lawyers, of course, are fortunate enough to argue before the Supreme Court of the United States. These few are not—as are British barristers—members of a small and well-trained cadre of men whose profession is oral advocacy; rather, they are merely those attorneys who have charge of a case in which significant legal issues lurk. But even the fact that a lawyer is on intimate terms with his clients and their concerns does not guarantee that he will employ the English language with the precision and eloquence necessary to move men to do justice. American legal education includes a course called "moot court," in which students prepare an appellate brief and argue a case to a panel of fellow students, a visiting jurist, or lawyer. Judged by the results, little else in the average lawyer's experience prepares him to endow oral argument with the clarity and grace demanded to make it a realistic means of ensuring some measure of equity for the poor and outcast.

In most cases, therefore, the Supreme Court explores the more obvious considerations, but the appearance of the decision-making process which argument represents is too often dull and uninspiring. This is regrettable, especially in cases involving pressing social issues, for without style the process of decision seems more bureaucratic than it may actually be. It evokes a feeling that the Court's views are mainly preconceived, and that argument is a search for justification rather than illumination.

Fortunately, there are exceptional lawyers who present elegantly spoken legal arguments, who respond to questions deftly, and at the same time manage to convey a feeling of life beyond the courtroom and of the stakes involved in the Court's decisions. Lawyers who knew Tony Amsterdam looked forward to the argument in Maxwell's case with a certain restrained optimism because he was such an advocate—and it would take inspired advocacy to persuade the Court to alter the settled capital case practices of some forty states.

Amsterdam's skill derived from familiarity with prior Supreme Court decisions and an exceptional capacity to anticipate questions. If he had any fault as an advocate, it was a tendency toward dense, complex sentences that were difficult for the uninitiated to follow. But during the two previous years he had argued challenges to capital punishment laws in Arkansas, Florida, California, New Jersey, Louisiana, and Texas. As a result, his expression of the complex issues had been much simplified, and by March 1969, his legal argument on the standards and single-verdict claims was polished and clear.

Hopes that Maxwell's case spelled the beginning of the end for capital punishment were also based on the character of the bench that would hear the case. Many observers felt that Amsterdam could persuade at least five and perhaps six members of the Court.

Chief Justice Earl Warren, since his appointment by President Eisenhower in 1953, had dignified the Court with a persistent concern for basic decency which, as former Solicitor General Archibald Cox has pointed out, often disturbed lawyers "engrossed by the intellectual and institutional side of the law." In his stately way, the Chief often fixed his eye on government lawyers appearing before the Court and asked, "Is that fair?" Warren had supported most of the Court's criminal procedure reforms and was blamed for all of them by a substantial segment of the public, but as a prosecuting attorney, attorney general, and governor, he had helped send many men to the California gas chamber. How this experience would affect his view of the case was a troubling question.

Justice Hugo Black, a member of the Court since 1937 and its senior judge in point of service, presented Amsterdam with an entrenched view of the Constitution at odds with his argument. Black believed that the Court was powerless to reverse state criminal convictions by finding a violation of the Due Process Clause of the Fourteenth Amendment unless the states had failed to accord one of the protections specified in the Bill of Rights. His consistent and oft-stated view was like a rock which an advocate could navigate around but never ignore. As Maxwell's contentions depended largely on a more flexible and open-ended view of the Due Process Clause—one which permitted the Court to act in the name of basic fairness—Amsterdam could anticipate Black's hostility. Additionally, Black had dissented in *Witherspoon* and commented negatively on the abolitionists' approach: "If this Court is to hold capital punishment unconstitutional, I think it should do so forthrightly, not by making it impossible for states to get juries that will enforce the death penalty."[3]

Even as a Washington corporation lawyer, Justice Abe Fortas had demonstrated great interest in criminal law reform. He had represented the defendant in a well-known case, *Durham v. United States,*[4] that had resulted in a change of the insanity test used by the District of Columbia courts. Later he had been appointed by the Supreme Court to represent Clarence Gideon in the famous right-to-counsel case. After Lyndon Johnson coaxed Arthur Goldberg into resigning his Court post in 1965 to become Ambassador to the United Nations, he appointed Fortas to replace him. With few exceptions, Fortas picked up where Goldberg left off and consistently voted in support of the constitutional claims of dissenters, blacks, and criminal defendants. In a landmark decision, *In re Gault,*[5] that imposed rudimentary procedural restrictions on state juvenile courts, he had taken a view of the Due Process Clause as sweeping as Justice Black's was narrow. LDF observers counted on Fortas' vote, but if their expectations were misplaced they might find out at oral argument: he had the pleasant habit of commenting on points raised at argument with thinly veiled approval or disapproval.

In contrast, Justice Byron White, who had stayed Maxwell's execution but dissented in *Witherspoon* and *Jackson,* had the habit of asking devilish questions—often befuddling logical conundrums. To many he seemed as cryptic on the bench as Fortas was blunt. White had been the Deputy Attorney General of the United States before John F.

Kennedy appointed him to the Court in 1962, and he often favored the prosecution in criminal law matters. His primary concern in several cases, however, had been whether the lower courts were equipped to give a defendant a fair opportunity to prove his case. White, for example, had written an important opinion requiring the states to give jury trials to criminal defendants.[6] If he viewed the role of the Supreme Court as ensuring that the lower courts gave a full and fair hearing to individual claims, it was possible that he would dislike the single verdict which LDF argued kept relevant evidence from the sentencing jury. Still it was difficult to expect support from a Justice who had written in his *Witherspoon* dissent that the Court "should restrain its dislike for the death penalty and leave the decision about appropriate penalties to branches of government whose members, selected by popular vote, have authority not extended to this Court."[7]

John Marshall Harlan, a member of the Court since 1955, came closest of any of its members to being the "great dissenter" of the Warren era. But if Harlan was, as journalists inclined to oversimplify often wrote, a judicial conservative, he was a special brand of conservative, one who mixed a keen sense of the institutional limitations of the Court with a healthy concern for due process and First Amendment values. Many lawyers thought that Harlan recognized better than Felix Frankfurter, his spiritual teacher, that there were occasions when the conservative judicial credo—restraint; honoring precedent; and deference to the states, Congress, and the executive branch—had to give way, but he was especially difficult to persuade that state laws were unconstitutional. Although Harlan violently disagreed with Black's view that the Due Process Clause of the Fourteenth Amendment imposed on the states the specific guarantees of the Bill of Rights and nothing else, his construction of the Due Process Clause could contain as meager fare as Black's. In Harlan's view, the courts might identify constitutional rights that the framers had not particularized in the Bill of Rights but only the most flagrant cases of foul play qualified as constitutional violations.

Everything Harlan did, he did well. His opinions were thoughtful and crammed with legal lore; his dissents often laid bare the flaw in a majority's reasoning. He was the Justice most esteemed by the Court's academic critics. Although his mind never seemed closed to anything reasonable, Harlan appeared a difficult man for Amsterdam to persuade that the settled capital case procedures of four-fifths of the states were unconstitutional.

Potter Stewart, an Ohio Republican appointed to the Court by President Eisenhower in 1959, was something of an enigma when it came to capital punishment. Stewart had dissented almost as frequently as Harlan from Warren Court criminal law decisions, but he had written the majority opinions in both *Jackson* and *Witherspoon*. He was, however, an active questioner and often became involved in a spirited dialogue with an attorney. As several Fund lawyers believed that his vote was essential to victory, Stewart would be watched closely during the argument.

The remaining three Justices, William J. Brennan, Thurgood Marshall and William O. Douglas, formed with the Chief Justice and Fortas the core of the Warren Court "liberal" majority during the late 1960's. Back in 1963, Douglas and Brennan had joined Justice Goldberg in questioning the constitutionality of the death penalty in rape cases. Marshall's experience as a defense lawyer in many racially-charged Southern capital cases contributed to the impression that he was hostile to the death penalty. Although none of the three had expressed a view on the single verdict or standards questions, they could be expected to support the Fund position in this case simply because their published opinions so often reflected a desire to provide the accused with a highly protective set of criminal procedures. Any question from them which suggested skepticism toward the LDF arguments for standards and split verdicts would place Amsterdam in a difficult position. But if Brennan,

Marshall, and Douglas were joined by Fortas and one of
the remaining five, Maxwell would win. Certainly Warren,
and perhaps even Stewart, seemed likely to go along.

Such speculations—for, in fact, they could be sure of
nothing—occupied the minds of LDF lawyers on March 4,
1969, as Amsterdam took his place at the counsel table.
Representing the party who was appealing from the decision of the courts below, he was to speak first. Amsterdam
would be followed by Albert W. Harris, Jr., the attorney
who had been his adversary in the California death case
(California had obtained special permission to argue orally
to the Court as amicus curiae), and then by the youthful
Arkansas Assistant Attorney General, Don Langston.

After Warren called out the name of the case—*Maxwell
v. Bishop*—Amsterdam stepped to the small lectern several
feet from the Chief Justice and immediately launched into a
description of how Arkansas law dealt with men accused of
rape.*

Death had been the mandatory punishment for rape until
1915, when the trial jury was also authorized to return a
verdict of life imprisonment. Over the years, the Arkansas
courts had defined the crime of rape so that it covered an
enormous range of factual situations: victims could be of
any age; may have been left harmed or unharmed; an
offender might be on intimate terms with, or a stranger to,
the ravished woman; the amount of compulsion necessary
to constitute rape ranged from verbal threats to brutal
assault. From this variety of factual situations, the jury
decided who would live and who would die. Thus, "the
penalty for rape in Arkansas is not really death but rather
subjection to a process of selection by individual juries
which can result in death."

---

* In order to aid the reader's comprehension of Supreme Court
argument, colloquy has been summarized and rephrased; quotation
marks indicate exact quotes from the Justices and the lawyers appearing before them.

Arkansas juries were instructed by the trial judge in the law defining rape before they decided whether to convict or acquit, but they were given no instructions whatsoever about the life-death choice they must make. The jury was not directed to any general inquiry such as "Would society be safe if this man were incapacitated in the penitentiary for life?" "Is he reformable or incurable?" The jury was not told, for instance, that because the defendant suffered from a mental illness or had no prior criminal record, the death penalty might not be appropriate. Nor was it told that certain matters, such as race, simply could not be considered. "For all a jury knows," Amsterdam continued, "the law considered everything relevant and nothing irrelevant."

At this point, Justice White interrupted to ask the first of a series of questions no less troublesome for being predictable. Suppose a judge did the sentencing: would he have any more standards to go on than a jury?

Unlike a jury, Amsterdam replied, a judge is a "professional sentencer" who develops a certain consistency of judgment when he sentences. But in capital cases, he conceded, there were usually no more sentencing standards available to the judge than to the jury.

Justice Harlan wanted to know if Amsterdam claimed that it was unconstitutional for a state to make the death penalty mandatory upon conviction of a capital offense.

Amsterdam turned to face Harlan, whose eyesight was almost totally impaired: "Making the death sentence mandatory would have none of the problems that Maxwell's case raises because there would be no individuating process, no choosing between men without rhyme or reason. It might, however, run afoul of other constitutional provisions, such as the Cruel and Unusual Punishment Clause of the Eighth Amendment, to make death follow upon conviction regardless of the facts."

Amsterdam resumed his description of Arkansas procedure in rape cases by focusing on the single verdict—the practice that required the jury to decide guilt and penalty simultaneously. He emphasized that if the defendant took the witness stand to plead that he should not die, every bad act in his life could be brought out on cross-examination.

Chief Justice Warren stared down incredulously. "Every act throughout his life?" he asked.

"There is a remoteness requirement," Amsterdam replied, "but it is insignificant." In one case, Arkansas had permitted a prosecuting attorney to bring up a twenty-year-old liquor violation. If, on the other hand, the defendant does not take the witness stand, he "goes to the slaughter like a dumb beast deprived of his best witness—himself—for only he can explain his motivation and he best can tell of the childhood circumstances that the jury may take into account as mitigation."

At this point, Amsterdam paused for an instant to emphasize that he was now addressing the main legal issue head-on. Of course the question was not whether this "Arkansas scheme may be unfair and unwise" but whether it violated the Constitution of the United States. "I believe that it violates the Due Process Clause of the Fourteenth Amendment, because it involves sentencing on a case by case basis by jurors who need not even discuss their reasons and who need not decide on a common ground; because each jury may condemn on a ground which is totally inconsistent with the reasons employed to determine the cases of other defendants; and because there need be no relationship between the purposes of having a death penalty and its imposition in any case. In short, there is an absence of the rule of law, of general principle. Life and death depend only on the shifting whims of the different men and women who sit as jurors."

Legislators have passed the buck, Amsterdam continued. They have decided that a mandatory sentence in all capital cases would be intolerable, but instead of identifying the characteristics which they want to lead to a death sentence, they have left the entire matter in the hands of each jury.

The result is that juries get away with the most flagrant actions without their verdicts being upset. An example was the record of racial sentencing by Arkansas juries in rape cases. The lower courts rejected the proof of racial discrimination offered in this case as insufficient, but they did concede that there was a great deal of evidence suggesting prejudice against blacks. Under a system without standards, however, it was extremely difficult to prove that a jury was discriminating.

Suddenly Amsterdam's voice seemed that of an angry prophet: "I think that this Court would not, for example, sustain an Arkansas sentencing procedure which provided that every man convicted of rape should roll the dice and if it came up 7 or 11 he would die; any other number, he would live.

"Actually, what Arkansas has done is worse. It is worse because I assume that the dice would not decide on the grounds of race, and it is worse because the 2 out of 12 chances are at least identical."

A moment later, Justice Fortas ruthlessly exposed a fundamental difficulty with Amsterdam's position. Could standards be drafted? If so, what would they be? These were questions Amsterdam had expected—they had been asked of him often by judges and journalists—but that did not make persuasive answers any easier to find. The last thing the Supreme Court wanted was embroilment in a continuing controversy over the constitutionality of complicated state laws in a wholly new area. But if the Court required standards, would it not have to pass on the validity and police the enforcement of those that were adopted?

Amsterdam's answer to Fortas' question sought to reduce this anxiety. It would be improper in this case, he replied cautiously, for the Supreme Court to set forth anything more than the *need* for standards. The standards ultimately adopted should reflect specific judgments by each state about the purpose and utility of the death penalty within its borders and rightly should be the work of a state legislature or judiciary.

The Model Penal Code, adopted by the distinguished American Law Institute, provided one approach to the drafting of standards that might be acceptable. The Code set forth aggravating and mitigating circumstances about which the judge instructed the jury in murder cases; it did not provide capital punishment for rape. The Code, Amsterdam continued, was an example of rules that guide and channel the vast discretion of the capital case jury. A state could also choose to require certain factual findings, for example that the defendant used a weapon, injured the victim permanently, or committed the offense on a person of a grossly disparate age, before a death sentence could be imposed. Each state might work out a different formula, but the Constitution requires that they attempt to draft standards.

Here Amsterdam summed up. "The point is that Arkansas has not done anything like this. It has said . . . whatever the jury does is acceptable."

Then it was Harris' turn. In order to obtain permission from the Court to argue as amicus curiae in a case arising from another state, Harris had cited the large number of men on his state's death row and the many pending challenges to California capital case procedure.

California and Arkansas, Harris began, both permit a jury to determine whether to impose a death sentence without any guiding standard or instruction, but there is one important difference between them: "California has a separate sentencing hearing or penalty trial before the jury at which the defendant could present any evidence he wished in mitigation and the state could present evidence in aggravation." In short, California had abandoned the single verdict.

Justice Fortas quickly inquired whether instructions were given to the jury at the end of this penalty trial.

Harris answered that only general directions on the duties of a juror were given; in California, as in Arkansas, there were no sentencing standards.

Harris could not agree, however, with Amsterdam's contention that the legislature was passing the buck to individual juries. "The fact is that it is impossible to set out in advance all the considerations which might relate to capital punishment." Kindness and compassion are involved in jury deliberations and no penal code or set of rules can assure mercy. "Most defendants," Harris reasoned, "would have better opportunities to seek a life sentence under the present system of jury discretion than they would have under any conceivable set of formal standards." Further, "it was not insignificant" that no state had yet adopted the Model Penal Code provisions. Perhaps, Harris' remark implied, the Code was merely the result of the lofty, but impractical, hopes of law professors.

Looking directly at Justice Stewart, Harris mentioned that the *Witherspoon* decision had assured defendants a fair shake at sentencing because now juries included persons with distaste for capital punishment.

Stewart immediately brought up a troublesome point. The transcript which recorded whether persons with scruples against capital punishment had been excluded when the jury was selected for Maxwell's 1962 trial was not part of the official record on file with the Supreme Court. Where was it?

In reply to a similar question, Amsterdam had told Stewart that he assumed it was still on file with the court of appeals which had heard Maxwell's last appeal, for that court had considered the transcript but had not made it part of the official record of the case. But Harris announced that he and Langston had the official transcript with them in Court.

Stewart then asked Harris whether, if a violation of *Witherspoon* were shown by the transcript, the Supreme Court could avoid the standards and single-verdict claims—

both of which raised novel and difficult issues—in Maxwell's case. Could the Court set aside the death sentence on *Witherspoon* grounds even though the question had not been formally raised?

Harris said that he had read the transcript and was sure that it revealed illegal selection of jurors.

Warren then interrupted to ask whether there was any objection to having the transcript read by the Supreme Court. Like Stewart's question, the Chief Justice implied that if Harris were right, the Court might choose to follow its policy of avoiding decision of difficult constitutional questions when a case could be decided on a narrower ground.

Amsterdam rose to say that he had no objection, but that he would like to speak to the question later, in the few minutes that he had remaining for rebuttal.

After Harris concluded, Don Langston argued for Arkansas. He was asked a number of questions about state criminal procedure, and some of his answers made the Justices chuckle. For instance, at Fortas' prodding, Langston conceded that as far as he knew, Arkansas judges never overruled jury decisions in capital cases. Though they might have power to do so, judges in Arkansas are elected, and they do not go around setting aside jury verdicts, because they think it would "look bad."

Langston argued that the real penalty in a rape case was death, and that a life sentence was actually mercy extended by the jury. The implication was that the jury merely extended clemency by not imposing the death penalty. He hammered home a point made by Harris: mercy required conscience, not standards; no legislature could provide compassion by writing a set of rules.

After Langston sat down, Amsterdam presented his rebuttal. This right of reply is the great test of an advocate because time is short (Amsterdam had three minutes) and often he must improvise to deal with arguments raised for the first time by his opponent.

California and Arkansas, Amsterdam began, admit that they have an arbitrary procedure. "They defend it simply on the grounds that it is necessary, that you can't do anything else. Both in reading their briefs and in hearing the oral argument, I was struck that I had heard this argument somewhere before. And so I looked around. I find that indeed I have.

"The argument that you have to allow arbitrary discretion so as to individualize on the facts of each individual case was originally written by William Paley in 1785. He was defending the English Bloody Code under which 250 crimes were capital, and he defended it on the ground that you couldn't get a narrower formulation. There was just no way in which you could cut down on some of those crimes by fixing standards. . . .

"Paley argued that 'the law of England was based on the wise policy of keeping in the net every crime which under any possible circumstances may merit the punishment of death and then letting individual circumstances ferret it out.' He concluded that 'the wisdom and humanity of this design furnish a just excuse for the multiplicity of capital offenses which the laws of England are accused of creating beyond those of other countries.'

"That was a justification for a code of 250 capital crimes."

But for the ticklish *Witherspoon* issue that had been raised, Amsterdam would have stopped here. Stewart's question, however, threatened to derail a carefully planned test case. If the Court were to examine the transcript, decide Maxwell's case on the basis on *Witherspoon,* and not agree immediately to reconsider the standards and single verdict claims in another case, the moratorium would be in grave danger.

For several reasons, the Fund's brief in Maxwell's case had not argued that *Witherspoon* had been violated. The petition for a writ of habeas corpus on which the appeal was based had been drafted two years before the *Wither-*

spoon decision and did not challenge exclusion of scrupled jurors; the Supreme Court generally refused to consider legal issues that had not been presented first to the lower courts; even if this appeal was lost, the *Witherspoon* violation could be presented to the federal courts in Arkansas. But now that several Justices had indicated interest in considering the selection of jurors in Maxwell's case, Amsterdam's obligation to his client meant that he could not suggest that the Court by-pass any potentially winning issue. The problem was that Fund lawyers represented other men whose interests were better served by obtaining a decision on standards and single verdict from the Warren Court. The Chief Justice had announced his retirement effective in June, and his replacement might shift the delicate balance of the Court on criminal law issues.

With only a minute of his time left, Amsterdam had to confront a dilemma that had troubled Fund lawyers from the day they had agreed to represent anyone on death row who sought their help: would obligations to individual clients clash with the interests of the whole class of condemned men?

Amsterdam's solution to the dilemma was ingenious. He told the Court that he welcomed consideration of the *Witherspoon* claim, but that at the same time he was forced to emphasize that an unconstitutional exclusion of jurors in Maxwell's case did not justify the Court's avoidance of the standards and single-verdict issues.

"Maxwell has been on death row in Arkansas since 1962. He has twice come within a few days of death. The last time to be saved only by a stay issued by Mr. Justice White of this Court." What many lower courts have done with *Witherspoon* is to vacate the death sentence but order a new penalty trial to determine whether the defendant should live or die. "It would be inhumanity second only to killing this man" not to resolve now "whether the State of Arkansas has any right to try him for his life under the unconstitutional procedures that we are challenging." In

short, Arkansas procedure " . . . is unconstitutional for
violation of the rule of law, and we hope that the Court will
reach and decide the issue in this case."

A week after the argument, Amsterdam, Himmelstein,
and I met to share our reactions. The basic legal argument
for sentencing standards and against the single verdict had
emerged unscathed. None of the Justices had publicly declared his agreement with our views, but none had explicitly
rejected them. Maxwell himself seemed out of danger.
Arkansas had come very close to conceding that he had a
Witherspoon claim that justified a new penalty trial. Ironically, however, his improved prospects caused some dismay, for if the Court decided to take advantage of the
Witherspoon issue to postpone consideration of the standards and single-verdict questions until another day, stays of
execution might become more difficult to obtain. In the past
two years, LDF lawyers had developed confidence in their
legal arguments and in the national network of capital case
lawyers. The press had begun to devote attention to the fact
that there had been no execution since June 1967. Abolitionist lawyers had successfully confounded the governors
of California and Florida, the states with the largest death-
row populations. But all of this would dissolve in the face of
silence from the Supreme Court of the United States.

9

Boykin

The same day in March of 1969 that Amsterdam, Harris, and Langston argued *Maxwell v. Bishop,* the Supreme Court heard the appeal of Edward Boykin, Jr., one of the few men on death row for a crime other than murder or rape. A twenty-seven-year-old black, Boykin had been indicted for committing a series of holdups in Mobile, Alabama during a two-week period in the spring of 1966.

Alabama was one of nine states that provided the death penalty as the maximum punishment for robbery, but all the others required the presence of aggravating circumstances before authorizing a capital sentence. After a brief conference with his court-appointed attorney, Boykin decided to plead guilty to five robbery charges. For all that the court records of the case showed, he never knew that his guilty pleas subjected him to electrocution.

Despite the admission of guilt, Alabama presented seven witnesses to a jury, simply to confirm that the crimes had in fact occurred. They described the holdups and identified Boykin as the culprit. The amounts taken in the robberies ranged from $150 to $373, and in each holdup he was armed. In one of the robberies he fired a shot that ricocheted and hit a girl in the leg, but the sole witness to this episode had testified that she did not think Boykin intended to shoot anyone.

After the jurors heard this testimony, the trial judge, Walter F. Gaillard, described their solemn duty to fix a punishment:

Now robbery [first degree] once again, gentlemen, is the felonious taking of money or goods of value from another against his will and without his permission by violence or by putting him in fear. That boils it down in a nut shell just what robbery is. Now, it carries from ten years minimum in the penitentiary to the supreme penalty of death by electrocution. I'll have the forms for you in just about one minute. One form has been written up here. If you decide not to give death by electrocution, of course, the form on the indictment, you can use that. On the other hand, gentlemen, there will be a form . . . if the jury finds the defendant guilty of the offense of robbery as charged in the indictment and fixes the penalty at death by electrocution. You will have that form. You can use either one form or the other when you arrive at your verdict.[1]

Less than an hour later, the jury returned with the form for five death sentences, one for each robbery.

The court-appointed lawyer soon dropped out of the case, and Boykin was without an attorney until his plight came to the attention of E. Graham Gibbons, of Birmingham. With the help of two volunteers from the North, Stephen Hopkins and John Flackett, Gibbons took Boykin's case without fee and appealed to the Supreme Court of Alabama.

On appeal, Gibbons included in his brief a claim that to execute for the crime of robbery was "cruel and unusual punishment in violation of the Eighth Amendment of the Constitution." Another argument for Boykin was brought out by three judges of the Alabama Supreme Court: that Judge Gaillard had erred by failing to make certain that Boykin understood the potential punishment before he pleaded guilty. A defendant could not make an intelligent decision to admit his guilt, they argued, unless informed of its potential consequences.

On February 8, 1968, the Supreme Court of Alabama rejected both arguments, with three judges dissenting on the guilty plea issue.[2] Six months later, the Supreme Court of the United States agreed to review the decision of the Alabama Court.

Boykin's appeal marked the first full Supreme Court consideration of a claim that capital punishment itself, as opposed to the manner in which death was inflicted, violated the Eighth Amendment. A case which did not involve homicide presented the Court with an excellent opportunity to narrow the use of the death penalty. It was imperative, therefore, that the Fund tell the Court why it thought Boykin's death sentence amounted to a cruel and unusual punishment. Even if the Justices chose to decide the case on the guilty plea issue alone, they would plainly be attentive to the Eighth Amendment question.

In December, 1968, Amsterdam went into seclusion to write an LDF amicus curiae brief in the *Boykin* case. For several weeks, he pondered means to invigorate the Eighth Amendment, a provision of the federal Constitution which was poorly conceived, rarely applied, and had never been used to restrict capital punishment.

In splendid vagueness, the Eighth Amendment provides only that "Excessive bail shall not be required, nor excessive fines imposed, nor cruel and unusual punishments inflicted." It is generally agreed that the Cruel and Unusual Punishment Clause was inserted in the Bill of Rights in revulsion toward earlier English law. As men of the Enlightenment, the Founding Fathers seem to have concurred in defining the "cruel" punishments they wished to prohibit as those with a decidedly medieval cast, involving torture or lingering death. They wanted to ensure that the penalties available to a democratic society would not include the barbarities of the past: disembowelment, the rack, the thumb-screw, pressing with weights, boiling in oil, hanging and cutting down alive, drawing and quartering, public dissection, castration, or burning alive (the latter a punishment reserved for witches and women who had killed their husbands.) Capital punishment, however, was a commonplace to men who lived at a time when lengthy imprisonment was novel.

The framers of the Constitution plainly believed in the legitimacy of the death penalty—they would have asked what alternative method of dealing with dangerous criminals was open to them—as well as a number of "minor" punishments, such as whipping, the pillory, branding of cheeks and forehead with a hot iron, and slitting, cropping, nailing, and cutting of ears. Although today such punishments would disturb most Americans, in the eighteenth century they were the common fate of thieves, drunks, fornicators, and other petty criminals. As for the death penalty, it was so common that the framers assumed that it would be employed. They provided in the Double Jeopardy Clause of the Fifth Amendment that no one should be subject for the same offense to be twice placed in jeopardy of *life* or limb. Once was quite acceptable in 1791.

The historical record does not tell us what meaning the framers of the Bill of Rights thought future generations would give to the phrase "cruel and unusual punishments." Although prohibitions against excessive punishment predated the Magna Carta (1215), the language of the Eighth Amendment was taken from the English Bill of Rights of 1689, where its purpose was vague. Some historians thought that the English Bill of Rights merely intended to eliminate torture; others, that it was primarily directed against legally unauthorized use of harsh penalties. Language prohibiting cruel and unusual punishments had been inserted subsequently in several eighteenth-century charters, constitutions, and protest documents with little comment and less explanation.

As best one can guess from the scanty evidence, the

Eighth Amendment seems to have been thought of only as a constitutional promise against a recrudescence of barbarism. Patrick Henry urged adoption in order to block "torturous, or cruel and barbarous punishment."[3] But the two members of Congress who addressed themselves to the proposed Eighth Amendment did not view it with favor. As Samuel Livermore of New Hampshire put it: ". . . it is sometimes necessary to hang a man, villains often deserve whipping, and perhaps having their ears cut off, but are we in the future to be prevented from inflicting these punishments because they are cruel?"[4]

One modern scholar, Anthony Granucci, has taken the position that the English Bill of Rights was in fact a response to irregular imposition of punishments "unauthorized by statute and outside the jurisdiction of the sentencing courts" rather than a reaction against torture.[5] But Granucci also concluded that the framers of the Bill of Rights did not themselves fully realize this history and were primarily concerned with a prohibition of barbarity.

Even less is known about the intentions of the framers in defining "unusual" punishment. The word had appeared inexplicably in a late draft of the English Bill of Rights; American Constitution-makers kept the word but never said why. Did unusual mean infrequent or exotic? Was it intended to mean anything different from "cruel"? Did it prohibit penalties not commonly in use in one state or country but common in others? What of the penalties that were not common anywhere, but perhaps not cruel—as in the first use of a more "humane" form of execution? What did the amendment say about common punishments which were more severely extended—e.g., a more lengthy prison term than usual, though jail for the offense was neither cruel nor unusual?

The dearth of historical answers to such questions meant that the prospects were meager for any contemporary use of the Eighth Amendment, much less use of it as a device to restrict application of capital punishment. Additionally, nothing said in early Supreme Court Eighth Amendment decisions looked toward eventual abolition. Although the Court did not decide explicitly that the death penalty was or was not cruel and unusual punishment, it had come close to approving capital punishment in the nineteenth century. Execution by public shooting in Utah, and New York's introduction of electrocution in 1890[6] had been upheld as constitutional methods of killing: neither involved the sort of manifest cruelty or lingering death which the Constitution proscribed. The electric chair was certainly unusual, but the Court approved its introduction because it was intended to minimize pain.

A 1910 Supreme Court decision, *Weems v. United States,*[7] broadened the use of the Amendment, but not in a way that permitted its general application to criminal penalties or directly affected the death penalty. Weems had worked as a disbursing officer for the Coast Guard in Manila at a time when the Philippine Islands were subject to the jurisdiction of the United States, and had been convicted of defrauding the government of 612 pesos which he falsely entered on the books as having been paid out to lighthouse workers. The sentence imposed under a provision of the Spanish Penal Code still in force for Weems's crime of "misrepresentation of truth" was fifteen years imprisonment while chained at ankle and wrist. Additionally, Weems was fined, sentenced to hard and painful labor, deprived of rights to parental authority, guardianship of persons or property, subject to surveillance upon release, and required to inform public authorities whenever he changed his domicile. For good measure, he was deprived of the right to hold office and to vote.

When Weems claimed that the statute authorizing such penalties inflicted a cruel and unusual punishment, the Court agreed. Considering the offense, the term of years at hard labor seemed excessive and several of the other penalties—especially chaining—were thought by the Supreme Court to be foreign to American concepts of justice. (This simply ignored Southern prison chain gangs.)

The Court's opinion conceded that what constituted cruel and unusual punishment was uncertain, and that "the terms imply something inhuman and barbarous—torture and the like . . ." Nevertheless, a prison sentence might be so disproportionate to the offense charged as to be unconstitutional, at least when combined with, to quote Professor Herbert Packer's characterization, "a good deal of laid-on unpleasantness offensive for its novelty as well as its severity."[8] In other words, a punishment need not be bloody or barbarous to be cruel and unusual.

In a dissenting opinion which Justice Holmes joined, Justice Edward D. White argued that the Cruel and Unusual Punishment Clause did not require proportionality between punishment and crime. Historical analysis of the Clause satisfied White and Holmes that it was intended only to prevent the legislative branch "from authorizing or directing the infliction . . . of cruel bodily punishments."

In a striking passage, Justice Joseph McKenna rejected such a narrow formulation of the framers' intentions:

Legislation, both statutory and constitutional, is enacted, it is true, from an experience of evils, but its general language should not, therefore, be necessarily confined to the form that evil had theretofore taken. . . . Therefore a principle, to be vital, must be capable of wider application than the mischief which gave it birth. . . . In the application of a constitution, therefore, our contemplation cannot be only of what has been, but of what may be.

McKenna proceeded to inquire whether the minimum sentence provided by the statute in question was excessive. He noted that the United States did not punish far more serious crimes, such as inciting rebellion, as severely as the Philippines punished "misrepresentation of truth"; and that the federal government punished an offense similar to the one committed by Weems by not more than two years imprisonment and a fine of twice the amount embezzled. These comparisons persuaded McKenna that the sentence inflicted on Weems was unconstitutionally excessive for the crime he had committed.

The Court's decision in the *Weems* case could be read broadly as authorizing the courts to measure the proportion between a sentence and the offense for which it was imposed. In short, the Court asked: did the punishment fit the crime? Or *Weems* could be viewed narrowly, as only restricting penalties foreign to American traditions.

The former interpretation presented judges with so much latitude that in the years following the *Weems* decision it was rarely employed. How much disproportion disqualified a punishment? What standards should be used to measure disproportionality? If an extremely harsh punishment might deter others from committing a specific crime, could it not be used? Was an especially heavy penalty for an offense prohibited, even though necessary to rehabilitate or incapacitate a dangerous offender? To compound these difficulties, just because a punishment fit a crime perfectly did not mean it was valid under the Eighth Amendment. As the Legal Defense Fund's brief in Boykin's case put it: "Court-ordered maiming is arguably proportioned to the crime of mayhem, but we have no doubt that maiming would be held to violate the prohibition of cruel and unusual punishments."[9]

The narrow view that interpreted *Weems* as dealing with exotic punishments also had its difficulties. In the few cases where it might be used, a prohibition of penalties developed in other countries froze the form of the criminal sanction by making experiment with different forms of punishment difficult to justify.

Neither a broad nor a narrow interpretation, however, was particularly helpful to lawyers seeking to have the death penalty declared unconstitutional under the Eighth Amendment. Death was plainly precisely proportionate to murder, for which it was most often imposed. Moreover, there was nothing alien in its use.

Because government has grown subtler and no longer employs the rack, the riddle that Amsterdam confronted was whether the Eighth Amendment could be given an interpretation which had significance for contemporary society, or whether it was to remain simply a remedy for obsolete or overwhelmingly repudiated wrongs. Thus, the utility of the Amendment as a device to test the constitutionality of modern criminal penalties necessarily implied a judgment concerning the nature of a written Constitution. Should the Supreme Court expand, revise, or interpret constitutional provisions to apply to contemporary evils? If so, would the judges not be "making" rather than "finding" the law? Was there anything wrong with this?

Lawyers once fondled such questions with the eagerness of young lovers, because the view that the Supreme Court took of how constitutional provisions ought to be construed determined the basic character of American political institutions. Today, such questions are still troubling (because as long as judges exercise great power the leeway they are given will be a matter of public debate), but it is generally accepted that the Constitution must be read with flexibility, in a manner meaningful to modern conditions, even though the result might shock the framers.

This does not mean, of course, that judges freely read the Constitution consistent solely with their personal views. A democratic society would crush a judiciary that tried. All "sorts of institutional habits and characteristics"—to quote Professor Bickel out of context—restrain the judges and ensure an orderly expansion or contraction of constitutional principles.

Supreme Court Justices, of course, exploit ambiguities of statutory language and legislative intent and take detours around previous decisions. But generally they still find support for their opinions in the evolution of the law. In short, personal conviction mingles with limited power, professional training, and the force of precedent. The Justices creep up on change, then crawl back to retrench. Time and again, for example, a new majority has declined to overrule a disliked rule and instead merely taken a restrictive view of the prior decision.

Stretching but not breaking doctrine forged in different times to meet the felt needs of the day is the greatest challenge of judicial review. The Eighth Amendment, however, had never been given an interpretative gloss which permitted its ready application to any contemporary punishment, much less the death penalty. The urge to invoke the Constitution to prohibit capital punishment immediately caught on the Amendment's broad language, narrow historical intention, and confusing implications. This primitive state of Eighth Amendment jurisprudence was one reason why the Fund's initial courtroom challenges to the death penalty emphasized procedural fairness in reaching the life-death decision rather than outlawing that decision itself. The Amendment offered little guide to the judges except one that they recoiled from with distaste, as had Judge Mosk in California: If you are shocked by a punishment, if it violates your own ethical standards, strike it down.

LDF lawyers found few helpful clues in what little had been said about the Eighth Amendment after *Weems*. In 1947, in the bizarre case of Willie Francis,[10] a majority of the Justices refused to interfere with Louisiana's second attempt to execute Francis after the electric chair initially misfired. According to Barrett Prettyman, Jr.'s gripping account of the state's first attempt to kill Francis in *Death and the Supreme Court*,[11] spectators saw the young Negro's "lips puff out and swell like those of a pilot undergoing the stress of supersonic speeds. His body tensed and stretched in such catatonic movements that the chair, which had not been anchored to the floor, suddenly shifted, sliding a fraction of an inch along the floor." Still, Francis lived.

After granting a short reprieve, the state decided to try again, but lawyers attempted to block the execution by claiming that to put Francis to death was cruel and unusual punishment. On June 10, 1947, the Supreme Court announced that it would not review the case, but the following day, according to Prettyman, a horrified Supreme Court clerk discovered that a mistake had been made and that the case "had been designated 'denied' instead of 'granted.' " After correction of the error, the case was restored to the Court's docket.

Ultimately, four of the nine Justices decided that Francis was merely the victim of an accident, not an attempt by the state to inflict unnecessary pain. Another four thought that "death by installment" constituted the very lack of civilized conduct it was the purpose of the Eighth Amendment to forbid. The deciding vote against Francis was cast by Felix Frankfurter, a rabid opponent of capital punishment, who concluded that to prohibit a second attempt at execution would be to impose his private opinion of what was shocking and uncivilized on the people of Louisiana. Rumor had it that Frankfurter believed the governor of Louisiana would commute the death sentence if the Supreme Court upheld it, but several months after the decision the state managed to accomplish what it had botched earlier.

In a 1958 case, *Trop v. Dulles,*[12] the Justices decided that it was cruel and unusual punishment to make loss of citizenship the penalty for desertion in wartime. In a key passage, the Eighth Amendment was said to take its meaning "from the evolving standards of decency that mark the progress of a maturing society." As a person who had lost his United States citizenship, Trop existed at the sufferance of the country in which he happened to find himself. Expatriation, the Court concluded, was merely a modern version of the barbarities of the past:

There may be involved no physical mistreatment, no primitive torture. There is instead the total destruction of the individual's status in organized society. It is a form of punishment more primitive than torture, for it destroys for the individual the political existence that was centuries in the development.

But a prohibition of banishment hardly opened the Eighth Amendment to broad application. In an opinion subscribed to by four members of the Court, Chief Justice Warren expressly warned that the death penalty was not cruel and unusual punishment—"in a day that it was still widely accepted."

The Supreme Court also had invoked the Cruel and Unusual Punishment Clause in a 1962 case called *Robinson v. California*.[13] Robinson had been convicted under a California law that made his narcotics addiction a crime, and the Court reversed his conviction after concluding that to punish a man for an illness that could not be relinquished voluntarily was unconstitutional. But in 1968, the Court had refused to apply *Robinson* to a Texas alcoholic who made a similar claim after conviction for public drunkenness.[14] Still, even if the *Robinson* decision could be considered viable, it offered abolitionists little help. They did not argue that the particular conduct involved in capital crimes—rape, robbery, murder, and so forth—was improperly labeled criminal; their goal was to remove a particular sanction, not to eliminate criminal punishment entirely for these offenses.

However, there were two aspects of the *Robinson* decision that could be employed to advantage in an argument that capital punishment was unconstitutional. The Eighth Amendment does not apply directly to the states; the Fourteenth Amendment does. *Robinson* established beyond question that the Fourteenth Amendment's Due Process Clause "incorporated" the Eighth Amendment, and therefore that the Cruel and Unusual Punishment Clause could be used to strike down state, as well as federal, laws. Secondly, as Jeffrey Mintz, one of Amsterdam's former students who worked for the Fund, put it in a memo:

Robinson reaffirms that "the Eighth Amendment recognizes changing standards and increased knowledge as one of the factors in determining its application."

According to the *Trop* and *Robinson* Courts, the Eighth Amendment prohibited criminal penalties that were uncivilized and indecent. If the consequences of loss of citizenship, for example, were shocking and extreme to modern sensibilities, Congress would have to find another punishment. But how could one argue that the death penalty contravened the moral standards of the American people when over forty states and the federal government authorized its imposition for some criminal offense?

In a democratic society, surely an enlightened public is capable of abolishing a penalty which does not meet generally accepted standards of decency. The whip and the brand had been discarded. The legislatures of nine states had abolished the death penalty, and five more had severely restricted capital punishment to offenses such as the murder of policemen or prison guards. Presumably, elected legislators more accurately reflected public attitudes than appointed federal judges. If, as the LDF amicus brief in the *Boykin* case posed it, the "question asked by the Eighth Amendment" is "whether our democratic society can tolerate the existence of any particular penal law that is on the books," the answer came back quickly: society has not yet determined that a penal statute that most elected legislatures have not repealed violates basic standards of decency.

If this was what the Eighth Amendment meant, if offered slight protection for a constitutional right. Judges could use it to strike down punishments only when the overwhelming majority of jurisdictions had abandoned a cruel penalty, but a few lagged behind; or when a few states introduced novel or inhumane punishments. It was all right for judges to use the Amendment to prohibit whipping by the one or two states that still occasionally employed it, but they were not authorized to prohibit an even more painful penalty that was more generally authorized by law.

Amsterdam's brief in the *Boykin* case propounded an imaginative theory of the Eighth Amendment to deal with such apparent contradictions and the absence of helpful precedent, as well as the amendment's murky history. His legal argument began with a rhetorical device. Assume an inquiry by a disinterested, nonlegal scholar. Free from the encumbrance of legal concepts, what would such a scholar observe about the death penalty and its contemporary uses?

He would learn immediately that roughly forty nations had abandoned capital punishment, and that it was in relative disuse in many others;

He would look at history and conclude—along with legions of writers, philosophers, and theologians—that the progressive abandonment of the death penalty marked the advancement of civilization. Capital punishment had always been associated with barbarism; its abolition with such democratic values as the sanctity of life, the dignity of man, and a humane criminal law;

He would see that the supporters of capital punishment were rarely found in the ranks of those who had studied human behavior—social scientists, penologists, psychologists, doctors;

Because few people could stomach witnessing an execution, he might conclude that legal killing was maintained in large part because of the secrecy involved, and that this suggested the states' shame at the process;

He would learn of the decay of the waiting man, the anguish of his family, and the enormous amounts of money spent on death case trials and appeals;

Finally, he would observe that capital punishment was justified primarily by the fear, unsupported by research, that without it murder would increase. Given the available evidence of its costs and utility, he certainly would conclude that the death penalty could be dispensed with.

But the very conclusion—the undesirability of capital punishment—that a scholar was free to reach, the Supreme Court of the United States could not find decisive, because the Justices are not authorized to simply convert their own views of what is wise policy into constitutional law. To be sure, the Eighth Amendment restricts legislative enactment of cruel penalties. It is not limited to prohibition of punishments that would have turned the stomachs of the framers of the Bill of Rights. *Weems* had established as much, for the Court had said that the amendment should be progressively interpreted, "not fastened to the obsolete but [to] acquire meaning as public opinion becomes enlightened. . . ." But surely an elected legislature is better able to measure the public's view of what is cruel than a court. If the death penalty violated contemporary values, would not the legislature remove it from the books? And if the legislature did not do so, how could a court justify itself as better able to judge the values of the community?

Answers to these questions constituted the great contribution of the *Boykin* amicus brief. The American people, Amsterdam argued, accept the death penalty *only* on the statute books—in theory, that is, but not in practice. The evidence demonstrates that Americans will not in fact tolerate its general, even-handed application. Our society accepts the death penalty, he contended, solely because it is applied "sparsely, and spottily to unhappy minorities." The numbers selected are so few, their plight so invisible, and their background so unappealing, that "society can readily bear to see them suffer torments which would not for a moment be accepted as penalties of general application to the populace."

The Eighth Amendment, then, is a constitutional measure of the allowable difference "between what public conscience will allow the law to *say* and what it will allow the law to *do*—between what public decency will permit a penal statute to threaten and what it will allow the law to carry out. . . ."

Take Boykin's crime of robbery, Amsterdam reasoned. There were over 200,000 such offenses known to the police in 1967, and many thousands were convicted of the crime.

But only an arbitrarily selected freakish few would find their way to death row. Could one easily imagine execution of even a tiny fraction of convicted robbers, say two a week, without widespread public revulsion?

If persuasive for robbery, the same analysis spelled out the ultimate rejection of death as a penalty for murder. Although over 15,000 homicides (not all capital crimes, of course) are committed each year in the United States, only about one hundred murderers are yearly sentenced to death, and only a handful of these would be executed. Between July 1, 1964, and December 31, 1968, for example, Georgia had sentenced 14 men to death out of 424 "eligible" convicted murderers (3 percent). Twenty-eight men were convicted of first-degree murder in Maryland between July 1, 1965, and June 30, 1966, but only 4 (14 percent) were sentenced to die. During the years 1946 through 1968, 5,034 persons were convicted of murder in Texas, and 139 (2 percent) sentenced to death.

The moratorium itself, and other pending proceedings in both the Supreme Court and lower courts, partially accounted for the decrease in actual execution, but the fact remained that the number of actual executions had begun to decline long before organized efforts to abolish capital punishment through the courts. In the 1950's executions averaged 72 per year, whereas from 1960 to 1965 the average was 19. By 1967, there were 435 men awaiting execution, and though no executions took place thereafter, the death-row census was only 500 by 1969. A nation of two hundred million that had executed only ten men since 1965 was hardly likely to find its moral sense unaffected by the wholesale killing that would follow nonarbitrary enforcement of capital punishment.

Hopefully, the *Boykin* brief charted a course enabling the courts to act against the death penalty in the name of a more acceptable constitutional standard than the transient sentiments of the judges as to what constituted the moral standards of the community. Measurement of community sentiment *was* a role of the elected legislature, Amsterdam's theory conceded, but it was the business of the courts to prohibit arbitrary use of a penalty. Courts must be sensitive to arbitrariness because only they deal with particular cases and are in a position to protect "the isolated individual."

The very rarity of execution permits the public conscience to "support laws enabling the individual to be [killed] . . . provided that arbitrary selection can be made in such fashion as to keep his numbers small and the horror of his condition mute." Legislators do not take account of the silent few. They respond politically and need not consider individual cases. "But it is the precise business of courts to take account of them," and "to disallow under the Eighth Amendment penalties so harsh that public conscience would be appalled by their less arbitrary application."

When the Supreme Court decided the *Boykin* case in June 1969, it passed over the Eighth Amendment claim and ruled that before a trial judge accepted a plea of guilty the Constitution placed an affirmative duty on him to inquire into the defendant's understanding of its nature and consequences.[15] Although Boykin won a new trial, the failure of the Court to reach the cruel and unusual punishment issue when a state sought to impose the death penalty on a robber—the most disproportionate use of capital punishment it was likely to face—was a sad omen. It probably meant that a majority of the Justices could not accept the Eighth Amendment argument. If the Court had originally decided to review the case in order to take a first step toward abolition, some Justices evidently had changed their minds. At best, the Court seemed uncertain of its course.

But though the Justices ducked the cruel and unusual punishment question, the LDF amicus brief was a landmark. The seed had been planted. Courts might be willing to put procedural restrictions on the use of capital punishment, but until the Amendment could be applied in a manner which avoided forcing appellate judges to see themselves as playing the role of Platonic guardians, judicial abolition would always be unlikely. It would be several years before the theory propounded for the first time in the *Boykin* case found an audience, but in 1969 one man's lonely act of intellection had discovered a clue to unraveling the mystery of the Eighth Amendment.

The *Boykin* brief was presented to the Supreme Court without fanfare or public notice, but LDF lawyers hoped that the view of the Constitution that it expounded might eventually become the legal basis for complete abolition. To sink in, however, the *Boykin* theory needed time. The power of Amsterdam's ideas would grow if the death penalty continued to be imposed in only a small proportion of all capital cases; if judges could be persuaded that even a moderate increase in its use, or in the public's actual experience of legal killing, would stimulate intense resistance. The much-desired victory in *Maxwell* would further restrict execution, and the continued moratorium might make legal killing seem all the more like a needless game of Russian roulette.

10

Haynsworth, Carswell, and Blackmun

The oral argument in *Maxwell v. Bishop* had been held in March 1969. Normally, the Court takes a preliminary vote shortly after a case is argued. Then the majority opinion and concurrences and dissents, if any, are written and circulated among the Justices for comment and final assent. Because Maxwell's case was complex, as well as consequential, no decision was expected until mid-June just before the Court cleared its docket and adjourned for the summer. But on May 14, 1969, an event took place that would postpone Supreme Court resolution of the issues involved in the case for two years: Justice Abe Fortas, one of the men whom LDF lawyers hoped would vote to require a split verdict or sentencing standards, resigned from the Court suddenly after conflict of interest charges were raised about payments he had received while a Justice from the family foundation of Louis G. Wolfson, an ex-client and convicted stock swindler.

The remaining eight Justices could have decided the case. If the eight divided evenly, Maxwell would lose his appeal because the effect of an evenly split vote is always to affirm the decision of the lower court.[1] In that event, the Court would not write an opinion and the case would not be considered a precedent. The eight Justices, however, were apparently unwilling to take any action affecting the fate of hundreds of death-row prisoners without the presence of a ninth Justice. On May 26, 1969, therefore, the Supreme Court published a brief order requiring reargument of *Maxwell v. Bishop* on October 13, 1969—at the beginning of the Court's next term—by which time, presumably, a new Justice would have been appointed to replace Fortas.

As Chief Justice Earl Warren was to retire from the Court in June, LDF's hopes for a favorable majority dissolved. Richard Nixon now had the opportunity to choose two of the men who would ultimately decide Maxwell's appeal—and the two whom he selected would replace men the abolitionists thought were in their corner.

Nixon's first choice, Warren Earl Burger as Chief Justice, brought to the Court a man with intellectual credentials and judicial experience on the Court of Appeals for the District of Columbia Circuit, but also one who five years earlier in the *Frady* and *Gordon* case expressed hostility to judicial interference in capital case procedure. While it is hazardous to predict the voting pattern of a Supreme Court Justice on the basis of views expressed before appointment to the high Court, Burger had come to public attention as an articulate dissenter from the reformist criminal procedure decisions of a court of appeals that had often gone further than the Warren Court in protecting the rights of suspects from the investigatory power of the police. In 1968, Nixon had actively campaigned against the changes prompted by these decisions and had cited the District of Columbia crime rate as an example of what happens when judges are too lenient. The Burger appointment—quickly confirmed by the Senate—was thought to be the first payment on his pledge to create a new conservative "law and order" majority on the Court, one that was unlikely to deny the public such comfort as it derived from the availability of capital punishment.

At the time Nixon announced Burger's selection, he set out the qualifications for a nominee in a manner that also made it unlikely that Fortas' successor would support judicial abolition. Nixon emphasized his preference for a "strict constructionist." The President was implying, Tom Wicker commented, that "a 'strict constructionist' is one who will abide by the Constitution while others"—loose constructionists—"are willing to distort it for their own social and political ends."[2] The rhetoric was shallow because a restrictive view of the Constitution might lead to a decision applauded by the political left in one case, by the political right in another; good law in some cases, absurd results in others. "The labels liberal and conservative," as Anthony Lewis put it, "do not determine how a man approaches the job of interpreting the Constitution."[3] But Nixon's meaning was clear. He used "strict constructionist" as code words for a judge whose views on the character of constitutionally required protections were less favorable to criminal defendants and minority groups than those of the majority which had dominated the Court during the Warren years.

Only mild surprise followed Nixon's nomination of Clement Haynsworth of Greenville, South Carolina, the fifty-six-year-old chief judge of the Court of Appeals for the Fourth Circuit, to replace Fortas. On an important Southern court Haynsworth had a lackluster record of enforcing civil rights guarantees. His criminal law opinions were a mixed bag, but far more progressive than might have been expected, given the meaning generally ascribed to Nixon's intention "to restore the balance of the Court." Still, his selection did not bode well for LDF's chances at the impending reargument of *Maxwell v. Bishop.* "Judge Haynsworth has rejected several anti-capital punishment arguments," Fred Graham wrote, "and has shown no abhorrence of the death penalty."[4]

Both Everett Dirksen (R., Ill.), the Senate Minority Leader, and Mike Mansfield (D., Mont.), the Majority Leader, were quick to predict that the Senate would confirm the Haynsworth nomination, and there was little reason to doubt their judgment. After all, the enemies of the

Warren Court were growing bolder and had been quieted
only by Nixon's election. In 1968 Congress had passed by a
lopsided margin, and Lyndon Johnson had signed, an
omnibus crime bill that included provisions designed to
emasculate several reformist criminal law decisions. Senate
liberals had only narrowly defeated an effort to divest the
federal courts of habeas corpus jurisdiction. Burger's confirmation had been accomplished simply.

But powerful opposition to Haynsworth developed. As
an appeals court judge, he had often voted against claims
raised by labor unions and their members. George Meany,
President of the AFL–CIO, joined Roy Wilkins, Executive
Secretary of the NAACP, and Clarence Mitchell, the
NAACP's skilled Washington lobbyist, in letting it be
known that they would go to the mat to stop Haynsworth.

Nevertheless, it was unlikely that the Senate would have
denied the President his choice of an experienced and
competent jurist if information had not come to light which
raised questions as to Haynsworth's sensitivity to the ethical
obligations of a federal judge. He had been a shareholder of
the Carolina Vend-A-Matic Corporation, which did substantial business with Deering Milliken, Inc., a Carolina
textile firm. In 1963, by a 3-to-2 vote, the Fourth Circuit
had decided a case between a Deering subsidiary, Darlington Mills, and the Textile Workers Union, in which it was
claimed that Darlington had closed a textile plant solely to
avoid unionization;[5] Haynsworth cast his vote with the
majority to uphold the company. Subsequently, the Supreme Court unanimously reversed the decision.[6]

In 1964, Simon Sobeloff, then chief judge of the Fourth
Circuit, a distinguished Republican lawyer and a former
Solicitor General of the United States, had reported to the
then Attorney General, Robert F. Kennedy, that there was
no evidence of wrongdoing on Haynsworth's part. But after
Haynsworth's nomination it was learned that he had eventually sold his interest in Carolina Vend-A-Matic for over
$400,000. At the time the case was argued before the

Fourth Circuit, he owned one-seventh of the company's shares, as well as being a director and vice president. Nevertheless, Republican Senators circulated a memorandum, prepared by Assistant Attorney General William H. Rehnquist, that the judge's interest in the case was so remote that he was duty-bound to participate.

By the time the Court reconvened in the fall, Haynsworth had not been confirmed, but he was still not thought to be in serious danger of losing in the Senate. Nevertheless, the Court indefinitely postponed argument in *Maxwell* and a number of other controversial cases.

As the weeks passed, additional disclosures clouded Haynsworth's prospects for confirmation. Haynsworth had purchased a thousand shares (worth $16,000) in the Brunswick Corporation at a time when a case involving that corporation was before the Fourth Circuit. He also owned shares in the Grace Steamship Co. and a Maryland insurance company, though he had voted in cases involving both. While it was extremely unlikely that Haynsworth would profit even if the companies won these cases, such incidents contributed to the impression that he had been careless in keeping his business dealings separate from his judgeship. Although Haynsworth's labor and civil rights records, and a desire to embarrass Nixon, explained why a number of Senators opposed him, the ethical questions raised by Haynsworth's participation in these lawsuits gave many Senators nonpolitical justifications for opposition to his appointment. Several conservative Republicans felt bound to vote against him because they had opposed Lyndon Johnson's 1968 nomination of Fortas as Chief Justice on ethical grounds and feared charges that they had applied a less strict moral standard to a Republican. Some Democrats probably saw Haynsworth's indiscretion as a golden chance to even the score for Fortas' resignation.

Incredibly, enough Senators were disturbed by Haynsworth's character to place the nomination in jeopardy, and so leading Republicans asked Nixon to avoid a showdown

by withdrawing the judge's name from Senate consideration. House Minority Leader Gerald Ford, however, attempted to frighten Haynsworth's opponents by claiming
that a higher ethical standard was applied to him than to
previous judicial candidates. If the Senate was to set a
higher standard, Ford said, he wanted to use it to scrutinize
the conduct of members of the Supreme Court and to
impeach Justice William O. Douglas. Douglas had been
president of the Albert Parvin Foundation, a philanthropic
organization, which received part of its income from a
mortgage on a Las Vegas gambling casino, but it was his
outspoken civil liberties opinions, his consistent "liberal"
vote, his most recent book, *Points of Rebellion*,[7] which
called the violence of radicals an understandable reaction
to American institutions, and his several marriages to much
younger women that made him Ford's target.

Senator Gordon Allott, a Republican from Colorado, one
of Haynsworth's staunchest supporters, tried a different
tactic. Allott implied that if not confirmed, the judge would
be destroyed and even forced to resign his court of appeals
post.

Senate debate opened on November 13, 1969, with
James Eastland of Mississippi, the Chairman of the Senate
Judiciary Committee, attacking the press for creating a
distorted impression of the seriousness of the ethical issue.[8]
On the same day, Vice President Agnew delivered his
famous speech accusing the media of slanting news by
permitting a clique of New York and Washington, D.C.,
executives, newscasters, and reporters to present biased and
unrepresentative views on national issues. The White House
exerted enormous pressure on Republicans to support the
nomination.

But the arm-twisting did not work. During the ten days
of debate that followed, as Senators took the floor to state
and explain their votes for the record, it became plain that a
majority would vote "no." Senator Jacob Javits (R., N.Y.)
voiced a common complaint when he lamented the fact that

all but three of Haynsworth's fourteen civil rights decisions had opposed the implementation of constitutional guarantees of racial equality. But Senator Len B. Jordan of Idaho, a conservative Republican, articulated the sense of the swing Senate votes when he charged that Haynsworth had given the *appearance* of impropriety, as important in evaluating a judge as whether or not there had been actual wrongdoing.

On Saturday, November 22, the Senate voted 55 to 45 against confirmation, 17 Republicans voting against the Administration. Nixon issued a statement of regret, but many thought that by Haynsworth's defeat he had gained an important political goal: the affection of voters who saw the President as thwarted by liberal proponents of judicial activism. Once again, the reargument in *Maxwell v. Bishop* was postponed by the Supreme Court.

It soon seemed that Nixon would emerge victorious with both a political victory and a far more certain "law and order" vote for the Administration. As if thumbing his nose at labor and civil rights opponents of Haynsworth, in January 1970 he announced the nomination of G. Harrold Carswell of Tallahassee, Florida. Carswell did not own a share of stock, but Senator Daniel K. Inouye (D., Hawaii) was to say of him, "The only good thing I've heard about Judge Carswell is that the next nominee will be worse."[9]

The good things about Carswell were few indeed; by comparison, Clement Haynsworth shone like a Holmes or Cardozo. Carswell's eleven-year record as a United States district judge was marked by consistent court of appeals reversal of his decisions in civil rights cases, a habit of discourtesy to lawyers representing unpopular clients, and an undistinguished series of judicial opinions.

Although six months earlier Nixon had elevated Carswell without opposition to the Court of Appeals for the Fifth Circuit, 457 lawyers, including several leading Eastern Republicans and numerous law teachers, signed a letter to the Senate stating that he lacked "the legal and mental qualifications" for the Supreme Court. In an assessment submitted in a letter to *The New York Times,* Louis Pollak, the dean of the Yale Law School, found a total lack of distinction in his opinions. But Carswell did not need such enemies with friends like Senator Roman Hruska of Nebraska. Hruska retorted, "Even if he is mediocre, there are a lot of mediocre judges and people and lawyers and they are entitled to representation . . . we can't have all Brandeises, Frankfurters and Cardozas."[10]

By the time the Senate voted on Carswell's confirmation, two law school deans supported him and twenty-three registered opposition. Two hundred former Supreme Court law clerks asked the Senate to reject the nomination, and thirty-seven law schools passed resolutions urging his defeat. An American Bar Association committee did find him qualified and refused to reconsider, but its decision led to a wave of protest from hundreds of lawyers, and criticism from local bar associations in New York, Philadelphia, and San Francisco.

The critics concentrated on the racist attitudes shown in Carswell's public record. In 1948, while running for public office in Georgia, he had made a blatant white supremacy speech. Further, he was an incorporator of a private club that took over Tallahassee's municipally owned golf course in 1956, after a court ruling that city-owned recreational facilities must admit Negroes. He denied any intent to avoid desegregation, but Neal Rutledge, a Florida lawyer and son of former United States Supreme Court Justice Wiley Rutledge, sent a telegram to Senator Birch Bayh (D., Indiana) in which he stated that it was common knowledge in Tallahassee at the time that the reason for setting up the private club was to exclude blacks.[11]

In 1963, when he was United States Attorney for the Tallahassee area, Carswell had chartered a nonprofit corporation to support Florida State University athletic teams.

Membership was restricted to "any white person interested in the purposes and objectives for which this corporation is created."[12]

In 1966, while a federal judge, he and his wife conveyed a lot by a deed that required the purchaser to bar nonwhites from buying or occupying the property.[13]

Carswell himself committed a blunder which may have contributed to his defeat. On the eve of his appearance before the Senate Judiciary Committee, two representatives of the ABA's Committee on the Federal Judiciary confronted him in his Washington hotel room with documents describing his role in incorporating the golf club. He conceded that he was an incorporator but denied any discriminatory purpose, and the next day the ABA committee found him qualified for the Court. In testimony before the Senate Judiciary Committee, however, Carswell denied being an incorporator, claiming that his memory of the whole matter was foggy and that he had not seen the records of the corporation in years.[14]

On April 6, 1970, the Senate seemed to be going along with the Administration when it voted 52 to 44 *not* to recommit the nomination to the Judiciary Committee for further study, a move that would have shelved it without forcing Republican Senators to go on record as opposing the President. But two days later, in a dramatic reversal, seven Senators who had opposed recommittal voted against the nomination, and Carswell lost 51 to 45.

Haynsworth had been rejected in an attempt to embarrass Nixon, to keep a judge with a weak civil rights record off the Court, and to compensate Democrats for whatever loss in prestige they had suffered when Fortas was forced to resign. But no one had claimed that Haynsworth was intellectually unqualified for the Court. If he had been indiscreet, the lapses were minor, and many lawyers who knew his record intimately thought that he had taken a bum rap.

Carswell, however, was rejected on his merits. In the end, the only thing that the Administration could assert on his behalf was party loyalty and Presidential prerogative. Ironically, the votes that defeated him came from Senators who were perfectly willing to see conservative judicial philosophy represented on the Court. A poor preliminary examination by the Department of Justice had failed to save them from the embarrassment of a judge who had served without distinction, and whose record on racial issues was offensive.

Curiously, the call for "law and order" which constituted Nixon's avowed purpose in putting a "strict constructionist" on the Court contributed to Carswell's defeat. Obedience to law requires respect for it. A judicial system staffed in a time of crisis by judges whose public record was so questionable would hardly command respect. A majority of Senators apparently agreed with *New York Times* columnist James Reston, who asked rhetorically: "how are we ever going to restore public respect in the institutions of the nation, if the highest officers of the nation don't lead the way?"[15]

For over a decade, the Supreme Court of the United States had borne a large share of the burden of remaking the moral order and readjusting political power to bring them both into step with the realities of black discontent, shifts in population, demands for personal expression, and humanitarian ideals. But an institution which tells white America it can no longer maintain the illusions that bound it together in the past—happy workers, grateful young, respectful niggers, a punitive criminal law—is the obvious focus of resentment. By 1970, the Court seemed exhausted by the effort of defending itself from its critics, and internally divided over whether to continue wholesale enlargement of constitutional protections or to retrench.

The struggles which defeated Nixon's first two selections for the Court caused a certain bitterness in those who treasure the Court's place in American government. If the man ultimately selected was really not so different from Clement Haynsworth, one had to wonder whether the stress was really worth it. Haynsworth was a decent man with a moderate record who might not have graced the Court, but certainly would not have disgraced it. Carswell, however, had no deep commitment to, or rigorous intellectual interest in, the processes of constitutional law. Hence, once Haynsworth was rejected, Carswell could not be accepted without a fight. But many thought that the long wait in confirmation, and the attendant bickering about the Court, unnecessarily injured what Louis Hartz, professor of government at Harvard, has called ". . . the remarkable power of the Supreme Court, a power resting on the notion that there is enough moral agreement in the political world to permit the adjudication of even its largest questions."[16] And if the Court did not feel confident in its moral leadership, it would surely hesitate before taking such a giant step as abolishing the death penalty.

Two days after Carswell's defeat, an angry President petulantly claimed that both Haynsworth and Carswell had been subjected to "vicious assaults on their intelligence, their honesty and character . . . falsely charged with being racist" solely because of their "philosophy of strict construction of the Constitution . . . and the fact that they had the misfortune of being born in the South."[17] His next nominee, he said, would be a man who would restore conservative balance to the Court, but he would not be a Southerner.

A week later, when Nixon nominated Judge Harry A. Blackmun of the Eighth Circuit Court of Appeals, there was a general sense of relief. Blackmun was sixty-one, a native of Minnesota, a boyhood friend of Chief Justice Burger, and barely known outside the Midwest. Those familiar with his work claimed that he was unadventurous and painfully slow at preparing written opinions, but he was also reputed to be a compassionate and studious judge.

Curiously, the code meaning of "strict constructionist" did not accurately characterize Blackmun. As a court of appeals judge, he often turned aside arguments for changes in the law by saying that the Supreme Court of the United States was the proper body to alter settled practice, but he had not always taken a narrow view of constitutional rights. In a case I had argued to the court of appeals in 1966, he had written a comprehensive opinion protecting black public school teachers in Arkansas from wholesale dismissal when black schools were closed.[18] A colleague of mine, John Walker, a leading Arkansas civil rights lawyer, thought that Blackmun's decision had saved hundreds of jobs. Nor could he be considered a "law and order" judge; his opinions reflected enough concern for procedural fairness in the criminal law to dispel thoughts that he might try to demolish the "due process revolution."

Thus, to most lawyers concerned with the Court, Blackmun seemed a prudent choice. For capital punishment lawyers, however, he was a disaster. Ironically, on his third try, Nixon had selected the federal judge who had most forcefully expressed himself against the Fund's arguments. Because he had written the Eighth Circuit opinion in *Maxwell v. Bishop,* Blackmun could not sit on the case as a Supreme Court Justice, and therefore, the Court remained with eight effective votes for the reargument. But the real problem was future cases, for Blackmun had committed himself, in a long opinion, to rejection of the standards and single-verdict claims. He could change his mind—if the issues were not ultimately resolved in *Maxwell v. Bishop*—but this was unlikely.

Apparently, there was confidence that this time Nixon's choice would be confirmed, and because Blackmun could not sit, there was no need to delay the *Maxwell* reargument any further. On Friday, April 17, 1970, Supreme Court chief clerk John F. Davis called Amsterdam at his Stanford Law School office to inform him that the Court would hear arguments in *Maxwell* within two weeks. Eight years after he supposedly raped a white spinster, close to three years since the last execution in the United States, and almost fourteen months after the Court had first considered this,

his third, Supreme Court appeal, the day of reckoning approached for William Maxwell.

Meanwhile, Judge Blackmun told an Associated Press reporter that he opposed the death penalty and would not be surprised if the Supreme Court declared it cruel and unusual punishment in "1970 or 1980." His court of appeals opinion in the *Maxwell* case, the story pointed out, had contained an important reservation: Blackmun found the case an "excruciating" one to decide because he was "not personally convinced of the rightness of capital punishment" and questioned whether it was "an effective deterrent."[19]

The newsprint on this story was hardly dry before Blackmun seemed to reverse himself. On April 29, 1970, before the Senate Judiciary Committee, Senator Hiram Fong of Hawaii asked Blackmun about the article, and the judge replied that while he was "not convinced of the rightness of capital punishment as a deterrent in crime," this was "part of a personal philosophy." The "rightness of legislation" was "an entirely different question." The imposition of the death penalty was "a matter for the legislature." If the legislature were to declare it a capital offense for a pedestrian to cross "the street against a red light this might be something else again. . . . [But] I start with the premise that this is basically a legislative discretionary matter."

Senator Fong asked, "And if the Legislature says that capital punishment should be imposed, you would follow that?"

Blackmun replied, "Certainly, with an exception perhaps in my pedestrian illustration."[20]

11

Maxwell (Continued)

The *Maxwell v. Bishop* reargument was finally rescheduled for May 4, 1970. Although the Court consisted of only eight Justices, it would still take a majority of five to decide the case in Maxwell's favor. If, as LDF lawyers had speculated, Warren, Fortas, Brennan, Douglas, and Marshall once had been the ingredients of a favorable majority, now with Warren and Fortas gone, Maxwell would lose unless he found two new votes. And even if Stewart were part of an earlier majority, another vote was still necessary to win. If the Court were split 4 to 4 in this case, it could, of course, grant review in still another case and reconsider the standards and single-verdict issues the following term. Such a move would prolong the moratorium for at least six months but it did not promise ultimate success, for Justice Blackmun, who would be able to sit on the next case, was likely to reject the contentions at issue.

The second round of argument in *Maxwell* presented Amsterdam with several perplexing problems. First, he had to handle the hot potato that had been raised during the 1969 argument concerning the application of the *Witherspoon* rule to the case. An examination of the 1962 trial record had turned up evidence that seven prospective jurors had voiced opposition to the death penalty in only general terms but had nevertheless been excluded from jury service. Should Amsterdam urge the Court to vacate Maxwell's death sentence on this ground alone? Or should the *Witherspoon* claim be presented as one of three issues, all of which should be decided?

Another question of great importance was how much emphasis to place on a 1969 Supreme Court decision, *North Carolina v. Pearce*.[1] In *Pearce*, the Court had ruled that when a defendant successfully appealed a criminal conviction and won a second trial, he could not be sentenced to a higher penalty than he had received after the first trial, unless the trial judge justified the higher sentence on the basis of the defendant's conduct *subsequent* to the first trial. The reasoning behind *Pearce* was simple. If trial judges imposed higher sentences after retrials, it would deter defendants from appealing to higher courts. As a result, trial court errors would go unnoticed and constitutional rights unprotected by appellate review. An appeal would force defendants to gamble: they might win new trials, but they might also be hit with a heavier sentence (to punish them for appealing) if subsequently reconvicted.

Although *Pearce* dealt with a special problem, it marked the first time that the Supreme Court had laid down explicit sentencing guidelines for trial judges to follow. It did not seem such a large step from requiring standards to guard against vindictive sentences by judges on retrial to requiring standards to guard against arbitrary sentences by juries in capital cases. But the Court clearly had not written *Pearce* with Maxwell's situation in mind. Should Amsterdam bring up *Pearce,* and if so, should he rely on it heavily?

Finally, even though this was the second time the case was being argued, there was uncertainty about what most troubled the Court's swing votes. Justices Marshall, Douglas, and Brennan were still counted on LDF's side. Of the remaining five, persuasion of Black and Burger would be difficult. That left Justices Harlan, Stewart, and White. At the first argument, each had asked several troublesome questions, but study of the stenographic transcript of the argument provided few clues to winning the two out of three votes necessary for a majority.

Because the Court had grown familiar with both the facts of Maxwell's case and the considerations that the Fund and the states of Arkansas and California, the amicus curiae, thought most important to the decision of the legal issues, Amsterdam's plan was to depart from his prepared argument at the first sign of a lead in the questions of the Justices.*

He began cautiously, like a boxer feeling out his opponent in the early rounds. There were four questions before the Court. The first two questions were the standards and the single-verdict issues—the issues that the Court initially had agreed to review in December 1968. The third question involved the claim of wrongful exclusion of jurors with scruples against sending a man to death from the jury that sentenced Maxwell to die in 1962—the *Witherspoon* claim. The fourth question was which of the first three questions the Court should decide.

Choosing the legal question to be decided was uniquely a matter of the Court's discretion, Amsterdam conceded, but he stressed that there were facts the Court should know.

First: There were 67 death cases on the Supreme Court's docket. Forty-five of the cases, coming from 18 states, presented either the standards or single-verdict questions.

Second: There were approximately 510 men on the death rows of those states which retained the death penalty. A decision on the standards issue would potentially affect 505 of them.

Third: Because five states, including California, the state with the largest death-row population, had abandoned the

---

* A reminder to the reader: As in the presentation of the original argument of the Maxwell case before the Supreme Court (Chapter 8), the colloquy has been paraphrased; exact quotes are indicated by quotation marks.

procedure whereby the jury decided guilt and sentence together, a decision on the single-verdict claim potentially affected 380 to 390 men.

Fourth: Prior to December 1968, when the Court agreed to review Maxwell's case, it had been difficult to obtain stays of execution for condemned men. Occasionally, it was even necessary to apply to Justices of the Supreme Court only several days before a scheduled execution; in fact, this had been necessary to save Maxwell's life. After the Court had agreed to review *Maxwell v. Bishop,* a dramatic change followed. Many state judges granted reprieves readily, and the governors of Arkansas, Massachusetts, and Washington had agreed to postpone all executions until a decision in the case had been reached.

Fifth: If the Court did not decide the standards or single-verdict issue now, *or* grant review in one of the many other cases pending before the Court which raised these issues, continued postponements would be difficult to obtain. Undoubtedly, executions would take place before the Court eventually decided the issues, because in recent years the highest courts of seventeen states (including those with the eight highest death-row populations) had rejected the need for standards, and the highest courts of eleven states had upheld the single verdict. Three federal courts of appeals—the Eighth, Ninth and Tenth Circuits—had rejected both positions. Plainly, then, these issues were of national importance and the Court should pass on them in this or in some other case.

The Justices had contained themselves through this opening statement, but the remainder of Amsterdam's hour was question-filled. The Chief Justice led the parade.

Chief Justice Burger: Isn't your burden here to show not that the procedures you seek are wise or sound, but that they are compelled by the Constitution of the United States?

Amsterdam: Our position is that due process of law requires that some legal standards govern a jury when it decides whether a man lives or dies, and secondly that the Constitution does not permit the states to whipsaw a defendant between his privilege not to take the witness stand and his right to present evidence rationally related to informed sentencing.

This position does not rest on a new-fangled concept of due process. We do not contend that the standards selected by Arkansas will be better for all defendants; for some they might be worse. What we contend is that Arkansas procedure lacks the first essential of due process: a regularized system of principles governing whether men live or die.

Justice Stewart: Did Arkansas merely extend mercy in 1915 when it changed from mandatory to discretionary capital punishment after conviction of a capital offense?

Amsterdam: No, what Arkansas did—along with the other states that kept the death penalty—was to say that in every case it is up to the jury to decide who lives and who dies.

Justice White: Several states permit juries to do the sentencing in noncapital cases; this is a practice much older than the twentieth century. Are you attacking all jury sentencing? Does your argument depend on the fact that the jury here was deciding the sentence in a capital case?

Amsterdam: My personal view is that any time a legislature gives the jury the right to make an important distinction among persons arbitrarily, the Constitution is violated. But one can distinguish between capital and noncapital offenses. A rape case may involve an enormous range of conduct, from a brutal attack by a stranger to forcible intercourse among persons who have a pre-existing relationship. I do not think the jury working within this enormous range can be given the absolute right to decide life or death. Why do we expect that twelve men off the street, who have never sentenced and never will again, can sort this out even-handedly?

Chief Justice Burger: But isn't the process the same when jurors determine negligence in an accident case?

Amsterdam: In such a case the judge instructs the jury about the legal standard of care. He tells them to decide if the defendant acted as a reasonable man under the circumstances. I would be surprised if research into such cases did not discover that there was a strong correlation between the presence of such things as faulty brakes and jury verdicts of negligence. But we did a study of sentencing in Arkansas rape cases and found that the death sentence was associated only with race.

Justice Hugo Black asked his first question and his tone suggested great hostility: Would your argument be the same if Arkansas had not changed its law in 1915 to make the death penalty discretionary?

Amsterdam: No. If the death penalty were mandatory, then our only argument would be that it was cruel and unusual punishment.

Chief Justice Burger: Don't all these statistics about racial discrimination suggest that legislative bodies have advantages over courts in this area?

Amsterdam: Certainly. That is why we think the Constitution requires that state legislatures direct themselves to drafting standards. This Court should not draft them. But no legislature has tried. None has even said it cannot be done. We think *they* should write the rules, but now there are no rules. It is like a roll of the dice. Now it is lawless.

Chief Justice Burger: Once you get standards, won't you be asking us to review them? You are not giving the legislature a blank check?

Amsterdam: Legislatures will have great freedom in drafting acceptable standards; this Court will have limited review over their penological judgments about sentencing.

In the 1930's members of the Jehovah's Witnesses came to this Court and said that police chiefs had denied them permits to distribute leaflets or to march. Local laws contained no standards governing police discretion to grant or deny the permits; if the police said "no," the answer was "no." Then this Court said that the Constitution required standards. Three years later, the Court had no trouble upholding a set of standards which permitted the police to disallow a parade that might have interfered with traffic. Over the years, the Court has had to reverse many convictions of leafleteers and marchers, but not because cities and states could not draft standards; rather, because fair standards would have allowed unpopular groups free access to the streets.

Justice Harlan: Suppose a state passed a law which provided that the jury could sentence on the basis of the evidence presented as to guilt. Would that be a constitutional standard?

Amsterdam: "I believe the Court will not set its foot on the primrose path" if it requires sentencing standards. First, Arkansas has not required anything of the sort suggested by Justice Harlan's question. Second, statutes are draftable that provide standards. The American Law Institute's Model Penal Code has a set. But if it were impossible to draft a statute that would bring the rule of law into this process, then I have no doubt what should be dispensed with. If the cost of capital punishment is lawlessness, the Constitution requires that it be abandoned.

Justice Black: Don't we assume that the jury comes to its job with some sense of the facts of life?

Amsterdam: The statistics do not support the contention that the jury sentences to death in only the worst cases. An Arkansas black has a fifty-fifty chance of getting a death sentence if convicted of raping a white woman. When the rape is intraracial, a defendant's chance of receiving a death sentence plummets to 14 percent.

Justice Black: Do you have statistics for other states?

Amsterdam: All the available evidence points to the same conclusion.

Justice White: Isn't sentencing without standards just as bad in non-capital cases?

Amsterdam: Where more is at stake, due process is more exacting.

Justice White: Isn't a great deal at stake with life imprisonment?

Amsterdam: One can distinguish between a judge deciding whether to sentence to ten or to fifteen years and a judge differentiating between life and death. In non-capital sentencing, rehabilitation is a factor; it is terribly difficult to know whether rehabilitation will take ten years or fifteen. But when we sentence someone to die, rehabilitation is irrelevant. The difficulties of sentencing in non-capital cases cannot be borrowed to justify arbitrariness in capital cases.

Last year, in *Pearce,* this Court prohibited judges from resentencing criminals to higher sentences after a second trial, unless they could point to antisocial conduct that occurred subsequent to the time of the first sentence. The theory was that the sentencing judge might be vindictive toward a man who successfully had appealed an earlier conviction. It is anomalous to require standards to protect a defendant in such a situation and not where racial discrimination is likely to have been practiced.

Justice White: Would you be satisfied with standards limited to race?

Amsterdam: No, because I am not worried as much by the obvious bigots as by the people who don't think they are racist. We cannot tell whether there is racial sentencing unless we have a method of control. Some sort of review is necessary. But in order to review the jury's decision, you need coherent standards against which judges can measure what the jury does.

Amsterdam's time was up but he had been interrupted by so many questions that Chief Justice Burger allowed him an additional ten minutes. He talked briefly about the single-verdict argument, emphasizing a position that might appeal to Mr. Justice Black. He was not relying on vague motions of fairness, Amsterdam insisted, but on the plight of a defendant forced to waive either his Fifth Amendment privilege against self-incrimination or his right to present evidence freely on the question of sentence.

Donald Langston, the assistant attorney general who had also argued for Arkansas in 1969, began his presentation with a subject Amsterdam had not mentioned. Maxwell's guilt was not strictly relevant to the legal issues, but Langston wanted the Court to know the facts of the rape. He proceeded to describe them in some detail. He also told the Court of the recent overwhelming defeat of a bill introduced in the state legislature to abolish the death penalty.

Justice White: Under Arkansas law, could the judge order a new trial if he disagreed with the sentence?

Langston: Well, he could order a new trial if he disagreed with the *guilt* verdict. Then there would be a whole new trial. But the statute providing for this has not been used.

Justice Marshall: How old is the law?

Langston: It is older than Arkansas' admission to the Union.

Justice Marshall: And you are an Assistant Attorney General and you never heard of it used in the history of the state?

Justice Harlan interjected: Could the question of this statute's application be certified to the Supreme Court of Arkansas so that they could tell us what the state law is?

Langston: I don't think so. The Arkansas Supreme Court does not give advisory opinions.

Langston took Amsterdam to task for injecting the racial issue. The Court, he pointed out, had not agreed to review the lower court's decision that there was insufficient evidence of discrimination. The real question, he thought, was whether the jury system was viable in a capital case. Arkansas assumed that a defendant's greatest protection resided in the good judgment and common sense of a jury, unencumbered by formal rules. As to the single verdict, although a few states had decided to separate the trial establishing guilt from that which would fix punishment, no one had ever suggested that they were constitutionally required to do so.

In response to questions from Justice Marshall, the only black man on the Court, Langston conceded that Arkansas judges did not tell jurors that they could not consider race. The matter was totally in the hands of the jury.

A question from Justice Black implied that the accused in a death case had sufficient protection and that standards were not necessary: If the judgment in a death case is contrary to the weight of the evidence, could the judge set it aside?

Langston: I think so.

Justice Black: Don't you know it?

Langston: Yes, I know it.

Justice Marshall: That would reverse the judgment of guilt, not solely the sentence?

Langston: Yes.

Chief Justice Burger: Isn't the sentence part of the court's judgment?

Langston: Of course.

Justice Brennan brought up another point: What happens when an accused takes the stand? Can he be asked about all past bad conduct or only criminal convictions?

Langston: He can be asked the same questions as any other witness. The defense, however, is entitled to have the jury told that his answer about his past misconduct is not to be considered evidence of guilt but only as affecting his credibility. The prosecution must take the answer given by the witness to questions about character; it cannot dispute what he says.

On this note, Langston concluded in order to permit Harris, again representing California, to use the remaining portion of his time for argument. As he had a year earlier, Harris made clear at the outset that California's interest in the case was limited to the standards question. California had abolished the single verdict and replaced it with a special sentencing proceeding at which the defendant can present evidence without waiving his Fifth Amendment right at the guilt trial. At the sentencing hearing all sorts of evidence, such as psychiatric records, can be presented to the sentencing jury. And under California law the state can bring out only prior convictions, not general bad conduct.

Justice Black: Are there any standards in California "in addition to those defining the crime"?

Harris: I believe that there are such standards, and that during the first argument in 1969 I too readily accepted the view that there were none. After the jury sentences to death, the trial judge has the power to reduce a sentence to life imprisonment if he feels that the death sentence is unjustified. The appellate courts do not have this power, but the Supreme Court of California can set aside the entire penalty proceeding because of errors in the judge's handling of the sentencing hearing. In such a case, the defendant wins a new chance to go before a sentencing jury. As California law now stands, a trial judge even has the power to set aside a death sentence because he opposes capital punishment.

"We think our procedure reflects a clear recognition of the problems involved in sentencing in capital cases." The jury is told to consider the background of the defendant, as well as all the evidence of the crime, although it is not essential that the jury find any aggravating circumstances before sentencing to death.

Justice Harlan: Then you do have standards?

Harris: Yes.

Justice Brennan: But the jury still has absolute discretion?

Justice Stewart interrupted: Then there is a clear legislative decision as to what should be considered?

Justice Harlan nodded.

And Justice Black chimed in: Isn't the jury the conscience of the community?

Before Harris could answer, White asked: Do California juries ever sentence in non-capital cases?

Harris: Rarely.

Justice White: Does the judge disagree often with the jury's decision about capital punishment?

Harris: Yes . . . If you list some of the factors which are to be considered, you exclude others. That is a problem with standards. If a standard is not listed, it cannot be considered, even though it may be relevant to the particular case.

On rebuttal, Amsterdam had only a few minutes and very little hope, for White, Stewart, and Harlan had appeared to accept Harris' view that California already provided legal standards of some kind. He stressed that Arkansas and California had vastly different capital case procedures, and that the merits of the California practice should be decided in a California case.

Amsterdam: The fact is that the procedure *in Arkansas* is lawless. Indeed, the California procedures suggest the defects of the Arkansas procedure. The statute Langston has mentioned, which supposedly permits a judge to set aside a death sentence, predates 1915, when capital sentencing was mandatory upon conviction of a capital offense. "It doesn't apply here because it was envisioned to be used in a day when capital sentencing was mandatory. In 1969, Mr. Langston agreed that it didn't apply."

The Chief Justice: Do you think that the large number of death-row inmates in California is accounted for by the fact that the single verdict has been replaced with a split verdict?

Amsterdam: Absolutely not. California is the most populous state in the Union. It has the most crime and for several years Governor Brown did not permit anyone to be executed.

Chief Justice Burger: Then statistics aren't very reliable in this area?

Amsterdam: No, they are subject to analysis. The only

reliable statistics directed to why the death penalty is imposed have to do with race, and they were put into evidence in this case.

It had been a rough session. Very little of the guarded optimism we had felt the year before about the prospect for the standards and single-verdict issues was left, and events of the spring of 1970 confirmed LDF's sense of impending defeat.

These were not auspicious times for the Supreme Court to be deliberating about any controversial reform, much less about making the death penalty more difficult to impose. Fortas' resignation, the embarrassment of the Haynsworth and Carswell nominations, and the attack on Douglas could hardly be expected to put the Justices in an adventurous mood. Significant alteration in criminal procedure seemed unthinkable at a time when the country apparently was relishing the politically tinged prosecution of eight radicals for riot and conspiracy to incite riot at the 1968 Democratic Convention. At the same time, the Justice Department under Attorney General John Mitchell was grinding out proposed legislation to detain federal defendants without any bail requirement, and attempting to subpoena the notes of newsmen who had interviewed militants.

Other Mitchell proposals were to relax proof requirements in perjury cases; limit the opportunity of defendants to raise constitutional objections to the admissibility of illegally seized evidence; overturn the Supreme Court's 1969 decision[2] that gave defendants the right to see transcripts of illegal electronic surveillance; authorize grand jury presentments critical of public officials without requiring that the grand jury charge them with crime; permit police searching for drugs to enter homes forcibly without announcing their purpose or requesting entry; and transfer authority to determine which drugs were "dangerous," and thereby illegal, from the Department of Health, Education and Welfare to the Department of Justice.

It was also a spring of bombings. On March 6, 1970, an explosion destroyed a Greenwich Village town house. Three occupants, white radicals who were thought to have been attempting to make nitroglycerine, were killed. Four people were charged in New York with planting explosives in office buildings. Seventeen were injured on March 22 by a pipe bomb that exploded at a Lower East Side night club, the Electric Circus. On March 28, a man was killed and another critically injured in a Lower East Side apartment where the police found live explosives and bomb-making materials. Shortly before the trial of black militant H. Rap Brown began in Maryland, the Dorchester County Courthouse, where he was to be tried, was destroyed. Later, two of Brown's friends were killed when their car blew up. In many cities, anonymous threats to bomb armories, office buildings, and transportation facilities were commonplace. Nixon's response was to propose legislation amending the federal criminal code to make the illegal transportation of explosives when death resulted a capital offense. It was enacted.[3]

In the wake of the invasion of Cambodia, universities closed, students took to the streets, and national guardsmen killed four on the campus of Ohio's Kent State University. At Jackson State College in Mississippi, state troopers opened fire without apparent provocation, killing two and injuring nine. Attorney General Mitchell denied a Marxist scholar entry to the United States to attend a professional meeting. Vice President Agnew talked of "the whole damn zoo" of "deserters, malcontents, radicals, incendiaries, the civil and uncivil disobedients." Because of all these factors, as the time approached for the announcement of the decision in *Maxwell v. Bishop,* political rhetoric of "law and order" was being interpreted by many Americans to mean justifiable violence by police against students and blacks.

Public attention was absorbed by fears of urban crime, student disruption, and massive school desegregation, and the nation was in the hands of a President who had been elected on the strength of his ability to convert these fears into votes.

The "strict constructionist" rhetoric which marked Nixon's search for a new ninth Justice betrayed little feeling for the Court as an institution. It seemed a piece of political public relations, an advertisement directed toward those Americans who Nixon's men thought controlled his electoral future. The sales pitch went something like this: "Your President is trying to keep down those who threaten you, to resist the forces of change invading the comfort of your lives." If this was a cruel hoax—because the Supreme Court could not turn back the clock to 1960 and wish away riots, Vietnam, campus rebellion, and Civil Rights Acts—it nevertheless might be good politics to make the Court one of the demons responsible for the ills of American society.

Into this mix the questions that were presented in *Maxwell v. Bishop* were dropped like grease on a hot skillet. No matter that the case affected only five hundred or so men on death row and would affect only the hundred or so sentenced to death each year. Reform simply cannot flourish in an atmosphere of fear, or where the belief that the criminal law will eliminate disorder and social conflict is widespread and promoted by politicians. Nothing could more strengthen the hand of such politicians than court decisions favoring rapists and murderers. The curbstone philosophy had it that just such sentimentalism as would produce judicial abolition was responsible for the stalemate in Asia, drugs, bombings, uppity blacks, and resentful youth. How could a Court made vulnerable by the risks of fifteen years of activism, and under vigorous attack from within the government itself, demolish the oldest panacea of them all?

12

Taking Stock

During the months that Nixon and Mitchell attempted to coax a new ninth Justice out of the Senate, lawyers mobilized against the death penalty were able to postpone every scheduled execution. In 1969, forty-six appeals in death cases were lodged in the Supreme Court; in 1970, thirty-eight more were filed. All were held in abeyance until the decision in *Maxwell v. Bishop*. Many of these cases involved defendants who had exhausted all other available avenues of legal redress; their high Court appeals bore silent witness that if Maxwell's sentence was affirmed, many executions might take place.

By 1970 the median length of time spent by prisoners on the death rows of American prisons was close to three years.[1] Some death-row inmates behaved like tormented animals, but most tried to convince themselves that they would never be executed. "The longer a man is kept on death row," Maryland prison psychologist Stephen Berman observed, "the less the idea of the death penalty bothers him."

The pressures of the long wait for reprieve or death were aggravated by cramped physical conditions, archaic and degrading security precautions, and the emptiness of days without activity. The health of death-row inmates was often viewed with indifference. According to one inmate, Edgar Smith, Jr., none of the twenty-four men in New Jersey's death house had seen a psychiatrist or psychologist since the first week he had arrived in prison. It was not surprising that many death-row prisoners became psychotic while waiting for execution.

Generally the condemned were not allowed to mingle with the rest of the prison population and were denied a number of the privileges available to other inmates. Officials only permitted visits from immediate family and lawyers. Some prisons provided television, radio, earphones, and reading materials, but Smith had to lobby for years to get a typewriter. In Colorado, death-row prisoners exercised in their own yard, but were not permitted to work in prison shops or even to attend chapel with other inmates.

In Louisiana, each inmate was allowed out of a 9-by-6 foot cell for fifteen minutes a day. During this period, he was supposed to bathe, wash clothes, and exercise. When he was hauled into federal court by Baton Rouge Legal Aid Society lawyers to justify the practice, Warden C. Murray Henderson pointed to a 1929 Louisiana law which required that death-row inmates be held in solitary confinement.[2]

At San Quentin, correspondence courses and television were the main activities, but many of the condemned men never emerged into the sunlight, as there was no outdoor exercise space for them; a population of over seventy-five walked in a heavily guarded corridor several hours a day. A proposal to install sun lamps on death row was rejected on the ground that prisoners might suffer from overexposure.

In preparation for the *Maxwell* reargument, Himmelstein and Lyons had surveyed the death-row population, and the leading cases, in most of the capital punishment states. The welter of problems and the variety of experiences that they recorded surprised even the lawyers who had been forced to cope with them.

Louisiana: With one exception, no death warrant had been signed since 1961. While thirty-seven blacks and six whites lived under barbarous physical conditions in the state penitentiary at Angola, Louisiana, Governor John McKeithen continued to follow the practice of his predecessors by declining to sign the papers necessary before an execution could take place. Some state courts followed suit by allowing death-row cases to remain on their dockets for years without holding hearings.

But a regime of de facto abolition has a capacity for caprice, and in one case, involving a rapist named Leon Brent, a death warrant was signed. However, Amsterdam had hurried to New Orleans and persuaded the Court of Appeals for the Fifth Circuit to stay Brent's execution pending completion of litigation in the state courts over the constitutionality of the state's administration of the death penalty and its discriminatory use in rape cases.[3] Thereafter, Louisiana had remained quiet.

Nevada. Before LDF intervention, Lester Morford III, a twenty-five-year-old itinerant ranch hand from Santa Rosa, California, came perilously close to death. Morford had murdered a honeymooning couple who had given him a ride while he was hitchhiking in 1962 when he was eighteen, and was scheduled to die on April 1, 1969. As he prepared once again to challenge his conviction in the courts, rumors circulated that the state legislature would not act on an increase in the salaries of state supreme court judges until his petition was dismissed. On March 14, the Nevada legislature passed a resolution supporting Governor Paul Laxalt's decision to cast his vote on the pardon board against commutation. On March 17, the State Senate passed a resolution disqualifying Nevada judges from hearing capital cases if they opposed the death penalty.

Shortly before the execution date, Douglas Lyons, then a University of California undergraduate, learned of the case and contacted Steve Ralston, LDF's San Francisco attorney. Ralston flew to Nevada to help Samuel Francovich, Morford's Reno lawyer, argue for a stay from Federal Judge Bruce Thompson. Meanwhile, Lyons and a group of

San Francisco Theological Seminary students built a large cross which they prepared to carry from Sacramento to Carson City to protest the execution. However, after considering Ralston's request, Thompson said it was "unthinkable" that the pardon board could not delay the execution until the Supreme Court ruled in *Maxwell v. Bishop.* Judge Thompson wrote: "It is horrifying that state government would refuse to stay the execution under these circumstances . . . We cannot allow the state to appear as an ogre anxious to kill."[4]

But the state *was* anxious to kill. Nevadans, said Laxalt, "want the sentence carried out and carried out with dispatch." They were "fed up with the mumbo jumbo" of continuous legal appeals. His mail, he noted, ran in favor of Morford's execution.

The following year, the case of another Nevada death-row inmate, Thomas Bean, captured the headlines. Bean had been convicted of an atrocious 1963 slaying, in which he had entered a young woman's apartment and twisted a rope around her neck while she was asleep. It was not clear if she was dead when he stabbed her with his knife and raped her. He then cut out her heart, cut off her head, tried to skin her like a carcass in a slaughterhouse, split the corpse from crotch to neck, and finally stuck her body in a hope chest. He casually listened to her phonograph records, and then took her sports car for a joy ride.

The Supreme Court of Nevada voided Bean's death sentence—though not his conviction—because of the state's noncompliance with *Witherspoon,*[5] but District Attorney William Raggio, the man who had prosecuted Bean, publicly criticized the decision: "judicial legislation at its very worst," said Raggio, "outrageous," "uncalled for." Raggio got so much publicity from the case that he ran for the United States Senate, but the decision stood, and a year later the Supreme Court of Nevada formally reprimanded Raggio for his conduct.[6]

Illinois. Although approximately thirty men were being

held for execution and voters seemed likely to reject a proposed state constitutional amendment abolishing the death
penalty, Illinois required only occasional assistance from
Fund lawyers. Defense lawyers in most capital cases were
highly skilled, and Elmer Gertz and Willard J. Lassers,
lawyers associated with the Illinois Committee to Abolish
Capital Punishment and the Illinois American Civil Liberties Union, kept a careful watch for any case that might
break the moratorium.

Colorado. The situation in Colorado was stable, Denver
lawyer Rollie Rogers informed Himmelstein. Cases where
execution was a serious threat were in the hands of able
counsel; several were pending on the Supreme Court's
docket. Still, Colorado had to be watched closely, for legislative abolition was unlikely. At one time it had been
thought that Colorado might become an abolitionist state—
as it had been from 1897 to 1901—but in 1966 the voters
had rejected a referendum eliminating the death penalty by
a 2 to 1 margin.[7]

To reporters who had interviewed them, Colorado's
death-row inmates provoked more sympathy and sadness
than desire for vengeance. Sylvester Lee Garrison, for
example, a black who had come to death row in 1960, told
an interviewer from a Denver newspaper about the years he
had spent watching television, reading the sports pages, and
corresponding with lonely women:

If I had known then, as I know now, that I was going to be
around these ten years, I would have tried to have arranged it
some kind of way to have been educated, but you don't know
how long you are going to be around, see? But they really don't
want to educate us here. We are not brought down here to be
taught and trained in the first place. We are brought down here
to be killed, see?

Joseph Segura, a fifty-eight-year-old trash hauler, represented by Professor Donald MacDonald of the University of

Colorado, was the most pathetic case of all. Segura became embroiled in a squabble with his wife over some tomatoes she had failed to can. When his twenty-seven-year-old son tried to protect his mother, Segura clubbed him to death with a baseball bat in a moment of rage.

Texas. Despite the efforts of Houston attorney Will Gray, who represented more than a dozen death-row inmates without compensation, Texas was a state where executions would certainly take place soon after the federal courts stopped issuing stays. Dr. George Beto, the influential director of the Texas Department of Corrections, was a progressive prison administrator who had greatly improved the quality of prison life and installed a number of sensible rehabilitation programs since his appointment in 1962. Beto might have been instrumental in abolishing the death penalty in Texas, but he believed that the state had a right to kill, so long as the death sentencing was done by judges instead of jurors.

One Texas case, involving Leon Spencer, a man who had a penchant for wife killing, having murdered his first and second, had caused LDF much anguish. Saving Spencer's life was difficult because the stenographer's transcript that recorded selection of his jury could not be located, and the state courts took the position that it was Spencer's burden to prove any irregularity.

Amsterdam, Himmelstein, and Michael Matheny, Spencer's Texas lawyer, unsuccessfully argued to a Beaumont federal district court judge that the *Witherspoon* decision placed the responsibility to prove error-free jury selection on the state. A stay pending appeal was denied on November 16, 1967, only two and one-half days before the execution. Himmelstein and Matheny set out for the airport with hurriedly prepared legal papers for a New Orleans court of appeals judge, but Matheny's car ran out of gas. Himmelstein jumped out. Without breaking stride, he ran onto the highway and forced an approaching motorist to bring his car to a screeching halt. Explaining that there was an emergency, Himmelstein pushed Matheny into the car and persuaded the startled driver to speed them to the airport, arriving a minute before their flight took off. Soon after they reached New Orleans, the appeals judge granted a postponement, and ultimately the Fifth Circuit Court of Appeals ruled that Spencer could not be executed until the state demonstrated that persons with sentiments against the death penalty had not been excluded from the jury in Spencer's trial.[8]

Florida. Most death penalty litigation in the state had come to a standstill awaiting disposition of Toby Simon's lawsuit on behalf of all death-row inmates; Judge McRae seemed disposed to postpone any action until *Maxwell* was decided. But one case did go forward. It was a classic proof of the abolitionist argument expressed in the remark, which some have attributed to Thomas Jefferson and others to the Marquis de Lafayette: "I shall ask for the abolition of the punishment of death until I have the infallibility of human judgment demonstrated to me."[9]

In 1960 Robert Shuler, twenty, and Jerry Chatman, twenty-three, both black, were convicted of raping a white woman and sentenced to die by a Lake County jury. Through years of litigation, Shuler and Chatman insisted on their innocence. Twelve years later, in 1972, a federal judge, Charles R. Scott, finally upset the convictions after finding that plaster of Paris footcasts introduced at trial had been fraudulently manufactured in the backyard of the Deputy Sheriff.[10] The police, Scott decided, had also suppressed exculpatory evidence: statements made by the victim soon after the crime that the man who raped her was in his forties or fifties and that she did not recognize Shuler (Chatman had not even been presented to her for identification). Long before, in 1965, Chatman had given up on his life. "I'm writting to you concerning a majar decision that I have made concerning my future," he told Simon. "I have come to the conclusion that I prefer to die rather than to live . . . So I ask of you Sir as my attorney to make all the arrangement with the governor so that I maybee executed as soon as possible."

Massachusetts. Fourteen men resided on death row at ancient Walpole Prison, but the unofficial state moratorium in effect since 1947 continued.

Alabama. Few states sapped the energies of the LDF staff as Alabama did. Local black lawyers were able but exhausted by a flood of civil rights litigation; state officials were hostile to abolition. For several years, Alabama death cases were dealt out to LDF's New York staff like so many playing cards. Each capital punishment lawyer was responsible for a resident of death row.

One Alabama case was particularly interesting, for it helped refute the argument that capital punishment saves the states money. Rather than having taxpayers support a killer in prison for the rest of his life, so the argument goes, society has a right to put him to death. Those who can justify disposing of a human being in this way are unlikely to be persuaded by any argument to the contrary, but the case of Caliph Washington illustrates that even when a defendant does not press the illegality of capital punishment, the state cannot execute him quickly or cheaply.

Washington was convicted of murdering a police officer in 1957, when he was seventeen, after he had been stopped on suspicion of possessing moonshine whiskey. In 1959 an Alabama court quashed the conviction because the prosecuting attorney had attempted to introduce a confession without giving Washington an opportunity to testify about alleged inconsistencies in the statement.[11] Washington was duly retried, convicted, and sentenced to death. This time the Alabama courts found no error, but in 1965 federal Judge Frank Johnson ruled that the state had improperly relied on the transcribed testimony of a witness rather than producing him at trial and giving Washington an opportunity to cross-examine.[12] The state appealed and lost.

At his third trial, held in 1970, Washington was convicted of second-degree murder and sentenced to forty years in prison. But he appealed again, and this time a state appeals court decided that Washington had been denied a fair opportunity to prove systematic exclusion of blacks from the Jefferson County, Alabama, juries.[13]

As the Washington case shows, any system of justice which continually monitors the reliability and fairness of trial courts costs dearly. The death penalty actually *adds* expense. Capital trials are elaborate affairs, with more security precautions, more prospective jurors, and more days of trial than usual. Haunted by the possibility of mistake, appellate courts bend the law to favor the condemned man; any error not deemed totally harmless is enough to justify a new trial. Capital defendants end up exhausting judges, jurors, and attorneys as often as legal remedies.

Maryland. On November 3, 1969, Governor Marvin Mandel calmed fears about several Maryland inmates when he issued orders that stays of execution would remain in effect until the Supreme Court decided *Maxwell v. Bishop* and the other capital cases before it. A year earlier, former Maryland Governor Theodore R. McKeldin had wept as he told state legislators of his "shame" at not commuting the sentences of four men executed during his first term. But McKeldin's plea for abolition was rejected by the lawmakers.

Arkansas. In Maxwell's state, Governor Winthrop Rockefeller declared his opposition to the death penalty and announced an official moratorium on executions until the legal questions involved in the case were settled. Arkansas' seventeen condemned men had spent a total of sixty-four years on death row in cells nine feet deep and six feet wide. Except on rare occasions—for court appearances and on New Year's Eve—the condemned were not permitted to leave their cells. Tom Murton, the controversial reformer who served briefly as superintendent of the Arkansas State Penitentiary, had ordered the electric chair, nicknamed

"Old Sparkie" by the inmates, removed from a concrete room at the end of death row. The chair was taken out by some trusties and was promptly "lost." Murton converted the room into an infirmary, and permitted inmates to mingle with the general prison population.[14]

New Jersey. Working closely with the state Public Defender, Amsterdam and Himmelstein shepherded several appeals through New Jersey courts to the Supreme Court of the United States. A critical question facing the high Court was whether New Jersey statutes—which required that a capital case defendant who did not contest his guilt be sentenced to prison—were covered by the Supreme Court's *Jackson* decision.

Edgar Smith, Jr., New Jersey's best-known death-row inmate, was not an LDF client. William F. Buckley, Jr., the conservative editor and author, had become interested when Smith wrote him that *The National Review,* Buckley's magazine, was not on the prisoner-approved reading list; he had subsequently helped Smith find a publisher for *Brief Against Death,* a moving account of the events which had brought him to death row. In the book, Smith claimed that he was innocent of the murder of a fifteen-year-old high school cheerleader, Victoria Zielinski of Mahwah, New Jersey. After years of litigation, a New Jersey federal court finally decided that Smith's 1957 confession was involuntary and that he was entitled to a new trial.[15] There followed one of the law's great ironies. Confronted with a choice between another murder trial at which he could again receive a death sentence, or a guilty plea which the State agreed justified immediate release on parole (at that point he had been on death row for fourteen years, six months, and three days—a record) Smith chose the latter. Insisting on innocence might have meant years more in prison or even execution; the price of freedom was admitting guilt. "Did you and you alone kill Victoria?" Smith was asked by Judge Morris Pashman. "I did," he replied. But

hours after his release, in a television interview, Smith insisted that he had only confessed because there was no other
way to obtain his freedom.

Georgia. This was a trouble spot. With a large number of
capital cases pending in the courts, Georgia had executed
more men since 1930—366—than any other state. During
the late 1960's, however, state officials were consistently
blocked from carrying out executions by Supreme Court
Justice Hugo Black, who had freely granted postponements.
Black may have disliked the Fund's legal arguments but he
believed that a condemned man could not be executed until
the Supreme Court conclusively determined the constitutionality of the death penalty. On March 26, 1969, a man
named James Thacker received a stay of execution from
Black, but officials at the Reidsville Prison facility did not
tell the trembling prisoner until April 2, only hours before
the scheduled execution.

Virginia. The Fund represented four of the seven men on
Virginia's death row, and with the help of a band of volunteer attorneys—Peter Rowe, Sterling Walker, Hugo Madison, Henry Marsh, and Philip Hirschkopf—had managed to
keep their cases bouncing up and down in local courts.
Jimmy Snider, Jr., a thirteen-year resident on Virginia's
death row, told a court that life seven feet from the electric
chair was "a living death." State attorney Edward S. White
dryly protested that Snider "is not qualified to testify that
the death penalty is cruel and unusual punishment as he has
not undergone it."

North Carolina. Here most death cases were handled by
a vigorous interracial law firm that LDF had helped set up.
Three of its members, J. LeVonne Chambers, James
Fergusen, and Adam Stein, made headlines by their defense
of one of the two women under sentence of death in the
United States, eighteen-year-old Marie Hill—a black
woman, who had been sentenced for a crime when she was
fifteen. She had been convicted of the brutal murder of a
Rocky Mount storekeeper, but when the facts of the teen-

ager's life of lesbianism and alcohol became public knowledge, her case attracted widespread sympathy.

In another important case, *Alford v. North Carolina*,[16] the Court of Appeals for the Fourth Circuit held that the Supreme Court's *Jackson* decision invalidated the death penalty provisions of North Carolina law. In November 1969 the Supreme Court of the United States heard the state's appeal, but on April 27, 1970, shortly before the *Maxwell* reargument, the Court set *Alford* down for another round of argument during the next term, the following autumn—an indication that a majority of the eight Justices could not agree on a result and that the Court was badly split on the death penalty.

Kansas. The two men awaiting execution obtained stays because of *Witherspoon*. One of them, Kenneth L. Kilpatrick, twenty-two, had pleaded guilty to the 1966 rape and murder of a seventeen-year-old girl *after* 36 of the 155 members of the jury panel had been excused because of scruples against the death penalty in apparent violation of the *Witherspoon* rule.[17] His case raised the particularly difficult question of whether a defendant could successfully claim that contemplation of trial by such a jury was enough to render a guilty plea involuntary.

California. With the greatest number of death cases, plus a state supreme court that had rejected the major legal arguments against the death penalty and a governor and attorney general who considered abolition misguided "do-goodism," California was the focus of much LDF energy. The state courts had slightly thinned out the death-row population by a liberal application of *Witherspoon*, but the future of the remaining inmates appeared to depend on what the Supreme Court of the United States did with the standards question.

Arizona. Tucson lawyer W. Edward Morgan seemed able to keep Arizona under control all by himself; he represented six of the eleven men on death row at the Arizona State Prison. Early in his career, he had worked for five years on the case of a Negro laborer named Arthur Thomas, until the Supreme Court of the United States, by a vote of 5 to 4, rejected his claim that Thomas' confession had been coerced.[18] Ironically, the Court accepted several of Morgan's arguments in the Thomas case almost a decade later in the famous *Miranda v. Arizona*[19] decision. But *Miranda* came too late to help Thomas: he had been executed in 1959.

Ohio. Twenty-four men were under sentence of death—including Fred (Ahmed) Evans, a black militant convicted of directing a conspiracy that resulted in the murder of three Cleveland policemen in a gun battle between police and black nationalists—but local lawyers had managed to obtain postponements pending Supreme Court resolution of the capital punishment issues.

Washington, D.C. In June 1969 District of Columbia Judge George L. Hart, Jr., sentenced Bernard J. Heinlein, a forty-one-year-old drifter, to death for the rape and murder of a skid-row woman. No execution had taken place in Washington since 1957, and Heinlein was the first man sentenced to death there since 1963. Given the rarity of the death sentence, Heinlein's lawyers, including Edward Bennett Williams, claimed on appeal that regardless of the experience of other jurisdictions, the death penalty was plainly unconstitutionally unusual in the District of Columbia.

Pennsylvania. Many of the twenty-one men under death sentences had resided on death row for years as governor after governor granted stays of execution. Anthony Scoleri, a nine-and-a-half-year veteran of the row, had become a frequent correspondent of Amsterdam's, writing the law professor about the legal problems of other inmates as well as his own case.

Despite the de facto moratorium, a Pittsburgh murder case aroused controversy when three black teenagers, including an eighteen-year-old girl, pled guilty on the expectation of leniency; they were sentenced to death, although the state had not asked for the death penalty. Byrd R. Brown, President of the Pittsburgh branch of the NAACP, termed the sentence outrageous, "a bitter symbol to thousands of black citizens across the state who know the swiftness with which the death penalty is meted out to black offenders and the reluctance of judges to attach a sentence of death to white offenders."

In 1969 Democratic leaders of the state House of Representatives asked Governor Raymond Shafer to delay all executions until the legislature considered abolition. Although no bill was reported out of committee, the state's attorney general, William G. Bennett, told the Pennsylvania Council to Abolish the Death Penalty that executions would cease until the Supreme Court clarified the law.

But clarification was not forthcoming. On June 1, 1970, the Fund heard the news from an excited Associated Press reporter: the Court had again postponed final resolution of the standards and single-verdict questions by disposing of *Maxwell v. Bishop* solely on the *Witherspoon* issue—the narrowest ground of decision available.[20] In a brief opinion, the Court analyzed several of the jurors' answers to questions about their beliefs and found a strong possibility that *Witherspoon* had been violated. In the event that Maxwell's death sentence had to be modified, a local federal court would be better suited to work out the details, and therefore the Court sent the case back to Judge Henley's court for a determination of whether in fact prospective jurors had been removed from the jury panel because of general opposition to the death penalty in violation of the *Witherspoon* decision.

No sooner did LDF lawyers digest the Court's brief opinion in *Maxwell v. Bishop* than word suddenly came by telephone that the Court had agreed to review two lower court decisions which also challenged the failure of the states to accord standards and split verdicts. For a short time, at least, the pressure on death row and its lawyers was eased.

One thing was plain from the Court's failure to decide the standards and single-verdict claims in the Maxwell case. Rather than treating capital punishment in its most exaggerated—and from LDF's perspective, most sympathetic—form (a rape case where there was great evidence of racial discrimination), the Court had selected cases where it was more difficult to present the legal arguments for restrictive procedures in a favorable context. One case—from California—involved a black, Dennis McGautha;[21] the other—from Ohio—a white man named James Crampton.[22] Both cases were sordid and vicious homicides.

McGautha was convicted of killing the husband of a Los Angeles market owner during a 1967 holdup which netted him a few dollars. Crampton, who earlier had been hospitalized for drug addiction, shot his wife while she sat on the toilet. Moreover, California came closer than any other state to providing standards to guide jury sentencing. As if to mock the contention that juries lacked the guidance to give appropriate sentences, McGautha, who had a long criminal record, had received the death penalty; his codefendant, who had no prior convictions, did not.

Neither McGautha nor Crampton, of course, claimed innocence. Both argued, as had Maxwell, that standardless jury sentencing was so open to caprice and discrimination in selection of victims as to deny due process; Crampton also argued that single-verdict sentencing was unconstitutional. Nevertheless, it would take a particularly dull sense of public relations to choose two such cases to announce a severe restriction on capital punishment. The facts of the two cases that the Court had selected did not augur well for the result sought by the anti-capital punishment lawyers.

13

"If the Death Penalty Is to Be Retained at All"

LDF represented many of the death-row inmates whose appeals had worked their way to the Supreme Court, but McGautha and Crampton were not among them. Their cases were in the hands of private counsel, but too much was at stake for the Fund to remain silent. An amicus curiae brief filed with the Court reiterated the arguments made in *Maxwell* and emphasized that by giving the jury few facts and absolute power, standardless and single-verdict jury sentencing encouraged racial discrimination. The full Court, including Justice Blackmun, heard oral argument in the two cases on November 17, 1970; Amsterdam remained in California, but Himmelstein, Lyons, and I shuttled to Washington for the proceedings.

Herman F. Selvin, a graying California advocate with a moving voice and a sharp mind, argued the case for Dennis McGautha. Selvin wandered over the law as if it were his backyard; his eloquence was impressive. But he had not spoken for long when it became apparent from the tone of the Justices' questions that the standards argument was a lost cause.

Arguing for California, Ronald M. George, a state deputy attorney general, emphasized, without being pressed, the points suggested by Harlan and White's ques-

tions in the second *Maxwell* argument. There *were* standards for the jury to follow, George insisted, because the
California jury was instructed to base the life-death decision
on the seriousness of the crime as it was brought out at trial
and at the separate sentencing hearing. Arbitrary sentencing would not be corrected by setting forth additional
standards: jurors could always disobey whatever instructions they were given by a judge.

In the second case, *Crampton v. Ohio,* John J. Callahan
of Toledo, Ohio, pointed to the dilemma that the single
verdict had presented Crampton—either to go to his death
without having spoken or else to take the witness stand,
forfeit his privilege against self-incrimination, and expose
himself to questions about past conduct which could destroy his credibility. Melvin L. Resnick, a Lucas County,
Ohio, prosecuting attorney, responded that the single-
verdict procedure was not unfair because mitigating evidence could be presented by witnesses other than the
defendant. The accused men who did not take the stand
simply made a tactical choice not to do so. To hold both a
guilt trial and a sentencing trial would add to the already
burdensome delays, costs, and complexities of capital cases.

The Court had asked Solicitor General Erwin Griswold
to present the views of the United States in the two cases,
and Griswold responded by endorsing the California and
Ohio position. In the politics of Supreme Court decision
making, the official position of the federal government, as
represented by the Solicitor General, is an important element. The Court is always less vulnerable to criticism,
especially from Congress, when the Administration in
power has put its prestige behind the wisdom of a particular
result. Staffed by exceptionally able lawyers, the Solicitor
General's office produces legal briefs of the highest quality,
and the government's brief in *McGautha* and *Crampton,*
written by Philip A. Lacovara, was no exception. Thus,
Griswold may have snuffed out what little chance was left

for the two procedural arguments when he announced that the decision to have unrestricted jury sentencing was a matter the federal Constitution left up to the states.

It was a quiet day in court—too quiet. Himmelstein and I agreed that our only hope was for a long gap between the argument and announcement of the decisions, months to plan what to do after the Court rejected the two procedural claims. This would leave only one major constitutional contention in LDF's arsenal: that the death penalty was cruel and unusual punishment. If the Court was willing to decide the Eighth Amendment claim, work had to begin on a definitive legal brief. If the Court declined, the lawyers would have to dig in and defend each case on its particulars, but the moratorium would end.

Fortunately, the number of men languishing on death row presented legal and ethical puzzles to officials other than Supreme Court Justices. The momentum of events increased in the months after the *McGautha-Crampton* arguments, making it imperative that the Court resolve the ultimate question of the constitutionality of capital punishment.

On December 11, 1970, the United States Court of Appeals for the Fourth Circuit (the federal court with appellate jurisdiction over cases arising in Virginia, Maryland, North and South Carolina, and West Virginia) startled the legal world by becoming the first federal court to hold a death sentence unconstitutionally cruel and unusual. Although the Fourth Circuit decision relied on Amsterdam's *Boykin* theory of the Eighth Amendment (that courts must "disallow under the Eighth Amendment penalties so harsh that the public conscience would be appalled by their less arbitrary application"), the rule which emerged from the *Ralph* case was inapplicable to most death-row prisoners, who had been convicted of murder rather than rape. In addition, it was likely to stimulate intense criticism of the *Boykin* approach.

Maryland had convicted William Ralph of rape in 1961. Ralph had broken into his victim's home and, armed with a tire iron, threatened her and her young son, asleep in another room, with death if she did not submit. Although the woman had been in real fear for her life, violence was not actually employed, and a physician who examined the woman shortly after the crime found no visible sign of trauma. After years of litigation, Ralph's court-appointed lawyer, Edward L. Genn of Washington, D.C., supported by Amsterdam—who presented the case for the Fund as amicus—argued the Eighth Amendment claim to the court of appeals.

Maryland replied that abolition was a matter for the state legislature, not the federal courts, but a three-judge panel of the court, composed of Judges Sobeloff, Haynsworth, and John D. Butzner disagreed.[1] They characterized the question involved in a manner derived from Justice Goldberg's 1963 *Rudolph* opinion: whether the state could kill a rapist who "has neither taken nor endangered life." The Court concluded that while death was not necessarily an unconstitutional penalty for all rapes, two factors coalesced to establish that Ralph could not be executed. First, death for rape was an excessive penalty: only a few jurisdictions authorized it, and even in these it was rarely used. Second, when "a rapist does not take or endanger the life of his victim" his sentence to death is "anomalous when compared to the large number of rapists who are sentenced to prison."

The *Ralph* decision was an important psychological breakthrough, but the Fourth Circuit's reasoning presented problems. By its own terms, the decision was inapplicable to many rape cases (and obviously to all murder cases), but critics would not be put off by its restricted scope. Moreover, other judges were unlikely to agree that Ralph had not endangered life simply because, fortuitously, the victim had been successfully threatened. Many would dispute that the state was obliged to measure each criminal penalty solely by the circumstances of a particular offense. By refusing to prohibit capital punishment for all forms of rape, the court appeared to concede that at least *some* rapes were deterred by capital punishment. If this were true, could not a state assume that punishing men like Ralph with death deterred other rapes? There were also "dangers to the life and health of the victim," such as trauma, possible pregnancy and "loathsome disease" (as one court of appeals judge observed when the state unsuccessfully sought a rehearing)[2] inherent in any rape. The court did not fully explain why the death penalty could not be used to protect women from such risks. But despite these difficulties, the *Ralph* court had demonstrated that at least in some cases capital punishment was sufficiently obnoxious to persuade hard-headed federal judges that room must be found in the Eighth Amendment to prohibit it.

At about the same time that the Fourth Circuit decided the *Ralph* case, Jack Himmelstein reviewed the situation of William Maxwell. After the Supreme Court returned Maxwell's case to the Arkansas federal courts, it had shuttled back and forth between the local federal district court and the Supreme Court of Arkansas. Despite the rather strong suggestion of a *Witherspoon* violation in the opinion of the Supreme Court of the United States, the Supreme Court of Arkansas found none. Meanwhile, Arkansas Governor Winthrop Rockefeller had lost his bid for reelection. Rockefeller had previously expressed opposition to the death penalty on taking office in 1967 by instituting a statewide moratorium on executions. At no time would he be more likely to act upon his beliefs and commute Maxwell's death sentence than in the two months during which he was a lame duck.

Himmelstein explored this possibility with George Howard, Maxwell's Arkansas lawyer, and Raphael Guzman, a professor at the University of Arkansas Law School, who had been studying the operation of the Arkansas prison system. Guzman called an administrative assistant on Rockefeller's staff and obtained an immediate expression of interest.

Several days later, a trial balloon floated in the Arkansas newspapers: the press reported that Rockefeller was considering a general commutation for all death-row inmates before he left office. When the leak was reported to Himmelstein, he immediately called Guzman and talked tactics: should Rockefeller be pressed to make individual decisions about the fifteen men on death row or to deal with them as a group? Should he be asked to commute the sentences of men who had received the death penalty but whose cases had not yet been reviewed by the Supreme Court of Arkansas? Himmelstein favored a mass clemency approach and urged organization of local lawyers to support it. As a fallback position, individual requests for clemency could be presented to the governor.

Guzman was not certain that Rockefeller would be willing to commute the sentence of every death-row inmate. He suggested that Himmelstein and Amsterdam meet with the governor's staff, and perhaps with Rockefeller himself, to discuss the pros and cons of clemency. Himmelstein thought that Arkansans would be far more effective lobbyists than outsiders, but when the potential national consequences of a mass commutation were described to Polester Hollingsworth, the governor's administrative assistant, he asked Himmelstein and Amsterdam to fly to Little Rock and make a formal approach to Rockefeller.

On the Tuesday before Christmas 1970, Amsterdam, Himmelstein, Guzman, Howard, Arkansas prison warden Robert Sarver, Lawrence Wilson, a former San Quentin warden, and several aides to the governor met at the executive mansion. While they waited for the governor to fill the conspicuously empty large black chair in the meeting room, Hollingsworth told Himmelstein that Rockefeller had thought of nothing else for days. He wished to commute all existing death sentences, but needed reassurance that it was the right and proper thing to do.

Finally Rockefeller entered the room, shod in a distinctive pair of cowboy boots, and took his seat. Turning to Guzman, he said, "You have done a study of this. Would you tell us the results?" Guzman made a short statement to the effect that he had carefully examined the records of five Arkansas capital cases and that the court costs in each were so enormous that it was not in the best interest of the state to continue to litigate the cases. Then he introduced Amsterdam.

Facing the governor across the richly polished table, Amsterdam ticked off the arguments against capital punishment. As he spoke, the governor began to nod. He seemed a man who was suddenly hearing from an authoritative source what he had been saying to others for many years. Tension filled the room as Amsterdam closed by alluding to the conventional practice of chief executives to grant clemency to condemned men in cases where two codefendants had received widely disparate sentences. "Disparate sentencing, however, is a characteristic of all capital cases."

The group sat in silence after Amsterdam had concluded. The next move was Rockefeller's. Finally he spoke. "Thank you very much. I had made up my mind, but what you were saying was so interesting that I did not want to interrupt you. But I have made up my mind. I have decided to commute them all. The only problem is . . ." he chuckled, "that you people cannot figure out exactly how many men are eligible."

The group laughed at the governor's joke. Himmelstein, who had sat rigidly throughout, sagged in his chair. The governor had taken the responsibility and made the decision. Suddenly the room was alive with happy people anxious to talk. A committee would work out the details, but all the men on death row were to receive executive clemency.

On December 29, 1970, Rockefeller formally announced

commutation of the sentences of fifteen condemned men to life imprisonment. He urged other governors to follow his example, "so that as a people we may hasten the elimination of barbarism as a tool of American justice . . . My position on capital punishment has been clear since long before I became Governor. I am unalterably opposed to it and will remain so as long as I live." He asked: "What earthly mortal has the omnipotence to say who among us shall live and who shall die?" And answered: "I do not."[3]

January 1971 brought other promising developments.

First, the National Commission on Reform of Federal Criminal Laws (headed by former California Governor Pat Brown) completed its proposed revision of the federal criminal code and recommended that Congress remove the death penalty for all federal crimes. Typically, the Commission was divided on capital punishment, with two members, Democratic Senators Sam Ervin of North Carolina and John McClellan of Arkansas, dissenting from the abolition recommendation.

The Commission's final report also gave a boost to the standards and single-verdict arguments. The proposed code contained an alternate provision (in case abolition was unacceptable to Congress) retaining the death penalty in cases of treason and intentional murder, but excluding offenders whose cases involved specified mitigating circumstances. If Congress kept the death penalty, the Commission also thought that a separate sentencing proceeding should be held "to exclude from the trial testimony relevant only to punishment and likely to prejudice the trial of guilt and sentencing."[4]

Secondly, on January 19 another lame duck, Pennsylvania Attorney General Fred Speaker, decided to act against the death penalty. Persuaded by a *Harvard Law Review* article in which Justice Goldberg and Alan Dershowitz, his ex-clerk, argued that courts had no monopoly on constitutional decision making,[5] Speaker instructed the superintendent of the state prison at Bellefonte to remove the electric chair from the Death Room at Rockview Correctional Institution and to convert the room into an office. "I am convinced," he wrote, "that the imposition of the death penalty constitutes 'cruel and unusual punishment' prohibited by the Eighth and Fourteenth Amendments to the United States Constitution . . . I believe deeply that our practice of killing criminals is both a disgusting indecency and demeaning to the society that tolerates it. In conscience I am compelled to speak out and to do what I can to stop it. The Death Room is an obscenity. Hopefully, legislation to abolish the death penalty will be enacted this year. In the meantime, I am unwilling to leave intact, as I depart my office, a cruel instrument of public vengeance."[6]

The new governor, Milton Shapp, opposed the death penalty, but he challenged Speaker's authority to order the electric chair dismantled: "It's up to the courts to make that decision, not the attorney general." Israel Packel, the governor's counsel, thought Speaker's directive meaningless because the electric chair could be returned to Rockview at any time. Nevertheless, Shapp promised that no one would be executed while he was governor. The new attorney general, J. Shane Creamer, repudiated Speaker's directive, but he made no effort to refurbish the Death Room, which in the meantime had been converted into a psychologist's office. Creamer also ordered Pennsylvania's twenty-four condemned men removed from confinement on death row and placed in the general prison population.

Next, in a bizarre decision later set aside by the state supreme court, the Alabama Court of Appeals ruled that because of an old Alabama statute specifying Kilby Prison, near Montgomery, as the place of execution, none could legally be held elsewhere.[7] As Kilby prison had been razed in 1967, no death sentence could be carried out. Even if the state attempted to restore the means of execution by building an electric chair in the new state prison at Atmore, no new law, the Court held, could operate ex post facto to authorize execution of men already on death row.

The Commission recommendation, the *Ralph* opinion, Rockefeller, Speaker, and even the decision of the Alabama Court of Appeals bolstered flagging spirits and demonstrated that public officials could be won over. But the prospects for success in *McGautha-Crampton* still looked bleak. Jack Himmelstein thought that the Supreme Court might announce its decision rejecting the standards and single-verdict arguments as early as April. As the winter waned, therefore, the flow of paper circulating between New York and Amsterdam's office on the Stanford University campus reached flood level.

On February 27, 1971, Amsterdam, Himmelstein, Nabrit, Lyons, Ralston, Jeffrey Mintz, Elaine Jones (a new Fund staff member) and I met in Greenberg's office to discuss a specific course of action in the event that the Supreme Court ruled against McGautha and Crampton.

Himmelstein stated that a decision was expected in April or May. If it was unfavorable—and all signs pointed in that direction—a general blood-bath might follow. It was possible that the Court would immediately grant review in a case raising the cruel and unusual punishment question, but this could not be assumed—and even if the Court did take such a case, victory was far from assured. It was imperative that a general emergency plan be developed.

Nabrit explained that Greenberg, who had not been able to attend the meeting, wanted to convene a second national conference on the heels of the *McGautha* and *Crampton* decisions to focus attention on the plight of death-row inmates. At the gathering, lawyers from around the nation would brainstorm strategy; the Fund would also make the point that the time had now come when abolition must succeed in the state legislatures. LDF also needed money for the battles ahead. Funds had never been raised solely for capital cases, but Greenberg thought he could persuade the

Rockefeller Foundation to foot the bill—about $20,000—for the conference and that the meeting itself might attract further support.

Several of the lawyers thought that such a conference was not worth the time needed to plan it. They did not want to repeat a general assembly like the one held in 1968, and argued for a small working parley, held without fanfare, even if inconsistent with public relations and fund raising. After an hour of debate, the group agreed to a compromise: a morning session for the press and foundation executives, followed by a day and a half of meetings devoted to pragmatic detail.

A tentative schedule was mapped out. Greenberg and Amsterdam would give opening addresses. Workshops would be scheduled for abolitionists and lawyers who expected to make clemency applications to state governors. Himmelstein and Lyons would put together a tentative list of people to be invited. If Michael Sovern, dean of Columbia Law School, consented, physical arrangements could be worked out to hold the conference there.

Elaine Jones agreed to research state laws in order to instruct conferees in how to block an execution if there was any claim of mental disorder. Lawyers with the Los Angeles firm of O'Melveny and Myers had offered their services and would update the *Witherspoon* argument. Mintz and I were asked to revise the cruel and unusual punishment argument. Himmelstein and Lyons were to strengthen the network of contacts that monitored execution dates. No longer would the Fund rely on volunteers: eight key men, each responsible for a region, would be paid to keep New York informed of imminent executions.

Ralston, Himmelstein, and Lyons took on the most important assignment of preparing a brief for the Supreme Court specifying the constitutional issues present in the hundred or so death cases pending before it. It was hoped that the Court might be persuaded to send many of them back to lower courts on *Jackson* and *Witherspoon* grounds,

even if *McGautha-Crampton* doomed the broader standards and single-verdict issues.

On March 22, Anthony Lewis, an influential reporter as
well as a former *New York Times* Supreme Court correspondent, dismally concluded in a column[8] that the United
States faced the brutalizing effect of a mass slaughter if
McGautha and Crampton lost their cases. For this reason,
Lewis observed cryptically, the two cases "have been considered at a high level in Washington," where "it has been
suggested that Attorney General Mitchell or the President
himself take the lead in urging some form of large-scale
clemency." While clemency was a state function, Lewis
predicted that state governors would welcome the support
of a conservative national Administration to deal "in a
humane way with a terrible problem."

What were the options? Governors could commute all
pending sentences while warning that in the future they
would enforce the death penalty; or they might permit a few
executions, but commute the most sympathetic cases. Both
courses maintained capital punishment while reducing the
number of actual executions, but both made execution seem
even more a matter of chance. Further, the latter alternative presented governors with extremely difficult choices
among individuals.

Although pessimistic about the Supreme Court's present
intentions, Lewis thought the decrease in use of the death
penalty reflected a movement of public opinion: "Perhaps
in a way, the prospect of mass executions will make more
people realize the dangers of killing by law."

Finally, on May 3, 1971, six years after the Fund had
begun to raise the issues in systematic fashion, the Supreme
Court announced its decision in *McGautha v. California*
and *Crampton v. Ohio*.[9] There were no surprises. The
Court ruled that the states might place the life or death
choice in the jury's or judge's absolute discretion, and that
the jury need not determine punishment at a separate

proceeding following the trial of the guilt issue. The vote was 6 to 3, with Harlan, Burger, Stewart, White, and Blackmun the majority, Justice Black concurring in the result, and Douglas, Brennan, and Marshall the dissenters.

Writing for the Court, Justice Harlan concluded that it was impossible to predict in advance the types of offenders who were worthy of death and those who were not: "To identify before the fact those characteristics of criminal homicides and their perpetrators which call for the death penalty and to express these characteristics in language which can be fairly understood and applied by the sentencing authority appear to be tasks which are beyond present human ability." He rejected the approach of the Model Penal Code, and that recommended in January by the National Commission on Reform of Federal Criminal Laws. Instructing the jury about aggravating or mitigating factors gave at best minimal control over the jury's exercise of discretion, he pointed out. Additionally, the factors enumerated in the model codes were not exhaustive. Their incompleteness suggested the "intractable" nature of the problem of drafting standards.

The states were "entitled to assume that jurors confronted with the truly awesome responsibility of decreeing death for a fellow human will act with due regard for the consequences of their decision and will consider a variety of factors, many of which will have been suggested by the evidence or by the arguments of defense counsel." The jury in *McGautha,* Harlan noted, had been able to distinguish between McGautha and his less culpable codefendant, who had received a life sentence. If the Court attempted to enumerate the appropriate factors, the result might be to inhibit rather than expand the scope of consideration, for no list could be comprehensive.

Crampton's claim that he was entitled to a separate penalty proceeding gave Harlan somewhat more difficulty, but he thought that the privilege against self-incrimination was not so broad as to include a right for defendants to limit the effect of their testimony to the issue of punishment. Crampton was entitled to bring to the attention of the sentencing jury matters particularly within his own knowledge, but the Constitution did not give him a right to be free of any adverse consequences which might result from his taking the witness stand, even if his testimony brought out evidence that supported the government's case.

The only passage in the majority opinion that was hopeful for the abolitionist cause merely suggested that the Court had not closed its eyes to the Eighth Amendment claim. It might well be, observed Harlan, that bifurcated trials and standards for jury sentencing were better means of dealing with the problems occasioned by capital cases "if the death penalty is to be retained at all." But the Supreme Court is bound by the provisions of the federal Constitution. They only require fair trials and respect for specifically enumerated rights of defendants. It is not irrational for the states to conclude, he wrote, that the compassionate intent of making the death penalty discretionary with the jury (rather than mandatory upon conviction) is better served by having guilt and punishment settled at a single trial than by focusing the jury's attention solely on punishment *after* determination of the guilt issue. If the jury considered sentence separately, it might more often sentence to death.

The Court's decision was expected, but Justice Hugo Black's short concurring opinion was not. Black began in a fashion famliar to readers of his opinions. He agreed substantially with what Harlan had written, but it was not proper in his view for the Supreme Court to inquire whether or not trials were "fair" if conducted without standards or split-verdict procedures. Federal judicial review, he went on, merely guarantees rights explicitly or impliedly set forth by the specific provisions of the Bill of Rights. This, and only this, is what "due process of law" means; it does not permit courts to reverse criminal convictions because of vague notions of "fairness." It is not enough that judges believe a procedure to have been unfair, arbitrary, or capricious.

Then Black dropped his bombshell by reaching out to observe that capital punishment did not violate the Eighth Amendment or the Fourteenth (which applied the Eighth to the states). In his view, the Cruel and Unusual Punishment Clause could not be read to outlaw capital punishment because at the time the Constitution was adopted the death penalty was in common use and authorized by law both in the United States and in the countries from which the first colonists came. He put it bluntly: ". . . it is inconceivable to me that the framers intended to end capital punishment by the Amendment. Although some people have urged that this Court should amend the Constitution by interpretation to keep abreast of common ideas, I have never believed that lifetime judges in our system have any such legislative power."

Black's reasoning was strong medicine. If followed, it meant that a variety of punishments in common use in 1791—whipping, lopping off of ears, branding, boring through the tongue, the pillory—were perfectly constitutional in the mid-twentieth century. But the most perplexing aspect of Black's opinion was that he need not have written it. The Court did not have the cruel and unusual punishment question before it in *McGautha* and *Crampton,* and Supreme Court Justices do not usually go so far out of their way to express personal views on constitutional issues.

Was there a message to the legal world in Black's concurrence that the moratorium would soon be over? Or, *mirabile dictu,* were his views an attempt to disperse clouds his trained eye saw looming on the horizon? There were no clues to be found. The Supreme Court conducts its deliberations in total secrecy; those who knew were not telling.

Justice Douglas wrote the opinion for the dissenters in *Crampton.* He believed that the right to be heard on the punishment issue included the right to speak for oneself, but this right could only be exercised by an unconstitutional surrender of the privilege against self-incrimination. If a defendant took the witness stand he could have his credibility impeached by admission of evidence establishing prior convictions for felonies or misdemeanors, pending indictments, prior convictions in the military service, dishonorable discharge, or other evidence establishing poor character. In Douglas' view it was almost sadistic to force the defendant to choose between the risk of silence and the perils of giving testimony. In the process, the single trial kept from the jury matters concerning the defendant's background and the character of his offense which were essential to the intelligent imposition of sentence.

Justice Brennan's dissenting opinion in *McGautha* barely suppressed his anger. He accused the majority of misunderstanding the legal argument for sentencing guidelines. Condemned men did not contend that due process required "predetermined standards so precise as to be capable of purely mechanical application." After wrongly assuming a need for "inflexible" legal standards, the majority went on to conclude that the California and Ohio legislatures were unable to put into words just when the state should kill some criminals, while others lived. Significantly, Brennan thought, the states had not argued that their legislatures were incompetent to draft standards.

If legislators were unable to formulate principles governing the life-death choice, the Court must still uphold McGautha's claim, Brennan said. The case involved a conflict between the rule of law and the power of government to kill. The concept of due process of law required that a responsible organ of state government, the legislature, make basic policy choices as to when death was appropriate. Otherwise life or death boiled down to the judgment of the official or jury wielding power at the particular moment.

At the time it seemed that the Douglas and Brennan opinions would be of interest only to scholars. After six years of litigation, the Supreme Court had finally and decisively rejected the two mainstays of the moratorium strategy. More importantly, it had refused an invitation to abolish capital punishment piecemeal. A ruling that required standards and split verdicts would have vacated virtually all existing death sentences and clouded the future of the death penalty for years to come. Would the Court now grasp the nettle and decide the ultimate question of a state's power to kill? The Fund quickly filed a previously prepared brief identifying those cases on the Court's docket with Eighth Amendment claims, making a back-to-the-wall plea for the Court to decide the cruel and unusual punishment issue.

The Court's intentions were uncertain, and enough was at stake for politicians to display caution. On the day that *McGautha* and *Crampton* were decided, Governors John Gilligan of Ohio and Marvin Mandel of Maryland announced that no one would be executed in their states pending resolution of the constitutionality of the death penalty. Ronald Reagan announced a wait-and-see policy. No one was eager to be the first to press the button.

Arthur Goldberg and Alan Dershowitz once again called on Congress to undertake an independent investigation of whether the death penalty violated the federal Constitution. The Supreme Court, they argued, had the last word on the meaning of the Constitution but since the Court had not spoken on the issue, the political branches of government must interpret the Constitution for themselves. Senator Philip A. Hart (D., Mich.) and Representative Emanuel Celler (D., N.Y.), Chairman of the House Judiciary Committee, promptly introduced bills in Congress to impose a two-year moratorium on all federal and state executions.[10] The purpose of the bills, according to Hart and Celler, was to provide breathing space for Congress and state legislatures to consider whether they should abolish or restrict capital punishment.

On May 15 and 16, the emergency conference planned in February to discuss post *McGautha-Crampton* strategy was held in New York City at the Columbia Law School. In a keynote address, Amsterdam told the group to capture public opinion and to present the issue not as "Shall we stop capital punishment?" but rather "Will we resume it?" Then over a hundred lawyers and abolitionists gloomily discussed the likelihood that the Supreme Court would consider the cruel and unusual punishment question. Workshops hassled over last-ditch strategy. Each conferee carried off several pounds of legal memoranda, prepared under Himmelstein's supervision, to be used if the Court refused to extend the moratorium.

But the emergency plans were shelved on June 28, after the Supreme Court gave notice that it would resolve the future of capital punishment. The Court published brief orders granting review in four cases (*Aikens v. California, Branch v. Texas, Furman v. Georgia, Jackson v. Georgia*), limited to the question: "Does the imposition and carrying out of the death penalty in this case constitute cruel and unusual punishment in violation of the Eighth and Fourteenth Amendments?"[11] *Aikens* and *Furman* were murder cases; *Jackson* and *Branch* were rape cases. All four defendants were black; all four victims were white. Fund lawyers were counsel in three of the cases: *Aikens, Furman,* and *Jackson.*

On the same day the Court sifted through the 118 capital cases pending before it, some involving more than one man, and vacated 30 death sentences on *Witherspoon* and *Jackson* grounds.[12] Three others were reversed for reasons having nothing to do with capital punishment. In another case, *Moore v. Illinois,*[13] the Court agreed to consider whether a lower court had watered down the *Witherspoon* ruling. In the remaining cases, the Court took no action. Stays of execution for 92 men (including McGautha and Crampton) continued in effect awaiting decision of the two murder and two rape cases.

Four days later Amsterdam, Falk, and five LDF lawyers met in San Francisco to set in motion the steps needed to prepare the *Aikens, Furman,* and *Jackson* legal briefs. The facts of the four cases in which the Supreme Court had chosen to decide the constitutionality of the death penalty did not simplify preparation of final arguments. Perhaps the Court was keeping its options open. It had selected one case involving a brutal multiple murderer, and another with an emotionally immature and mentally deficient defendant who had killed inadvertently. One rape was accomplished by violence, the other by threats.

Earnest James Aikens, Jr., had been sentenced to death for the murder of Mrs. Mary Winifred Eaton, a white woman in her sixties, but he had also been convicted at the same trial of the earlier murder of Mrs. Kathleen Nell Dodd; for the Dodd killing, he had received a life sentence only because he was seventeen years old at the time of the homicide. At Aiken's punishment trial, California had also introduced evidence that he had committed a third murder and a forcible rape in 1962.

According to the state's version of the facts, Aikens broke into Mrs. Eaton's house during the middle of the day, forced her into a bedroom, bound, gagged, and then raped her. He then stabbed her to death with a bread knife. Her husband testified that seventeen dollars had been stolen from the house. In the Dodd killing, the pattern was similar. The victim was a twenty-five-year-old white housewife, the pregnant mother of two small children. Aikens had entered her home during the late evening, stole sixty dollars from a drawer and a butcher knife from the kitchen. Mrs. Dodd was led out to an area close to her home, raped, and stabbed to death.

The facts of the Georgia murder case were unpleasant, but the defendant, William Henry Furman, did not arouse the same intense disgust as Aikens. Intent on burglary, Furman had entered the home of twenty-nine-year-old William Joseph Micke, Jr., the head of a household with five children. At about 2 A.M., Mr. Micke went downstairs to investigate, and Furman fled, but while running from the house he tripped over the cord of a washing machine on the back porch and his gun discharged, hitting Micke through a closed, solid plywood door.

Although Micke's killing was accidental, or at least committed without intent to kill, Georgia law authorized the death penalty when a killing took place during the commission of a felony. State psychiatrists who had examined Furman found him sane enough to stand trial, although mentally subnormal and suffering from psychotic episodes.

In the Georgia rape case, Lucious Jackson, Jr., an escapee from a prison work gang, had been convicted of the rape of a twenty-one-year-old white woman in 1968. The woman discovered Jackson hiding in her baby's closet; he then held a pair of scissors to her neck and asked for money. When he saw a five-dollar bill, he put the scissors down. She grabbed them, they began to struggle and Jackson raped her. The victim emerged with bruises and abrasions, but was not hospitalized.

Elmer Branch, a twenty-year-old Texan, slipped into the room of Mrs. Grady Stowe, a sixty-five-year-old white woman, surprised her in bed, and raped her. Although Branch pressed his arm on Mrs. Stowe's throat when she tried to yell, he did not threaten her with harm and had no weapon. After the assault, he requested money. Mrs. Stowe gave him the contents of her purse; Branch then left after the two held a brief discussion of the victim's feelings toward black people. The records of the Texas Department of Correction showed that Branch had an IQ of 67.

On July 21, 1971, E. Robert Seaver, the new chief clerk of the Supreme Court, informed each lawyer appearing in the four Eighth Amendment cases that oral argument had been scheduled for the first day of the next term of Court, Tuesday, October 12, 1971. "As you can readily see," he wrote counsel, "this schedule will require that there be no delay in filing the briefs and records in these cases."

Research and brief-writing assignments had been quickly parceled out. By July 23, in a long, involved, and brilliant progress report—only a portion of which is reproduced here—Amsterdam summarized the major themes of the LDF legal arguments:

(1) Hugo Bedau has agreed to send JH [Himmelstein] within 10 days:
   (a) a 10-page review of the sociological literature on deterrence, with references.
   (b) a 10-page memo on the world history of capital punishment, focusing on . . . the progressive abandonment of the death penalty . . . ;
   (c) a brief memo on the role of scientists and learned men in that history, stressing the enlightened character of abolitionists;
   (d) some notes on humanistic literature . . .
JH will ask Hugo if he can expand (b) to include an intellectual history of the struggle about capital punishment; identifying the arguments made for and against it at various stages, and the identities of the makers.

(2) [We must] . . . design an economic cost analysis of the administration of capital punishment.

(3) As per my discussion with Doug Lyons on 7/22, DL is doing
   *(a) a memo on published descriptions of executions;
   (b) some notes on humanistic literature to add his reflections to [Bedau's] in point (1) (d) *supra*.

(4) The following memos will be assigned within the LDF office:
   (a) . . . the major conceptual approach to an argument that the Eighth Amendment is concerned with the psychiatric state of the man who undergoes a punishment: i.e., that a punishment which might constitutionally be applied to *A* may be unconstitutionally cruel and unusual punishment as applied to *B;* and,

* Note: I am not clear whether Doug's memo (a) will include descriptions of the psychological sufferings of men on death row awaiting execution, as well as gory execution scenes . . .

specifically, that it violates the Eighth Amendment to kill persons of diminished mental capacity . . .

(b) . . . recent Eighth Amendment developments in non-capital cases in the lower courts, with emphasis on the themes of (i) evolving character of Eighth Amendment invalidations of penal practices that were widely accepted in 1791; and (ii) the nature of the tests applied to determine whether a penalty is cruel and unusual.

(c) . . . (i) An exhaustive review of [Supreme Court] Eighth Amendment decisions, involving two parts: (A) analyses of each case, including the issues; the holding; the language used to define the Eighth Amendment test, standard or approach employed to judge the constitutionality of penalties challenged as cruel and unusual; and any references made by the Court to interpretative aids (constitutional history, English history, world history, etc.); and (B) analyses of the support which the cases lend to [the following theories] (1) the Eighth Amendment standard is dynamic, not static; it evolves, and may condemn in 1971 what it permitted in 1791; (2) rarity of application of a penalty is a major (or at least a relevant) consideration in branding it cruel and unusual; (3) enlightened conceptions of "decency" and "human dignity" are the measure of the Amendment; (4) judges look to enlightened contemporary moral standards, with some independence of legislative judgment, in applying the Eighth Amendment to test legislation; (5) punishment which is disproportionately severe is unconstitutional under the Eighth Amendment, so that a penalty which might be constitutional for crime A may be cruel and unusual for crime B; and, in particular, death is disproportionately severe for rape; (6) punishment which is "unnecessarily" harsh violates the Eighth Amendment, so that courts must consider whether lesser penalties would not equally serve the end supposed to justify a harsher one; (7) the psychiatric state of the person upon whom a punishment is imposed is relevant . . . ;

and (8) mental suffering, as well as physical suffering, is relevant . . .

(d) . . . A history of the punishments in common use in the Colonies, England and other "civilized" nations in 1791, to show that banishment, dismemberment, flogging, stocking, branding, etc. were widespread, for the purpose of demonstrating that the death penalty cannot be sustained in 1971 upon the theory that it was commonly used at the time of adoption of the Eighth Amendment without also asserting that these horrors are all equally constitutional. (Also it might be useful to have a separate, brief memo demonstrating that *public* executions were the order of the day in 1791, and that our present unobvious executions are a product of a later era.)

The one thing that is not covered in this list [and] which is a high priority item is a memorandum on the rarity of death sentences and of executions in the twentieth century. . . . How about this one, Jack?

Lawyers, law students, and consultants funneled this research through Himmelstein to Amsterdam in California. By July 28, he was in high gear:

Dear Gang:

I will be sending you all portions of the piecemeal drafts of the briefs in *Aikens, Furman* and *Jackson* as I crank them out from time to time. Although we now have an extension until August 26 to file the three briefs, time pressure is going to be intense. If you have any comments, suggestions or concerns with the pieces of the drafts that you receive, please let me know at the earliest possible time. I doubt that we are ever going to be in a position where I can send you the completed drafts in final form; but I shall try to get all the sections into your hands as early as I can.

AGA

On August 18, Jeffrey Mintz arrived at the Stanford campus in Palo Alto to help Amsterdam finish the *Aikens,*

Furman, and *Jackson* briefs, which were due in Court eight days later. He presented Amsterdam with several thick files stuffed with research memoranda prepared by LDF's New York staff, spread out his papers in an empty seminar room, and set to work.

As *Aikens, Furman,* and *Jackson* were paupers, unable to pay the costs of Supreme Court litigation, a government-paid printer would prepare the final version of the briefs from a typed manuscript supplied by the lawyers. For the next week, Amsterdam and Mintz arrived at the law school early each morning and remained until well into the night. Pages were typed and retyped. Law student helpers ran errands, proofed copy, and checked legal citations. Two Berkeley lawyers prepared last-minute memoranda on special aspects of the cases, and each day additional material arrived from Himmelstein in New York.

Amsterdam was still writing late Wednesday afternoon, the day before the deadline. An exhausted secretary was sent home; Mintz, Amsterdam, and two law students finished the typing. By 10:20 P.M., they had completed Xeroxing, collating, and packaging the final manuscript. Mintz grabbed the package, rushed to the San Francisco airport, and put the parcel on the last plane that arrived in Washington in time for a former student of Amsterdam's, who was then working for the District of Columbia Public Defender, to pick up the briefs at the Washington airport and deliver them on schedule to the Supreme Court.

14

Powell and Rehnquist

As the October date set for oral argument of the death penalty cases approached, the Supreme Court received thick answering briefs from California, Georgia, and Texas. They relied heavily on the by-now-familiar position that abolition was up to the states. The framers of the Constitution, they argued, plainly did not intend to end the death penalty. Court decisions (most recently *McGautha-Crampton*) had not questioned its constitutionality. The states were given wide latitude in choosing criminal penalties; there was nothing foreign to American tradition in making death the price for serious crime. Evolving community standards did not make capital punishment unconstitutional. The evidence at most showed not a desire for abolition, but for limited retention. New York, for example, punished killing police officers with death. If the Court held that capital punishment was repugnant to civlized standards of conduct, limited retention to protect the police would be impossible.

The Texas brief in *Branch* raised a more controversial justification: that retribution was a legitimate end of criminal punishment. "The view is still widely held that for some particularly serious and offensive crimes no penalty short of death adequately satisfies the community's sense of just retribution."

According to the Texas brief, experienced law enforcement officers thought the death penalty deterred murder. They were "virtually as one in their conviction that the death penalty is a superior deterrent." In armed robbery cases, it was "common knowledge," according to Georgia, that robbers used unloaded weapons to avoid capital punishment. Even if the Justices believed that death was no more effective a deterrent than life imprisonment, the states reasonably might hold a different view. A state could keep the death penalty, Texas contended, "as a warning to all would-be murderers and rapists," though it actually applied the penalty in only the most serious cases.

Texas and Georgia argued that the death penalty for rape was not applied discriminatorily. The rape rate was higher among blacks than whites; studies in Denver and Philadelphia indicated that the incidence of rape among whites and blacks was one to twelve. If the rate were one to twelve in the South, then the disparity in the numbers executed was less persuasive of discrimination than seemed at first blush. Georgia claimed that in the 1960's the same proportion by race of those convicted were executed. In any event, statistics for the 1930's through the 1960's were "too far removed" to have validity. Racial attitudes in Georgia had changed.

These views were hotly contested by legal briefs submitted to the Court on behalf of individuals, organizations, and one state. Supreme Court cases affect far more people than the parties formally before the Court; those who wish to present their views submit amicus curiae briefs. Issues of consequence always attract a large number of amici, and the four death penalty cases were no exception. Aside from the State of Indiana, the amici offered the Court a grab bag of reasons why they felt capital punishment violated the Eighth Amendment.

A group of governors and ex-governors (Edmund G. Brown (California), David F. Cargo (New Mexico), Elbert N. Carvel (Delaware), Michael V. DiSalle (Ohio), Philip H. Hoff (Vermont), Theodore R. McKeldin (Maryland), Endicott Peabody (Massachusetts), Grant Sawyer (Nevada), and Milton J. Shapp (Pennsylvania), described in graphic detail the physical pain suffered by those executed.

A group of correctional administrators and prison wardens (James V. Bennett, Clinton T. Duffy, Lawrence E. Wilson, Robert Sarver, Harry C. Tinsley) argued on the basis of personal experience that poverty, ignorance, and minority racial status distinguished those sentenced to death. Capital punishment wrongly foreclosed the possibility of rehabilitation, and it discouraged capable men from entering the field of corrections.

Luke McKissack, a lawyer who represented three men on California's death row, including Sirhan Sirhan, emphasized that the states could implement the aims of the criminal law by means less severe than the death penalty.

An Ad Hoc Committee of Psychiatrists for Evaluation of the Death Penalty discussed psychological torture. Time spent on death row amounted to additional punishment of condemned men, often resulting in "brutal mental deterioration." The group reached three major conclusions: first, since crimes are committed for reasons other than a rational consideration of the consequences, the death penalty is not an effective deterrent; secondly, ". . . strong psychological reasons exist for believing that capital punishment serves to legitimize killing as a solution to human problems and actually to incite certain warped mentalities to kill"; and thirdly, the death penalty has a brutalizing effect upon society that apparently stimulates more homicides than it deters.

A scholarly brief from the Synagogue Council of America and its constituents (The Central Conference of

American Rabbis, the Rabbinical Assembly of America, the Union of American Hebrew Congregations, the Rabbinical Council of America, the Union of Orthodox Jewish Congregations of America, the United Synagogue of America, and the American Jewish Congress) canvassed ethical arguments against the death penalty and traced their roots in ancient Jewish tradition.

A large group of religious denominations and leaders (The National Council of the Churches of Christ in the United States of America; the American Friends Service Committee; The Board of Social Ministry, The Lutheran Church in America; The Church of the Brethren; The Council for Christian Social Action of the United Church of Christ; the Disciples of Christ; the Presiding Bishop of the Episcopal Church in the United States; the General Board of Christian Social Concerns of the United Methodist Church; the Greek Orthodox Archdiocese of North and South America; the American Ethical Union; the United Presbyterian Church in the United States of America; the National Catholic Conference for Interracial Justice; and the National Coalition of American Nuns) interspersed ethical objections with a judicious sprinkling of gruesome execution scenes.

A group representing the major religious groups in the State of West Virginia (the West Virginia Council of Churches, the Christian Church Disciples in West Virginia, and the United Methodist Church) also focused on physical and mental cruelty.

The NAACP, National Urban League, Southern Christian Leadership Conference, Mexican-American Legal Defense and Educational Fund, and the National Council of Negro Women argued that historically white American society had imposed harsher punishment, including capital punishment, on minority group members. They urged the Court to evaluate the death penalty within the context of a prior history of official and nonofficial racial violence, and suggested that post-1930 execution figures could only be explained as a vestige of pre–Civil War laws that authorized heavier penalties on racial grounds.

The National Legal Aid and Defender Association, an organization primarily concerned with the legal rights of indigents, stressed that condemned men were invariably poor.

The lengthy brief of the American Civil Liberties Union, written by Gerald Gottlieb, included an elaborate and well-documented argument that adequate alternatives to the death penalty existed with which society could defend itself, and that life on death row awaiting execution, and the execution itself, were indistinguishable from medieval torture.

A short brief from the State of Alaska testified to the success of that state's experience with abolition.

Only the State of Indiana joined California, Georgia, and Texas in favoring retention of the death penalty. A brief written by its attorney general, Theodore L. Sendak, quoted extensively from his speeches, and told the Justices that if society finds the death penalty repugnant, legislation or a constitutional amendment was the appropriate means to change the law.

While lawyers for the condemned, the states, and the interested peppered the Court with paper, an unexpected development led to postponement of the October 12 oral argument. Within a period of six days in September 1971, Justices Hugo L. Black, eighty-five, and John M. Harlan, seventy-two, resigned from the Supreme Court for health reasons; in three months both men were dead. The resignations meant that for the first time in thirty years an American President would have two Supreme Court vacancies to fill at the same time.

Given Nixon's attitude toward the Warren Court's civil rights and criminal law decisions, this unexpected opportunity to name two new Justices (four in all) might have shattered hopes for abolition. But while journalists had misunderstood Justice Black by describing him as "liberal" and oversimplified Harlan by labeling him a "conservative," neither would have been likely to vote to abolish the death penalty. Black, of course, had made known his position in *McGautha-Crampton*. Harlan's attitude was far more difficult to discern but he had written the Court's opinion in both cases. At the most, therefore, the retirement of Black and Harlan cost abolition one vote. If, however, the Justices were badly split on capital punishment, as Fund lawyers surmised, the two new appointees might exercise a decisive influence on the Court's key middlemen, Justices Stewart and White.

Because two of Nixon's past nominees had failed to win Senate confirmation, LDF lawyers hoped that he would propose one Justice who was not antagonistic to the Warren Court record in order to ensure confirmation of a second candidate less acceptable to the Senators who had defeated Haynsworth and Carswell. The President quickly shattered such wishful thinking of a trade-off. A White House aide was quoted as saying, "The next Court will be known as the Nixon Court, not the Burger Court or the Warren Court."

Several weeks after the Black and Harlan resignations, the White House leaked to the press the name of Congressman Richard H. Poff of Virginia, a man whose appointment would fulfill Nixon's longstanding pledge to name a Southerner to the Court. But a Poff nomination threatened a repeat of the Haynsworth and Carswell affairs. He had never voted for a civil rights bill, and in 1956 he had signed two anti–civil rights manifestoes drafted by Southern Congressmen. Abolitionists noted that Poff had served as vice chairman of the National Commission on Reform of Federal Criminal Laws that had recommended legislative abolition for federal crimes earlier in 1971, but there was no evidence that he believed the Supreme Court should end the death penalty or that the states were constitutionally forbidden to execute.

There were many who, after careful study of his legislative record, concluded that Poff would have given the White House more trouble than it bargained for, and that the next nominee would be *worse*. Nevertheless, Poff became a victim of the same coalition that had defeated Haynsworth and Carswell. Bishop Stephen G. Spotswood, the Chairman of the National Board of the NAACP, announced that the Association opposed the nomination; George Meany called Poff a racist. On October 2, apparently fearing another Senate debacle, Poff abruptly withdrew his name from consideration.

During the weeks that opposition to Poff gathered steam, the White House had leaked its interest in Lewis F. Powell, Jr., of Virginia, a former president of the American Bar Association. Initially, little attention was paid to Powell's name, newsmen preferring to concentrate on rumors of appointment of a woman to fill the second vacancy. With the growth of feminist political activity, journalists speculated that Nixon wished to be viewed as seriously considering the nomination of the first woman Associate Justice. Among the names dropped were Sylvia Bacon, a superior court judge in Washington, D.C., and Mildred Lillie, a state court judge in California.

While the President reportedly searched the country for a qualified woman, West Virginia's Democratic Senator Robert Byrd replaced Poff as the leading candidate for the other Court seat. This time the Administration's strategy seemed unbeatable. Because he was a powerful congressional politician and the Democratic Whip, the clubbiness of the Senate protected Byrd from a bitter floor fight. But like so many other Southern and border state politicians, Byrd had the past to explain. He had once organized for the Ku Klux Klan and like Poff had voted against civil rights legislation. Even in a 1965 Senate speech, he sounded as if he had not left the Klan view of the world behind: "Poverty is blamed for the riots. Yet poverty-stricken whites outnumber Negroes in America, but they are not rioting . . . We can take the people out of the slums but we cannot take the slums out of the people."[1]

Byrd had another liability that embarrassed even his warmest supporters: he had only graduated from law school (after six years as a part-time student) in 1963, had never tried a case, and had never obtained a license to practice law. "Being a lawyer," Byrd retorted incredibly, "is not an absolute requisite to serving on the Supreme Court."

After the Haynsworth and Carswell defeats, Attorney General John Mitchell announced that the Administration intended to consult the American Bar Association prior to making future Supreme Court nominations. Consistent with this new policy, on October 13, the President requested the ABA Committee on the Federal Judiciary to consider the qualifications of six candidates. The list included Judges Bacon and Lillie; two Southern appellate court federal judges, Paul Roney of Florida and Charles Clark of Mississippi; Hershel Friday, a municipal bond lawyer from Arkansas; and Senator Byrd.

The reaction against the "Nixon six" was strong and predictable. Those on the list who were known at all had distinguished themselves by representing Southern officials in segregation cases (Friday, Clark) or opposing civil rights legislation (Byrd); those who were not well known (Lillie, Bacon, Roney) seemed simply too undistinguished to sit on the Court. The academic community was particularly disturbed by the intellectual quality of the candidates. Twenty-five members of the Harvard Law School faculty signed a statement declaring that "at least half" of the six did not measure up to minimum standards for a Supreme Court nominee. A majority of the Stanford law faculty pronounced all six unsatisfactory.

Although the President had named six potential candidates, the Justice Department instructed the ABA committee to limit its inquiry to Friday and Lillie. Mrs. Lillie had been criticized because of her anonymity, and because higher courts had reversed her rulings too often. Friday's role as counsel to the Little Rock, Arkansas, school board certainly did not help him. The Arkansas *Gazette,* an influential Little Rock newspaper, announced its opposition: "Much of the legal labor of Herschel Friday over the last dozen years has been turned to the purpose of keeping black children out of white schools." But the ABA committee administered the *coup de grâce* when it voted 11 to 1 that Lillie was unqualified, and defeated 6 to 6 a motion to record the committee as "not opposed" to Friday. The President was not, of course, bound by the votes, but without ABA support both nominations would result in long, drawn-out battles in the Senate, with eventual confirmation in serious doubt.

Nixon's reaction was swift. The day after the committee rejected Friday and Lillie, he replaced them with men not on the list of six. On October 21, he told a national television audience his choices: Lewis F. Powell, Jr., a name mentioned but ignored, and William H. Rehnquist, a totally unexpected nomination. Neither man had been cleared with the ABA committee. Ominously for anti–capital punishment lawyers, Nixon assured the nation that his nominees believed as he did that it was time for the "peace forces" to assert themselves over the "criminal forces."

Powell was a sixty-four-year-old commercial lawyer. After college and law school at Washington and Lee University, and a short period of study for an advanced degree at Harvard, he had joined a Richmond law firm. In 1964 he won election as ABA President, and even critics of his nomination to the Court admitted that he had done a good job.

Between 1952 and 1961, as Chairman of the Richmond school board, Powell played the role of "racial moderate." He was responsible for keeping the city's schools open at a time when most Virginia public schools were closed to thwart court orders; on the other hand, he did little to stimulate integration. In 1971 he had written an amicus curiae brief in an important Supreme Court desegregation case, *Swann v. Charlotte-Mecklenberg Board of Education*,[2] at the request of Virginia Governor Linwood Holton. In the brief, Powell criticized federal court orders requiring substantial public school integration because they speeded the flight of whites to suburbs.

Powell's public statements and published articles argued that the Supreme Court had handicapped the police: "The pendulum," he wrote, "may have swung too far in affording rights which are absued and misused by criminals."[3] In 1967, as a member of the President's Commission on Law Enforcement and Administration of Justice, he signed, along with six other Commission members, a minority report critical of Supreme Court criminal procedure decisions. The report called for a constitutional amendment to permit the use of voluntary confessions, even if they were given by persons not advised of their rights to remain silent and to talk with a lawyer.[4]

Still, Powell's confirmation was assured. His social and political views hardly disqualified him in the eyes of most Senators, and no one spoke of him as other than a man of integrity. Also, he had served both Democratic and Republican administrations and was regarded as a leader of the legal profession. The labor and civil rights coalition was uneasy, but concluded that it would have to live with Powell. Along with some Senate liberals, the AFL–CIO and the NAACP decided to concentrate on defeating Rehnquist.

At the time of his nomination, William H. Rehnquist, forty-seven, was the Assistant Attorney General in charge of the Justice Department's Office of Legal Counsel, a position which might be described as chief legal advisor to the Attorney General. Born in Milwaukee, he had graduated from Stanford University, received an M.A. in history from Harvard, and returned to Stanford, where he received his law degree two years later, graduating first in his class. Following law school, Rehnquist clerked for Supreme Court

Justice Robert H. Jackson; thereafter, he moved to Phoenix, Arizona, and became immersed in Republican politics.

In 1964 Rehnquist vigorously opposed the passage of a Phoenix city ordinance requiring all public establishments to serve anyone, regardless of race, on the ground that it infringed property rights. It was alleged, but never proven, that he organized campaigns in 1962 and 1964 to challenge the eligibility of black voters in Phoenix. In 1967 he fought a move to eradicate de facto segregation in the Phoenix public schools: "we are no more dedicated to an 'integrated' society," he argued, "than we are to a 'segregated' society."[5]

As Assistant Attorney General, Rehnquist demonstrated what opponents of his confirmation characterized as "insensitivity" to civil liberties, a charge all the more bitterly lodged because he was not an intellectual lightweight like Carswell. He defended government surveillance of political groups, insisting that "the First Amendment does not prohibit even foolish or unauthorized information gathering by the government."[6] He justified dragnet arrests by Washington police of thousands of persons (bystanders as well as protestors) at a May Day 1971 anti–Vietnam War demonstration by declaring that the police "have the authority to detain individuals during an emergency without being required to bring them before a magistrate and filing charges against them."[7]

Faced with the prospect of an extremely conservative and bright Justice who would be on the Supreme Court for years, civil rights and labor organizations, liberal academics, and Senators mobilized to block Rehnquist's confirmation. In addition to the AFL–CIO and the NAACP, the United Auto Workers, the Leadership Conference on Civil Rights, the National Legal Aid and Defender Association, and the National Bar Association (a black group) announced their opposition.

Senator Bayh, a leading Senate critic, attempted to

equate Rehnquist's views on segregation with Carswell's: "A sophisticate like Bill Rehnquist, arguing persuasively that our society is no more dedicated to integration than segregation can perhaps persuade a wide audience. But wipe away the rhetoric and their views are identical."[8]

A strongly worded statement by several members of the Senate Judiciary Committee (Senators Kennedy, Bayh, John V. Tunney, and Hart) called on the Senate to vote against confirmation because Rehnquist's record "on issues involving the Bill of Rights . . . on surveillance, wire-tapping, inherent executive power, criminal procedural safeguards, dissent by public employees, and more—is a profoundly disturbing one. . . ."[9]

A group of activist law professors and law students worked to block Rehnquist's confirmation by providing liberal Senators with a critical analysis of his public positions and writings, but the Administration acted to defuse their efforts. FBI agents questioned Amsterdam, Professor Gary Orfield of Princeton University, and Professor Laurence H. Tribe of Harvard Law School, "possible" opponents of the Rehnquist and Powell nominations. The agents inquired whether the professors had gathered any information on the nominees, whether they intended to study the choices, and whether they planned to oppose them.

But Rehnquist had vocal supporters. Dean William H. Pedrick of the Arizona State University Law School and Dean Phil C. Neal of the University of Chicago Law School both endorsed the appointment. In Neal's judgment, Rehnquist's appointment "would add great strength to the Court."[10] In a letter to Senator James Eastland (D., Miss.), Chairman of the Senate Judiciary Committee, Professor Benno Schmidt, Jr., of the Columbia Law School, who had worked with Rehnquist in the Justice Department, expressed the view that the nominee was "unusually open-minded and free of reliance on dogma in dealing with constitutional questions."[11]

Schmidt touched a sensitive nerve when he argued that opposition to Rehnquist on the basis of his political views was inappropriate. Many liberal Senators who had disliked Carswell's politics were able to oppose him ostensibly on the grounds of blatant racism and judicial incompetence. Although the same Senators disliked Rehnquist's "right-wing political philosophy," most felt that they could not honestly vote to reject his nomination simply because they disagreed with his views. Rehnquist was neither a blatant racist nor a mediocre thinker. Arguments that he was closed-minded and lacked basic fairness were easily characterized as a smoke screen hiding dislike of his politics—which probably included support of the death penalty.

The ABA Committee on the Federal Judiciary unanimously found Rehnquist's credentials satisfactory, and a majority voted him "one of the best qualified available." The Senate Judiciary Committee recommended confirmation by a vote of 12 to 4. The majority saw "a man who fully understands and believes in the guarantees of individual freedom embodied in the Bill of Rights." Although Bayh and Kennedy took their case to the Senate floor, their efforts failed. On December 10, 1971, Rehnquist was confirmed by a vote of 68 to 26; four days earlier the Senate had confirmed Powell 89 to 1, with Senator Fred Harris (D., Okla.) the lone dissenter.

15

Closing In

"The California Supreme Court is to the courts what U.C.L.A. is to basketball."

ANTHONY G. AMSTERDAM

Senate deliberations had caused the Justices to delay hearing the four death penalty cases until January; the several months' postponement turned out to be a critical break for the abolitionists.

The new turn of events began late one afternoon in early December 1971, when Jerome Falk received a call from G. E. Bishel, the clerk of the California Supreme Court. Bishel explained that in January the court was going to hear still another appeal in the case of Robert Page Anderson, the same man whose challenge to the California death penalty the court had rejected in 1968. Anderson had won a new penalty trial on *Witherspoon* grounds, but the trial court had resentenced him to death. Anderson's lawyer had died. The court, Bishel continued, intended to reconsider the cruel and unusual punishment issue and to schedule the case for argument at the earliest convenient date. Would Falk or Amsterdam be willing to represent Anderson, file a brief, and argue the case?

After he recovered his composure, Falk quickly told

Bishel that Amsterdam would argue the case, but that since Amsterdam had never been admitted to law practice in California, he himself would accept appointment as counsel of record. Falk had barely put down the phone when he realized that the Supreme Court of California apparently was rushing to decide Anderson's case before the Supreme Court of the United States handed down its ruling in the four Eighth Amendment cases.

The oral argument was held January 6, 1972, two weeks before the United States Supreme Court hearings. Questions from the bench revealed a sympathetic court, confirming Falk's feeling that something was afoot. But in 1968, he reflected, the Court had appeared friendly and had gone on to reject the cruel and unusual punishment claim.

After argument of Anderson's case, attention turned to the Supreme Court of the United States. The four death cases were scheduled for hearing on Monday, January 17, 1972. First, the Court would listen to lawyers in the two murder cases, *Aikens* (from California) and *Furman* (from Georgia). In both, Amsterdam would argue for the condemned men. Ronald M. George—the state's lawyer in *McGautha*—represented California, and Mrs. Dorothy Beasley of the State Attorney General's Office spoke for Georgia.

In *Jackson v. Georgia,* the first of the rape cases, Mrs. Beasley also served as the state's counsel; Jack Greenberg represented Jackson. In the final case, Melvin Carson Bruder of Dallas, Texas, argued for Elmer Branch, and Charles Alan Wright, a distinguished University of Texas law professor, for the state. Each case would consume an hour, with thirty minutes allotted to a side.

Amsterdam prepared himself for the arguments on the West Coast and flew to New York on Friday to consult with Himmelstein. Greenberg wrote out a draft of his argument on Friday, and on Saturday morning gave a mock presentation to a group of Fund lawyers who played the role of Supreme Court Justices. This ritual of preparation, called a "dry run," was standard operating procedure for LDF lawyers appearing before the Court. Jostled by questions and comments, Greenberg refined his approach during the rest of the weekend.

On Sunday, both men took a train to Washington, along with Amsterdam's wife, Lois, Greenberg's wife, Deborah— both lawyers—and two of Greenberg's children, then retreated to rooms in the Sheraton-Carlton Hotel. The two men agreed that Greenberg would present the death penalty for rape as a geographic and racially restricted phenomenon and thereby "unusual"; Amsterdam would tackle the history and meaning of the Eighth Amendment and press the Supreme Court to act against the death penalty rather than defer to elected legislatures.

The following morning Amsterdam sat at the counsel table lost in thought as he waited for the Justices to enter. Next to him, Himmelstein flipped through a file. Greenberg stood nearby chatting with Jack MacKenzie, the Washington *Post*'s Supreme Court correspondent, and Bobby Hill, Jackson's Georgia lawyer. Charles Alan Wright, a tall patrician-looking man sat next to Crawford Martin, the Attorney General of Texas. Solicitor General Griswold shook hands with several visiting attorneys. Fund lawyers crowded the section reserved for members of the bar. Tourists filed neatly into pews behind the lawyers' section.

At 10 A.M. the Justices stepped from behind the curtains at the front of the courtroom. The nine men seated themselves in high-backed swivel chairs behind the long bench. Several opinions in pending cases were announced, and new members were welcomed to the bar of the Court. After what seemed to me like hours—actually only twenty minutes after the Justices had entered—the Chief Justice called the first case, *Aikens v. California*. Amsterdam rose and stepped to the lectern directly in front of Burger.

The four cases that the Court is to hear, Amsterdam began, involve the claim that the death penalty is cruel and unusual punishment. They include two rape and two murder cases, and a range of facts. Many considerations have been canvassed in the briefs. But the nub of the issue before the Court is the scope and wisdom of judicial review of state legislation requiring that particular crimes be punished with death. Forty-one states and the federal government at present provide the death penalty for some criminal offenses. The judgment of these legislatures is entitled to enormous respect, and judicial review of the decision of elected representatives to maintain capital punishment is difficult. But it is inevitable. The very existence of the Eighth Amendment is proof that legislatures are not totally free to set punishments. Because of the vagueness of the Cruel and Unusual Punishment Clause, the critical question is the test to use in applying the Amendment.

We do not argue, continued Amsterdam, that anything which shocks the consciences of particular judges violates the Constitution. That is too subjective a standard. We contend that the proper measure is objective: whether a punishment *if evenhandedly applied* would be unacceptable to contemporary standards of decency.

This is the proper Eighth Amendment test for three reasons. First, it takes account of the differences between courts and legislatures. Courts are concerned with the way a penalty operates in individual cases; legislatures look only to its general availability.

Justice Stewart: Are there any mandatory death statutes left?

Amsterdam: Very few, and most are obsolete . . . The second reason is that this test assigns a proper function to the Eighth Amendment. In a democracy, a generally applied but repugnant penalty would quickly be wiped off the books. A selectively applied penalty, however, one only used on the ugly, the poor, and the black, is not likely to provoke public revulsion. Selective, infrequent use of a penalty sterilizes the political processes of change, and explains why we have the Eighth Amendment in the Constitution in the first place.

Thirdly, our theory of the Cruel and Unusual Punishment Clause does not invite subjective judgments by judges about penological policy. In fact, it is an alternative to such an approach. The states concede that some criminal penalties which kill—say boiling in oil—are unconstitutional. But in Eighth Amendment terms, what is the difference between boiling in oil and electrocution or gassing? The states do not say, other than to assert that some penalties which kill are "horrible," while others that kill are not.

Justice Stewart: What do you say to the argument of the states that capital punishment was permitted at the time the Constitution was adopted, and also at the time the Fourteenth Amendment was adopted in 1868? Their position is that because the Constitution prohibits denial of life *without* due process of law it permits capital punishment when due process of law has been accorded.

Amsterdam: The Constitution says that if death is to be a penalty, then the condemned must be chosen by fair procedures, but it does not say that we must always have capital punishment. The language which became the Eighth Amendment was first put in the English Bill of Rights because of the seventeenth-century perjury trial of Titus Oates. Oates was not sentenced to a barbarous penalty but to an unprecedentedly harsh one—stripped of the rights of clergy, whipped, pilloried, fined, and imprisoned for life. It was a selectively harsh penalty. In 1967 the President's Crime Commission reported that the most striking characteristic of modern use of the death penalty was its rarity.

The death penalty was rarely used even before the moratorium of the late 1960's. We averaged 20 or so executions a year in the early sixties, down from 175 in the fifties. In 41 states, we now have a total of about 100 death *sentences* a year.

The Court had been more silent than usual. The faces of the Justices showed intense concentration. A light on the lectern indicated that Amsterdam's time in the first case had elapsed.

Ronald M. George, the California deputy attorney general, took his place facing the Justices. In one respect, at least, he agreed with Amsterdam: the critical question is whether the people of California or the Justices of the Supreme Court decide what sorts of criminal penalties the state is permitted.

Justice Douglas: Do you have any statistics describing the kind of people who are executed?

George side-stepped: The question is not who is executed but whether the legislature could reasonably believe that capital punishment deters.

Justice Stewart interjected: Is that the sole criterion?

George: Yes, so long as execution is carried out in a humane manner.

Justice Stewart: But burning at the stake would be a deterrent?

George: The Eighth Amendment, however, prohibits unnecessary pain.

Justice Stewart: Then it is your argument that if death is a deterrent and "no more pain is inflicted in imposing it than is necessary to kill, it's okay?"

George: Yes, because "cruelty means something more than death; it means something barbaric—but death is not barbaric."

Justice Marshall: Does the meaning of cruel and unusual change?

George: A form of punishment is unconstitutional that inflicts wanton pain or is unusual—not customary for that offense.

Justice Marshall: "Then or now?"

George: "Then." Words do not change their meaning every day. If they did our standards might regress, as happened in Germany during the 1940's. Boiling in oil might become the vogue . . . The Fifth Amendment [Double Jeopardy Clause] sanctifies the death penalty by its very terms.

Justice Stewart: Would you argue that the arm of a thief

could be cut off because the Fifth Amendment's Double Jeopardy Clause talks about not placing people twice in jeopardy of life or *limb?*

George: I do not think the framers of the Fifth Amendment were talking about taking off a limb but of corporal punishment generally . . . Even by Mr. Amsterdam's standards death is not cruel and unusual punishment. Forty-one states have it on the books; polls support it; some religious leaders support it. Capital punishment is part of our moral and theological heritage, sanctified as a legitimate form of punishment by a thousand years of use. Eight states have abolished and then changed their minds. California and the federal government recently added new capital offenses. No other nation has abolished judicially—although a great deal has been made by Aikens' lawyers of what happens in places like Mozambique and Lichtenstein. Juries in this country are the conscience of the community and they have continued to bring in death verdicts. There is even evidence that they have brought in more in recent years.

Justice Stewart interrupted: Could that be because they do not believe that the death penalty will be carried out?

George: No, jurors will not violate their oaths. Another flaw in the abolition argument is the assertion that "withering away" will not be reflected in legislation. When a man is having trouble with a naturalization matter, Congressmen have private bills enacted. This proves anyone can get legislation.

Justice Marshall: Is this on that level?

George: I think it instructive. The main point is that Mr. Amsterdam and his co-counsel have set themselves up as the guardians of evolving standards of decency, and they are asking this Court to set itself up as a super legislature. It is the state legislatures that should decide whether some men are unrehabilitable and should be killed, or if death deters crime. There is no discrimination against the poor, the sick, or the black in California. Only a small proportion of all murderers are sentenced to death—the Sirhans, the Mansons, the Aikenses. Juries are being discriminating, rather than discriminatory.

When Amsterdam returned to the lectern in the second murder case, *Furman v. Georgia,* he began by recalling one of the questions Stewart had asked in the *Aikens* case. Justice Stewart, he explained, had inquired whether if a punishment served a legitimate state purpose—say deterrence —it was immune from Eighth Amendment challenge. A legislature could plainly conclude, Amsterdam answered, that boiling in oil deterred crime. It was nonetheless unconstitutional. There was more to the Amendment than a requirement that criminal penalties deter. Forty-one states have the death penalty on the books but they do not use it. This is part of a world trend.

Chief Justice Burger: How did other nations abolish?

Amsterdam: Some by legislation, some simply by not enforcing the penalty.

Burger: It is not usually done by court decisions?

Amsterdam: Courts rarely have that power in other nations.

Justice Burger changed tack: Could the Supreme Court abolish death for murder, but permit the states to retain it for a more specific crime—say killing a prison guard?

Amsterdam: If a legislature passed a narrow statute directed to a specific evil, we would have a different case. The problems with statutes dealing with police and guards is that we have not had enough experience with them. But we have experience with general murder and rape statutes and have learned that there are approximately a hundred death sentences imposed each year. Only one out of every twelve or thirteen capital trials results in a death sentence.

Justice Rehnquist: Does your one in twelve or thirteen statistic include cases where the prosecuting attorney does not ask for the death penalty?

Amsterdam: It is difficult to know, but in many jurisdictions the prosecutor cannot control what the jury does.

Rehnquist: Do your figures include judge-imposed sentences?

Amsterdam: The statistics do not discriminate between judge and jury. But even pre-*Witherspoon* juries, with the scrupled jurors removed, refused to condemn in the overwhelming majority of cases. In a nation with a crime scare, and growing population, only a few are executed. Consequently, there is no pressure for the legislature to do anything about the death penalty.

Justice Marshall: How can you say it's so few if California has 105 people on death row?

Amsterdam: The number reflects an accumulation of many years; only one man has been executed in California since 1963.

The Chief Justice: If there are seven hundred people on death row is that not strong pressure on legislatures?

Amsterdam: The pressure will only tell if execution is resumed. Public sentiment will not be activated by an announcement that several "ugly" men will be executed at some future time.

Justice Stewart wanted to make certain that he understood Amsterdam's position: Even if rational people conclude that the death penalty is a deterrent, that it is not administered with unnecessary pain, that there are criminals who are not rehabilitable, that it is less expensive than prison, it still violates the Eighth Amendment?

Amsterdam: Exactly. Even if the ends are legitimate, the means are limited by the Constitution.

Mrs. Beasley began her reply by urging the Court to confront a threshold question of its power. The Fourteenth Amendment speaks of depriving a person of life if due process is accorded. By reading the Eighth Amendment to restrict state power in this area, the Court would be rewriting the Fourteenth.

Justice Marshall broke in: Then the states could boil in oil?

Beasley: No, that would violate due process.

Stewart leaned forward, impassive. Powell, as he had throughout the argument, looked at a pile of papers in front of him. Douglas looked querulous. Justice White rocked softly in his chair, his face ashen. Was he in a bad mood, did he have the flu, or did the cases trouble him?

Justice Douglas: Could Georgia impose death on all murderers except those that made over $50,000 a year?

Beasley: That would violate due process. That is discriminatory.

Justice Douglas: So cruel and unusual punishment carries with it a discrimination component?

Beasley: Yes.

Justice Douglas closed in: "Who does Georgia execute?"

Mrs. Beasley hedged: Discrimination would violate the Equal Protection Clause but not the Eighth Amendment, and anyway it is not proved. No state or federal court has decided that it is cruel and unusual to kill a murderer. The test is whether a punishment shocks the conscience, and this one does not.

Amsterdam spoke briefly in rebuttal: Juries are indeed the conscience of the community, but what they have done is to impose death rarely. Well, then, one may ask, why not leave them alone? The answer is that men get caught in the net of death unintentionally or because of race. Take this case. It was a horrible crime, but also a common felony murder; there was nothing to distinguish it from scores of cases where the defendant is given a life sentence.

In the third case, *Jackson v. Georgia,* Greenberg's task was to make abolition attractive for an offense which did not involve the taking of life, without going so far as to suggest that the Court should retain the death penalty for murder. He restricted himself to pointing out considerations especially relevant to the cruel and unusual punishment argument in rape cases.

Under any definition of the word, he thought, killing a man is cruel; the real question is whether it is unusual. The death penalty is plainly unusual for rape. Only Southern states authorize it. Even in the South, it is usually applied only to blacks who rape whites. Death as punishment for rape is rare in the international community—one study found three countries that permitted it. It is restricted racially: of 455 executions since 1930 for the crime, 405 of the men killed were black; of 73 men now on death row for the crime, 62 are black, one is an Indian, and one a Mexican. In Georgia, 58 of 61 rapists executed since 1930 were black. A black Georgian convicted of rape has a 38-percent chance of receiving the death penalty; but if a Georgian convicted of rape is white, his chance is one-half of one percent.

There is no need for a death penalty for rape. It is disproportionate to the offense and it does great mischief—for it tells minority group members how little the majority values their lives.

Greenberg was asked few questions. If the Court was interested in a split ruling—making death permissible for murder but not for rape—would it not have questioned Greenberg more thoroughly?

For the state, Mrs. Beasley sought to avoid any direct discussion of the racial history of Georgia's rape statute. She observed that the statistics do not reflect the present practice; they are unpersuasive; and they do not explore the factual circumstances of each case. At any rate, discrimination does not establish cruel and unusual punishment but is a violation of the Fourteenth Amendment's Equal Protection Clause—a claim not before the Court. Greenberg was really attacking the jury system, she implied. The way to deal with prejudice is by pre-screening jurors with questions and rooting it out.

Justice Stewart: The petitioner is not claiming a denial of equal protection, only the unusualness of the death penalty.

Beasley: Other countries and states still authorize a life sentence for rape; thus it is a serious crime. Is the difference between life and death so great that death is disproportionate for rape and life imprisonment is not?

Justice Marshall: But there is no death penalty in Georgia for shooting a man who does not die—even if you make him a vegetable.

Justice White interjected: If Georgia executed one in every hundred men convicted of rape would that make it an unusual penalty?

Beasley: It would be unusual but not constitutionally unusual.

Justice Stewart: Do you mean that unusual means exotic, not infrequent?

Beasley: Yes, that is the point.

In the last case, *Branch v. Texas,* Melvin Carson Bruder sailed through the Texas statistics and repeated some of those brought out by Greenberg: blacks have a 78 percent chance of getting the death penalty; whites (including Mexican-Americans), 22 percent. Texas procedure also violated the Constitution, according to Bruder, because the prosecutor is permitted to decide whether or not to seek the death penalty.

Justice Rehnquist pounced: Is that not true elsewhere?

Bruder: I do not know.

Justice Rehnquist: Prosecutors generally have the power to decide what offense should be charged, don't they? Doesn't this power always give them the ability to affect the authorized sentence?

Bruder: The point is that in Texas prosecutors do not seek death when whites are charged with rape.

Charles Alan Wright was the last lawyer to speak. The professor from Texas—an authority on federal criminal law—was the states' big gun. Texas Attorney General Crawford Martin told a reporter that he had retained Wright specially to defend the death penalty in *Branch* after hearing secondhand that Chief Justice Burger had "expressed an interest as to how Charles Alan Wright felt about the issue."

Surprisingly, Wright did not address his remarks so much to the legitimacy of death for rapists—the issue in *Branch*

—as to the question of the constitutionality of capital punishment for any offense. In a manner that could be appreciated fully only by members of the academic legal community, Professor Wright seemed set upon refuting Professor Amsterdam's earlier argument. Justices, audience, courthouse, all seemed to dissolve as if two scholars were having the issue out at a faculty meeting.

Wright: If one allows that capital punishment is permitted for any crime—like assassination of a President or bombing a 747 airplane—it is not inherently cruel. Capital punishment could not be prohibited for homicide, but permitted for these crimes, because these other offenses are still more rare. How can we say that murderers in general cannot be punished with death because it is cruel but that some murderers can be so punished? There is, moreover, no disproportionality in killing murderers. We execute few people, but this does not prove that we are not being selective.

Justice White: Would you be troubled if we only put one out of the hundred rapists to death?

Wright: Not under the Eighth Amendment. That would be a due process or equal protection question, but by putting a few people to death we simply keep the death penalty credible.

Justice White: So rarity becomes relevant at some point, but your position is that we have not reached that point yet?

Wright: Infrequency is one element of unusualness but not the only element. Some punishments would be prohibited even if applied frequently. Insofar as discrimination is raised by these cases, race may have been a factor in past sentences, but, if so, it was a factor in all criminal sentencing—not just sentencing in capital cases.

With Wright's argument in *Branch,* the long day in Court was over. But as with both *Maxwell* arguments, *McGautha* and *Crampton,* there was much to ruminate over before a decision would be announced, most likely in June. Except that if the abolitionists lost this time, the campaign against the death penalty probably was finished. Individual inmates might assert legal rights particular to their cases, but abolition in the courts rested on the Supreme Court's decision in these four cases.

On the basis of past performance, Brennan, Douglas, and Marshall were with us; Burger and Blackmun were not. Rehnquist's questions and background strongly suggested hostility. That left Powell, Stewart, and White, two of whose votes were necessary for an abolitionist victory. Powell was rumored to have been a supporter of the 1967 National Crime Commission recommendation that stopped short of urging abolition but criticized retention of the death penalty when it was rarely used. He had not asked a single question in four hours of argument.

Stewart and White, on the other hand, had asked many. Their questions mostly had probed difficulties in the position of the states. Still, only Stewart's voting record—in *Witherspoon* and *Jackson*—was at all encouraging. In both cases, White had dissented. But if only Stewart was persuaded, the score was five to four, with death row on the short end.

Fortunately, events relieved the tortures of a numbers game. The same day the Supreme Court heard the four Eighth Amendment cases, the Supreme Court of New Jersey announced an abolition decision. Under New Jersey law, a defendant who pleaded *non vult* (no defense) was guaranteed a maximum sentence of life imprisonment; the trial judge could not impose a death sentence. But if he pleaded not guilty, a jury *could* impose a death sentence.

In 1968 the New Jersey Supreme Court had decided that this scheme did not run afoul of *United States v. Jackson,* on the ground that a defendant could not avoid capital punishment, as in *Jackson,* simply by waiving a jury trial; he also had to plead *non vult,* the equivalent of a guilty plea, before he escaped the death penalty.[1] The court thought that if the *non vult*–life sentence rule induced guilty pleas to first-degree murder in order to avoid capital punishment, then no one who was charged with a capital offense could plead guilty to *any* offense, even to a lesser, non-capital, offense such as manslaughter or robbery. The state often would accept a guilty plea to a lesser non-capital offense in order to avoid the burdens involved in going to trial in capital cases. Defendants frequently went along with such an arrangement in order to avoid the death penalty. If LDF was right, the New Jersey Supreme Court argued, the state was coercing a guilty plea from *every* defendant charged with a capital crime who chose to plead guilty to a non-capital offense. As a consequence, it would be necessary for every defendant in a capital case to go to trial—a practical impossibility.

The Fund and New Jersey's Public Defender disputed the state court's reasoning and appealed to the United States Supreme Court. Three years later, in the wake of *McGautha-Crampton,* the Supreme Court sent the New Jersey case back to the state court with a cryptic suggestion in a brief directive that the New Jersey scheme for imposition of the death penalty was unconstitutional.[2]

In light of the Supreme Court's action, six of the seven members of the New Jersey court felt bound to void the death sentences in all twenty pending state death cases and to rule out capital punishment in the state unless the legislature passed a new statute which did not offer the prospect of escape from the death penalty by a guilty plea.[3] In a scathing concurring opinion, Joseph Weintraub, the Chief Justice of the state court, criticized the United States Supreme Court for deciding the Jersey cases without holding oral argument or writing a clear opinion. Whatever Weintraub's views on capital punishment, he was plainly angry at the use of federal power to interfere with matters he thought properly the state's concern.

Weintraub's objections to the Supreme Court's terse order had some validity. Recent Supreme Court decisions hardly suggested that the Court disapproved of plea bargaining. *Brady v. United States*,[4] *Parker v. North Carolina*,[5] and *North Carolina v. Alford*,[6] decided in 1970, rejected arguments that guilty pleas entered in capital cases were coerced because the risk of death *always* encouraged a defendant to seek to exchange a plea of guilty for a life sentence. It was not unreasonable for Weintraub to demand an explanation of the difference between the three 1970 decisions and the New Jersey situation.

Lawyers have criticized the manner in which the Supreme Court administers its vast caseload, arguing that by doing too much the Justices are diluting the quality of their work. But if time pressure explains why New Jersey did not receive its day in court, there is more to the matter than Weintraub's objection, serious as it may be. Hurried action by the Supreme Court could work in the defendant's favor in a capital case, but it might also result in erroneous affirmance of a death sentence. "To say that human judgment is fallible in capital cases as it is fallible everywhere else," Professor Charles L. Black, Jr., has commented, "is the exact equivalent of saying" that men will be mistakenly put to death.[7]

While New Jersey backed into abolition, a month later the Supreme Court of California gave it a warm embrace. By a 6-to-1 vote, the court brushed aside its 1968 decision in Anderson's case on the ground that· then it had considered only the federal Constitution's ban on cruel *and* unusual punishments and not the state Constitution's independent prohibition of cruel *or* unusual penalties.[8]

The Court's opinion, written by Chief Justice Donald R. Wright, a Reagan appointee, was long but straightforward. To appraise capital punishment one must look to contemporary practice, not to the nineteenth century, when vigilante justice and public hangings made it commonplace. The California Constitution measures the cruelty or unusualness of a criminal punishment by "evolving standards of decency," or it would still permit lopping ears and boring tongues.

Opinion polls reflect support for capital punishment, and juries still occasionally impose it, but the reaction of a public far removed from the actual experience of the death penalty tells little about the feelings of an informed public, one constantly confronted with the reality of capital punishment. Infrequent application of the death penalty suggests that people who are familiar with the facts have repudiated it; "What our society does in actuality belies what it says with regard to its acceptance of capital punishment."

The death penalty destroys a man after a long delay and a selection process more primitive than torture. As administered at present, it is lingering death. Intolerable delays are caused by the process of judicial review. But defendants' insistence on receiving the benefits of appeal does not make the long wait any less barbaric. Further, capital punishment "degrades and dehumanizes all who participate in its processes. It is unnecessary to any legitimate goal of the state and is incompatible with the dignity of man and the judicial process." We have no "sympathy for those who would commit crimes of violence," but society "diminishes itself whenever it takes the life of one of its members."

With one exception, the court concurred in the judgment —ordering life sentences for the 102 men and 5 women on death row. Justice Marshall McComb was the only dissenter. He thought, as he had in 1968, that the question was for the legislature.

To make up the court's majority, Justices Burke, Sullivan, and Mosk, all of whom had voted to uphold the death penalty in Anderson's 1968 case, joined Justices Peters and Tobriner, who had dissented then. Why had the three changed their minds? Why had Wright, Reagan's first appointee to a court he had often bitterly criticized, joined them? And, the most interesting question of all, why had the Supreme Court of California chosen to act at a time when the Supreme Court of the United States was about to decide whether the death penalty was cruel and unusual punishment in four cases, one of which was from California?

Edward L. Barrett, Jr., a University of California (at Davis) law professor, has supplied a possible answer.[9] The changed composition of the Supreme Court of the United States, Barrett speculates, made it appear unlikely to the California judges that the Court would use the Eighth Amendment's Cruel and Unusual Punishment Clause to abolish the death penalty. As the California legislature also showed no sign of acting to abolish or to restrict the death penalty, the Supreme Court of California found itself in an intolerable position. If the Supreme Court of the United States rejected abolition under the federal Constitution, the California court would be hard pressed to justify abolition on the ground that the California Constitution required it. The court would then be put to the choice of sending over a hundred men and women to their deaths, or continuing "the process of delays, reversals, and retrials" which had produced the exquisite psychological torture of the years spent awaiting execution.

"The first alternative," according to Barrett, "would be difficult to choose as a humane matter, yet only that alternative would create pressure for legislative change. The second alternative would aggravate the process of converting the death penalty into a refined form of torture and would increase public disrespect for the administration of criminal justice."

There was a hint of Barrett's conclusion in Chief Justice Wright's opinion, which suggested that the death penalty was considered a liability by those who knew most about it. What judges, jurors, and prosecutors did—regardless of what they said—was to avoid using the death penalty whenever possible. By reducing its use, they had reduced its justification. Relative disuse was inherent in modern administration of the death penalty. It was not watery sentiment by permissive jurists, but an historical trend; it reflected a community judgment on the nature of taking life. Nothing else could explain the actions of so many persons in so many different cases.

The California abolition decision may have expressed a dislike of taking human life that public officials and jurors held and acted upon in most cases, but it was not so welcome a ruling that it won official approval. The court's decision had barely been announced when Governor Reagan condemned it: "This decision makes a mockery of the constitutional process involved in establishing laws in California. . . . If it goes unchallenged, the judicial philosophy inherent in this ruling could be an almost lethal blow to society's right to protect law-abiding citizens and their families against violence and crime."[10]

Evelle Younger, California's attorney general, agreed with Reagan and threatened to take Anderson's case to the Supreme Court of the United States. But this was a political ploy, not a legal one. Since the state supreme court had decided that death was "cruel or unusual" under the *state* constitution, federal law was not involved. The Supreme Court of the United States has no power to review the decision of a state court on a question of local law, unless federal law requires a different result than the one reached by the state court. But nothing in the federal Constitution requires a state to retain the death penalty. The only real option open to Reagan and Younger was to drum up support for amendment of the California Constitution.

Even more important than the considerable impact of the decision on California was the message to Washington—as the state court itself had foreseen by hurrying the announcement of its ruling. The California Supreme Court had a "reputation for clarity and sound scholarship" and for legal trailblazing.[11] Many of its landmark decisions had been adopted later by the United States Supreme Court. What it said counted heavily in the legal world. Moreover, California was the most populous state in the nation, the state with the largest death-row population, and among its condemned were such controversial figures as Sirhan Sirhan and Charles Manson. Despite a governor who thought the death penalty an affirmative good, and a recent history of shocking prison killings, the California court— with a Reagan-appointed chief justice writing the opinion— had become the first state court to conclude that capital punishment could be dispensed with and that the courts should risk intense criticism to prohibit it.

The Justices of the United States Supreme Court could not fail to be influenced by the California decision. The question was whether the ruling carried enough weight to tip the scales. Even in the face of this development, most people were certain that the Justices intended to uphold the death penalty.

16

Cruel and Unusual

"We are not simply concerned to determine when violence 'works'; we are equally concerned to judge its rightness and propriety. . . . The most difficult task for those who would limit or eliminate violence lies in avoiding those situations in which men believe violence to be legitimate. And that remains the perennial challenge to political philosophy, to legislators, and to the law."

WILSON CAREY MCWILLIAMS

Despite the groundbreaking action in California, there was no shortage of rumors that the Supreme Court intended to uphold the death penalty. A well-known reporter claimed privately that he had been tipped off by an especially reliable source; another said he had learned from a politician's aide that Justice Stewart's critical swing vote would be cast to support the states. LDF lawyers first heard that an adverse ruling would be announced on a Thursday in mid-June, then on a Monday; first that abolition would lose by a vote of 6 to 3, then by a margin of 5 to 4. Both days came and went but no decision was forthcoming.

The gossip was disturbing, not so much because the lawyers believed it—they all knew that Supreme Court personnel were extraordinarily tight-lipped—but because it conformed so closely to their own estimate. The Burger

Court was not yet the Nixon Court, but its performance had been markedly more restrained than in the years when Warren was Chief Justice. *McGautha-Crampton* was an ominous sign that the Court was not preparing the nation for abolition.

Another disturbing sign was that Nixon's four appointees inclined toward voting as a block in criminal law cases. During the 1971–72 term several criminal procedure decisions had already cut back on rules framed in the 1960's to protect defendants. Juries, the Court decided, need no longer be unanimous in reaching a verdict in criminal cases.[1] Suspects now were entitled to the assistance of lawyers only at identification line-ups held after formal charges were lodged[2]—a ruling which gutted one of the Warren Court's most spectacular innovations.[3] In another decision, the Court turned down a claim that the Army's surveillance of civilian political activity invaded freedom of speech and assembly.[4] The majorities in these cases had been formed when Justices Stewart or White had joined the four Nixon appointees. Given the composition of the new Court and the result in *McGautha-Crampton*, it was not overstating the matter to say that a victory for abolition would rank among the greatest surprises in American legal history.

Time seemed to be running out on the moratorium. On June 7, the Court granted an LDF motion to dismiss the appeal of Earnest Aikens, Jr.[5] Because the Supreme Court of California had declared the death penalty unconstitutional under the state constitution, Aikens no longer faced execution, and the cruel and unusual punishment question in his case was moot. But over 900,000 Californians signed petitions circulated by police, district attorneys, corrections officers and their wives to place restoration of capital punishment by state constitutional amendment on the ballot at the November election. Two states that had abolished the death penalty, New Jersey (judicially) and New York (through legislation) showed signs of backlash: restoration bills cleared the New Jersey Senate 22 to 10 and failed by a slender margin in the New York Assembly. Elsewhere, Montana rejected by a 2 to 1 margin a state constitutional amendment that would have eliminated the death penalty.

With such news at their back and worse probably on the way, Fund lawyers half-heartedly plotted the steps they would take after announcement of the expected ruling in the three remaining cases that the death penalty was not cruel and unusual punishment. Marvin Wolfgang had been asked to ready rape-study results for use in several Southern states. Himmelstein and LDF staff lawyer Lynn Walker devised a new *Witherspoon*-type argument for cases where the prosecution had systematically employed peremptory, rather than "for cause," challenges to exclude jurors whose responses to pretrial questions indicated that they had scruples against the death penalty. A plan was in the works to halt the execution of any man with a mental disorder. The prosecution-proneness argument would finally get its day in court: the Louis Harris study of the attitudes of scrupled jurors had been completed and, along with research findings published by Edward J. Bronson[6] and George L. Jurow,[7] indicated that jurors who were not opposed to the death penalty were significantly more likely than scrupled jurors to favor the prosecution.

If the reasoning of the expected Supreme Court decision left room for argument that the death penalty was cruel and unusual punishment under any possible set of findings or facts, the lawyers would attempt to establish them. An adverse decision would no doubt reject evidence gleaned from published research, so emergency strategy called for in-court testimony about deterrence, death-row suffering, and the pain of execution from a parade of witnesses with first-hand knowledge.

In a nine-page memorandum, Himmelstein outlined these as well as other suggested tactics to salvage a portion of the death-row population: pleading with a group of concerned governors for simultaneous announcement of a death-row amnesty; efforts to enact the Hart-Celler moratorium bill in Congress; and a repeal campaign in state legislatures. He gathered promises of help from cooperative law firms, ACLU lawyers, and friendly law professors. Audrey Fleher drew up an organizational chart designating each strategem and the lawyers responsible for it. Amsterdam scheduled a meeting of key personnel in New York for July 4. After seven years of battling, the lawyers would not yield a man to the executioner without a struggle.

On paper the emergency plan looked as good as could have been expected, but Himmelstein was pessimistic. He felt as if he were being asked to hold together a cracked egg. "Of course we'll try everything," he shrugged, "but within six months after an adverse decision there will be an execution."

Such was the doomsday frame of mind on June 29, 1972, when shortly after 10 A.M., the Supreme Court convened for the last scheduled time during the 1971–72 term of Court. Set for announcement were many important decisions. The Justices entered; took their seats behind the bench. The crowded courtroom grew silent.

Moments later, Chief Justice Burger's resonant voice read a brief Court order disposing of the *Furman, Jackson,* and *Branch* cases. "The Court holds," Burger announced, "that the imposition and carrying out of the death penalty in these cases constitutes cruel and unusual punishment in violation of the Eighth and Fourteenth Amendments."[8] Justices Douglas, Brennan, Stewart, White, and Marshall, the Chief continued, support the judgment; each has filed a separate opinion explaining his reasons. Justices Blackmun, Powell, Rehnquist, and Burger himself had dissented.

Fantasy had become reality. Against every expectation, by the slimmest of margins, the future of the death penalty in America had been irrevocably altered.

Lawyers dashed to a room reserved for members of the bar of the Supreme Court to scan the posted opinions. They found that capital punishment had been abolished conditionally; there remained certain circumstances where it might be retained.

Within minutes the story began to appear on every major wire-service ticker. Calls jammed the LDF switchboard. Lawyers and secretaries produced transistor radios. General disbelief. Numbness. Tears in people's eyes. Slowly smiles replaced gaping jaws; laughter and embraces filled the halls. "This place looks like we just landed a man on the moon," Lyons shouted into a phone.

News broadcasts brought the first words of praise and scorn. Washington Governor Dan Evans said it was about time: "States that have the death penalty have not had less crime than those states that have not had it." Lester Maddox, Georgia's lieutenant governor, called the decision "A license for anarchy, rape, murder." New York Police Commissioner Patrick Murphy was cagey—"a step in the right direction," he thought—but Atlanta Police Chief John Inman deplored the loss of a "definite deterrent to major crimes."

Ken Brown, an official of the California Correctional Officers Association, lost no time urging a national drive to amend the Constitution. "We're in kind of a state of shock," said Brown. Jere Beasley, Alabama's lieutenant governor, said with disgust: "A majority of this nation's highest court has lost contact with the real world." A disappointed Memphis police chief, Bill Price, predicted that people who "hesitated to pull the trigger before just might go ahead and do it now."

Texas Prison Director George Beto commented that "The death penalty some years ago lost its deterrent effect . . . only swiftness and sureness of punishment are deterrents to crime; severity is not." Brevard County, Florida, Sheriff Leigh S. Wilson said; "I have a jail full of people who didn't think about their punishment before committing their crime." Edwin LaVallee, superintendent of New York's Clinton Prison, remembered that "witnesses would clamor" to attend an execution, "but if there was more than one they didn't want to see the second one. They would close their eyes. They wouldn't look."

By the time the evening papers were out, a few congressmen had proposed an amendment to the Constitution in order to permit the death penalty. Several state legislative leaders said they would ask for laws sentencing convicted murderers to life imprisonment without possibility of parole. Georgia State Representative Sam Nunn, Jr., a candidate for the United States Senate, announced that the decision justified forcing federal judges to face the voters every six years. Not to be outdone, the New York *Daily News* urged state legislators to readopt the death penalty with all its "old time" severity in order to see "what the Supreme Court does about that."

In his *New York Times* column, Tom Wicker predicted "a flurry of state laws requiring, for instance, mandatory death sentences" for vicious rapes, killing police officers or prison guards. President Nixon told a news conference that he hoped the Court's decision did not bar the death penalty for kidnaping and aircraft hijacking. Ronald Reagan speculated that the ruling would not interfere with a death sentence in the case of "cold blooded, premeditated, planned murder." But Jack Greenberg issued a statement asserting flatly: "There will no longer be any more capital punishment in the United States."

Soon after the first shock waves subsided, LDF lawyers turned to the printed opinions, which had been rushed from Washington. They knew that they had won, but they wanted to know precisely *what* they had won and how. The Court had stopped somewhere short of total abolition. How much distance remained?

Usually, a majority of the members of an appellate court agree on an opinion written by one individual judge, giving reasons for the decision of the court. Frequently, however, members of the majority join together to reach a particular result, but fail to agree on the reasoning that supports it. If they feel strongly enough about publicizing their differences with the majority opinion, such judges write concurring opinions separately setting forth their views. If the vote of a concurring judge (or judges) is necessary to make a majority, the concurring opinion must be consulted in order to discover the legal principles which the case has decided. The area of agreement between the concurring judge or judges and other members of the majority represents the rule of the case which judges in the future will feel bound to honor as precedent.

In the three cases, officially reported under the name *Furman v. Georgia,* the opinion of the Court was merely a short paragraph, designated "per curiam" (for the Court) rather than as written by a particular Justice. The per curiam opinion declared that imposition of the death penalty in the cases constituted cruel and unusual punishment and ordered lower court judgments reversed insofar as they imposed a death sentence, but it told nothing of the reasoning of the Justices who reached this result. In 120 other death case appeals pending before the Court, the Justices entered similar orders. There was, therefore, no opinion of the Court expressing agreed-upon reasons for the abolition decision; each Justice had written a concurring opinion stating separate reasons for his vote.

Thus, in order to learn what had been decided and how, and what the decision held for the future, one was obliged to pore over the approximately 25,000 words written by the concurring Justices—Brennan, Marshall, Douglas, Stewart, and White—and then to calculate the broadest ground of decision agreed to by all five. Although the implications of the decision were derived in this manner, the views of the four dissenters—constituting four opinions totaling approximately another 25,000 words—were also of more than academic interest. The dissents might illuminate the meaning of the majority opinions, as well as expose flaws in their reasoning.

All five Justices in the majority seemed to agree that the Constitution prohibited execution of the 631 men and 2 women held on the death rows of 32 states. These included 547 murderers, 80 rapists and 4 armed robbers; of which 351 were black, 267 white, and 13 of other racial backgrounds. All were entitled to new sentences of life imprisonment, to a term of years or, in a few cases, to new trials. The precise disposition was up to the state courts. Of course, laws punishing murder and other previously capital offenses could still be enforced so long as the death penalty was not imposed as punishment.

Two of the Justices, Brennan and Marshall, concluded for a variety of reasons that capital punishment violated the Eighth Amendment regardless of the crime or circumstances involved. The remaining three members of the majority—Douglas, Stewart, and White—believed that the death penalty was cruel and unusual punishment because of the arbitrary and capricious operation of laws that permitted juries and judges to select the men and women who were to be executed from all those convicted of a capital offense. All five agreed that the Eighth Amendment prohibited capital punishment when it was imposed so rarely that it could not serve any valid social purpose, be it deterrence or retribution.

The reasoning of Douglas, Stewart, and White did not reach the handful of crimes that carried a *mandatory* death sentence, such as spying for the enemy in time of war, a federal offense; assassination of the President or a state governor in Ohio; murder committed by a life-term prisoner in Rhode Island; and murder during the commission of a forcible rape in Massachusetts.

Little else was certain. Readers of the opinions wondered immediately whether Congress and state legislatures could remedy the constitutional defects identified by Douglas, Stewart, and White and reinstitute the death penalty. This was not an easy question; an answer required close analysis of each of the nine opinions filed by the Justices.

There was, however, little doubt about the view of Brennan and Marshall that the Constitution prohibited *any* form of capital punishment. Brennan gave several reasons for his conclusion. The Eighth Amendment protects the "dignity of human beings," but killing totally and irrevocably destroys human dignity. In contrast, a convict loses some but not all of his rights and remains a member of the human family. The death penalty degraded human beings, and this alone would render it unconstitutional if it had not been a long-standing form of punishment. But there was more, Brennan thought, that could be said against capital punishment. When a country of 200 million rarely inflicts an unusually severe penalty, the inference is strong that the penalty is unfairly and irregularly applied, that it runs counter to community values, and that there is a deep-seated reluctance to employ it. The notion that because people fear death the most, the death penalty is a superior deterrent to crime only applies to those who think rationally about committing capital offenses. Criminals are not so refined in their calculations that they distinguish among different penalties, but even a rational person contemplating murder or rape would hardly be dissuaded by the slight possibility that he might be executed in the remote future. Only swift and sure punishment deters crime, but these are the qualities capital punishment most noticeably lacks.

Justice Marshall arrived at the same conclusion as Brennan by a slightly different route. Alone among members of the majority, Marshall thought the word "unusual" in the Eighth Amendment of no importance, the result of an historical accident. But the death penalty was unconstitutionally cruel because it was unnecessarily harsh.

Marshall also found that the death penalty was unconstitutionally cruel because it was morally unacceptable to the American people. Demands for vengeance are common, but the Eighth Amendment was put in the Constitution to protect us "from our baser selves." It takes more than a pollster's mention of the death penalty to gauge public sentiment. He was convinced that capital punishment would offend the sensibilities of most Americans if they knew that it was no more effective a deterrent than life imprisonment; that most murderers who have been released from prison become law abiding; that the death penalty itself may stimulate criminal activity; that it is imposed discriminatorily; that there is evidence that innocent persons have been executed; and that the death penalty wreaks havoc on the criminal justice system.

Unlike Brennan and Marshall, Justices Douglas, Stewart, and White did not directly tie their votes to a view of contemporary moral standards. Instead they focused on the practical results of the present discretionary sentencing system.

Douglas thought that the Court was "imprisoned" by its 1971 *McGautha* holding that juries and judges had complete freedom to pick those who received the death penalty. He had dissented in that case because untrammeled sentencing discretion resulted in capricious selection of the condemned. But now that *McGautha* was on the books the Court had to confront whether the end result of a standardless sentencing system violated the Eighth Amendment.

It is impossible to deny, Douglas argued, that as presently administered the death penalty dooms blacks, the poor, and borderline mental defectives; "The Leopolds and Loebs are given prison terms, not sentenced to death." The Cruel and Unusual Punishment Clause leaves no room for penalties that are not evenhandedly applied; it was intended to forbid discrimination, as well as torture. The Constitution prohibits laws which exempt from a penalty anyone, say, making more than $50,000 a year, or which only condemn blacks who never went beyond the fifth grade, or the unpopular or unstable; laws that work the same results in practice have no more sanctity.

Justice Stewart also focused on the operation of discretionary capital sentencing laws, but where Douglas saw discrimination, he saw randomness. "These death sentences are cruel and unusual," he judged, "in the same way that being struck by lightning" is cruel and unusual: They have been capriciously, freakishly, and wantonly imposed.

By making the death penalty completely discretionary with jury or judge, the states themselves do not consider the death penalty essential to accomplish their legitimate interest in deterring criminal activity, preserving the peace, or inducing the public to forgo "self help, vigilante justice and lynch law." It follows that the death penalty is cruelly excessive. It is a uniquely harsh penalty that goes beyond what the states themselves have determined must be done to deal with crime. Nothing is plainer, Stewart continued, than that the death sentence is so infrequently imposed that it is an unusual penalty. The handful selected to die are chosen without rhyme or reason—unless the reason is race. Many murderers and rapists just as reprehensible as the condemned are sent to prison instead.

Stewart's view was echoed by Justice White. Where the legislature leaves sentencing up to the jury or judge, the "legislative will is not frustrated if the penalty is never imposed." Under the present system of discretionary sentencing, death is ordered so infrequently—even for atrocious crimes—that the odds are high against imposition and execution in any particular case. A penalty imposed so infrequently, White reasoned, ceases to serve the ends that are supposed to justify it. It is no longer a credible deterrent; nor does it satisfy community needs that criminals receive their "just deserts." "Seldom-enforced laws become ineffective measures for controlling human conduct." When such slight public purposes are served, killing becomes "pointless" and "needless."

Several common themes characterized the response of the four dissenters, the Nixon appointees, all of whom announced that they agreed with each other's position. They took a narrow view of the Eighth Amendment and disputed the empirical data on which the majority had based conclusions about public opinion, infrequent and arbitrary enforcement, and the relative deterrent value of the death penalty. Most prominently, they stressed that legislative bodies, rather than courts, should sift the available evidence and reach a decision whether or not to abolish the death penalty.

Burger, for example, concluded that the Eighth Amendment prohibits punishments of extreme and barbarous cruelty "regardless of how frequently or infrequently imposed." A man "awaiting execution must inevitably experience extraordinary mental anguish," but the suffering is not materially different from what was experienced by the condemned man two hundred years ago. The long wait on death row is an ordeal, but if the Constitution proscribes severe emotional stress, then capital punishment would have been impermissible in 1791.

Burger chided Brennan and Marshall for misreading the attitudes of the American people. Execution by modern methods, he felt, is not a punishment like burning at the stake, which everyone feels is repugnant. When a hundred or so death sentences are handed down each year and 15 to 20 percent of all convicted murderers are sentenced to death, it is hyperbolic of Stewart and White to speak of the rate of imposition as "freakishly rare." Further, by striking down a penalty because it is not thought necessary to achieve the ends of the criminal law, the Court breaks too sharply with prior decisions. The Eighth Amendment asks the courts to make moral judgments based on society's sense of decency, not to replace legislators.

Burger thought that Brennan and Marshall strained the facts when they asserted that the death penalty was not a deterrent superior to imprisonment. The Chief Justice's reading of the published literature revealed an "empirical stalemate" that cannot be resolved by casting the burden on the state to prove deterrence. If challenged, the states cannot prove conclusively that life imprisonment is a more effective deterrent than a twenty-year prison term, or that a ten-dollar parking ticket is more effective than a five-dollar fine. The available evidence regarding deterrence is subject to interpretation; such questions, therefore, are for legislatures, not courts.

For Blackmun, death cases induced an "excruciating agony of the spirit." He abhorred the death penalty and found it antagonistic to a lifetime's training and experience. His home state, Minnesota, had long survived without it. While he rejoiced at abolition, he could not agree that the Court had acted properly. The majority had misread history and constitutional law. Prior decisions never suggested that capital punishment was unconstitutional. To assert that the death penalty violates contemporary standards of decency flies in the face of the fact that the laws of four-fifths of the states provide for it. Members of Congress are as sensitive to human dignity and as aware of what is compatible with community values as are members of the Supreme Court, but between 1961 and 1970 they had passed several new capital punishment laws by lopsided margins.

The most scathing attack on the majority opinions was written by Justice Powell; he felt that they rejected history, brushed aside precedent, invalidated a staggering number of statutes, and poached on territory that the Constitution allotted to legislatures. He disputed the Brennan-Marshall conclusion that the death penalty cuts against the grain of community standards by pointing to the regular failure of abolition bills and the defeat of abolition referenda at the polls. Enough death sentences are meted out to show that capital punishment is far from repudiated in the eyes of jurors or lower court judges. In the last five years, twenty-five state courts have rejected cruel and unusual punishment claims.

It is pure speculation to say that if people knew more facts about capital punishment they would be revolted, Powell noted. His own speculations yielded different results. Highly publicized murder cases, senseless assassinations, and shocking multiple murders hardly provoke revulsion at the death penalty; the cry of the people is quite the contrary.

Powell admitted that the death penalty may fall more on the disadvantaged, but reasoned that this is merely a tragic by-product of social and economic deprivation. He discounted the possibility of racial bias: "The segregation of our society in decades past, which contributed substantially to the severity of punishment for interracial crimes, is now no longer prevalent in this country." Lastly, the evidence is simply too weak to show that legislatures are acting irrationally by keeping the death penalty. Many may decry their failure "to abolish the penalty entirely or selectively, or to establish standards for its enforcement," but impatience with slow, even unresponsive, legislatures is no justification for judges to intrude upon their powers.

What concerned Rehnquist most was the Court's failure to observe the limits of its authority. The Supreme Court, he warned, exercises no "roving commission" to declare laws unconstitutional "upon notions of policy or morality suddenly found unacceptable by a majority." Appointed judges must exercise restraint; else they will impose their own views of "truth and justice upon others." If a legislative act is mistakenly upheld, the error at least leaves standing the expression of the popular will voiced by the legislature. A mistake by the Supreme Court in declaring unconstitutional a legislative act imposes by fiat the views of judges whose connection with the popular will "is remote at best."

The first question arising from this welter of opinions is whether the decision voids every death penalty statute which authorizes discretionary selection of the condemned. New York, for example, authorizes, but does not require, the death penalty for the murder of police officers and prison guards; and the federal government permits capital punishment for several narrowly defined offenses like aircraft piracy and assassination of the President or a member of Congress. Do such laws fall to the judicial ax along with the general murder and rape statutes involved in the three death penalty cases?

While Douglas, Stewart, and White did not specifically address themselves to the constitutionality of narrowly defined capital crimes, their reasoning left little room to reconcile such laws with the Eighth Amendment. Douglas most plainly condemned all discretionary capital punishment, reserving only the question "Whether a mandatory death penalty would . . . be constitutional." Stewart, while concluding that the "case is a strong one" for the Brennan-Marshall position that "the death penalty is constitutionally impermissible in all circumstances under the Eighth and Fourteenth Amendments," found it "unnecessary to reach [that] . . . ultimate question." Like Douglas, he thought that the ultimate question would be raised when mandatory death sentence statutes came before the Court. Justice White agreed that the discretionary aspect of capital punishment rendered it unconstitutionally cruel and unusual. He also reserved decision on the question of the constitutionality of "statutes *requiring* the imposition of the death penalty for first degree murder, for more narrowly defined categories of murder or for rape. . . ." While this language is subject to interpretation, a fair reading supports rejection of any form of *discretionary* death sentencing.

Stubborn legislators might contend that the selection process could be purged of the arbitrariness that was the basis for Douglas, Stewart, and White's apparent rejection of all discretionary statutes. Burger's dissent suggested that states wishing to retain the death penalty could try to sort out the most culpable offenders or "worst" offenses by "providing standards for juries and judges to follow in determining the sentence in capital cases, or by more narrowly defining its crimes for which the penalty is to be imposed." Burger was aware that no jurisdiction had drafted such standards, but a few—New York's police killer statute being the most prominent example—have defined capital offenses in so particularized a fashion that it could be argued that they represent aggravated offenses where the death penalty could still be regularly imposed.

But as Burger was quick to see, unless such statutes carry a mandatory death sentence upon conviction, there is no assurance that they too will not be applied in a "random and unpredictable manner." Six Justices (Harlan, Burger, Black, Stewart, White, Blackmun) had agreed in *Mc-Gautha* that sentencing standards in capital cases—whether provided by jury guidelines or by a legislature's narrow definition of a crime—were constitutionally unnecessary, in large part because attempts "to identify before the fact the cases in which the penalty is to be imposed have been 'uniformly unsuccessful.' " The implication seems to be that even assuming narrowly drafted offenses or suitable guidelines, the likely prospect is that juries or judges will use their discretion in as freakish a manner as they have in the past.

States might argue that insufficient experience with sentencing standards justifies their right to experiment with them. Ironically, in trying to uphold discretionary capital punishment laws, the states would then find themselves mouthing a portion of LDF's unsuccessful argument for standards. Despite their previous opposition, defense lawyers, on the other hand, would hammer home the points relied upon by the majority (which included Stewart and White) in *McGautha:* that workable standards are impossible to draft, that they are unlikely to reduce caprice, and that they may mislead the jury. So long as *McGautha* remains on the books, it is probable that the Supreme Court will not permit an experiment with sentencing standards where the price of error is human life.

The other potential response of states—or Congress—that wish to retain the death penalty is resurrection of the mandatory capital punishment statutes that most American jurisdictions abandoned in the nineteenth century. Presumably, legislators will seek to define aggravated and premeditated murders, rapes, or kidnapings in a fashion that satisfies them that everyone convicted of the crimes deserves to die.

Such statutes face formidible obstacles, both political and constitutional. Although police and correctional officers' unions can be expected to mount vigorous lobbying campaigns, for the first time abolition-minded legislators have only to block rather than to enact legislation. Conscientious lawmakers will have to face serious ethical questions in any legislation which threatens to bring about a rate of execution unknown to post–World War II America, and which dooms the killers of tomorrow while assassins and multiple murderers of the past are protected from execution by the Constitution. In addition, regardless of what they say for public consumption, some governors do not want the death penalty back. Officials may divert pressure for restoration into efforts to pass more stringent restrictions on the grant of parole.

Correctional administrators often feel that the death penalty stifles both prison reform and attempts to sell rehabilitation programs to legislators, who hold the purse strings, and to the convict population. Capital punishment, as Professor Charles L. Black, Jr., puts it, tends "to make every other form of treatment . . . however brutal, seem less than extreme."[9] Undoubtedly, some wardens will oppose mandatory death statutes.

On the merits, the argument against a system which requires the jury to acquit or send to death is powerful. "Individual culpability," Burger had commented, "is not always measured by the category of the crime committed." But the future of such laws in many legislatures depends a good deal on how hard state prosecuting attorneys push for them. The prosecutors' position will depend partially on the extent to which the absence of the death penalty affects plea bargaining. Unless the overwhelming proportion of criminal defendants plead guilty, the criminal justice system cannot work. Courts are capable of giving trials and appeals to only a fraction of the total number of men and women charged with crime. As the Supreme Court recognized in its 1968 *Jackson* decision, the death penalty exerts a unique pressure on defendants charged with capital crimes to plead guilty in exchange for a lighter sentence. So long as prosecutors were empowered to trade a prison sentence for a guilty plea, they could keep the number of pending capital cases within bounds. But with the threat of a possible death sentence now removed, those jurisdictions which depend on plea bargaining to move serious cases along will attempt to induce a sufficient number of pleas by promising a term of years instead of a life sentence. If prosecutors conclude that the rate of guilty pleas has remained unchanged without the threat of capital punishment, they may be willing to forgo new death penalty legislation. A truly mandatory capital punishment law would not permit prosecutors in their discretion to offer lighter sentences or lesser charges in exchange for a guilty plea. And one thing is certain about such a law: no lawyer will plead his client guilty to a crime carrying an automatic death sentence.

Much might also turn on whether the majority or the dissenters in *Furman* stated the better case. The moral force of the majority decision is diluted by five separate —though not incompatible—opinions. Many of the darts tossed by the dissenters scored points, but that does not necessarily win the game. The Court, they insisted, had intruded into an area of policy making reserved to bodies directly responsive to the voters. All four believed that Congress and state legislatures are better suited to decide whether the death penalty is morally unacceptable. Elected representatives should rightfully judge disputes about deterrence, and evaluate claims that the condemned are a randomly selected few whose offenses are no more heinous than those committed by offenders who have received prison terms.

The line taken by the dissenters is a familiar theme to constitutional lawyers. The landmark Supreme Court decisions of the last two decades spelling the end of segregation laws, malapportioned legislatures, and state immunity from the strictures of the Bill of Rights have been subjected to the same criticism. But these decisions were a response to deeply rooted social conflicts that elected representatives had not addressed. The Court did not rush to judgment in disregard of the political process when it dealt with racial discrimination, the number of representatives rural-dominated legislatures allocated to cities and suburbs, or police practices. In each of these areas the interests that the Court protected could not mobilize sufficient power to engage the political process. The ins had no intention of granting concessions to the outs.

So it was with the death penalty. Professor Barrett has put it well: "The public cannot be expected to be aroused over a form of punishment which is seldom carried out. . . . Furthermore the death row experience is well-hidden from public view, so that public sentiment on the subject does not reflect the psychological tortures of the punishment."[10] All the public sees is that the courts reverse a large number of death sentences, and that years pass before judges permit an execution to take place. This is chalked up to coddling criminals rather than understood as a reaction by the courts to the very nature of the death penalty, and the ambivalence it provokes.

If the Supreme Court had refused to consider the constitutionality of the death penalty in *Furman,* capital punishment would have survived without any governmental institution evaluating its utility or morality in principled fashion. If the Supreme Court had deferred to the political process on capital punishment, it would have been deferring to a void. No greater breeding ground for contempt of law and government is imaginable than a legal system which permits killing without ultimate confrontation of evidence that the killing has become unequal and unnecessary.

Once the Court decided to meet the constitutional issues head on, weighing the evidence inevitably involved close questions. If the death penalty did not respond to deep human or social needs, it would have withered away without need of intervention. Either way the Court ruled, it could not escape criticism that it had wrongly read the historical or empirical record.

Two additional considerations lend potency to the majority reasoning. First, judged by a cost-benefit test, the abolitionists stated the stronger case. Whether the evidence was sufficient to meet the constitutional standard of cruel and unusual punishment is another matter, but even the dissenters said little in praise of the death penalty. Its constitutionality was defended with vigor and the majority reasoning was belittled, but the dissenters did not claim that legal killing was a positive contribution to mankind. Burger and Blackmun, for example, noted that if they were legislators they would vote to abolish or severely restrict the death penalty.

Secondly, the Court was not entering an area where legislators had superior expertise. As Byron White commented, the Justices have "daily exposure to the facts and circumstances of hundreds of federal and state criminal cases involving crimes for which death is the authorized penalty." Ten years of this exposure had persuaded White that there was no meaningful basis to distinguish the few cases where the death penalty was imposed from the many serious cases where it was not. Legislators might dispute White's conclusion, but none could contend that Supreme Court Justices had insufficient experience with the operation of the death penalty.

The many issues joined by the majority and dissenting opinions will receive a thorough airing in the press, the law reviews, and in legislative chambers. On the heels of the decision, Professor Sanford Kadish of the University of California at Berkeley commented that it was "ironic," if not "bizarre," that the death penalty might be administered in the future without the individualized treatment "one would have thought to be the requirement of a sensitive civilized society." Kadish's colleague, Jesse Choper, said of the dissents that "It is much easier to talk about judicial self-restraint and deference to legislative judgment when you know you don't have the votes to send 500 or 600 people to death." Harry Subin of New York University thought that mandatory capital sentencing laws would prove unworkable: "We provide for mandatory prison sentences in the narcotics field, but prosecutors and judges do everything in their power to avoid using them because they do not permit individualized punishment." Outspoken Michigan Law Professor Yale Kamisar thought the death penalty ". . . badly battered, and almost dead—but not so dead that the next Nixon appointee cannot breathe some life back into it."

Efforts were quickly mounted to bring back the death penalty. The Delaware and North Carolina Supreme Courts ruled that *Furman* only forced those states to excise *discretionary* capital sentencing provisions from their laws, leaving them with mandatory capital statutes. On November 7, 1972, California voters approved by a 2-to-1 margin a state constitutional amendment restoring the California legislature's power to enact capital punishment laws. Several weeks before the announcement of the *Furman* decision, when it had become clear that this referendum would appear on the November ballot, Amsterdam had thrown himself into a campaign to organize opposition to the measure. During the week prior to the *Furman* decision, he scheduled a meeting for July 7, at which representatives of the abolitionist forces in the state would begin planning overall political organization and strategy. When *Furman* was announced on June 29, most of the invitees called to ask whether the meeting would still be held as scheduled. Amsterdam read the Supreme Court opinions, decided that there was still room for state legislatures to pass capital punishment legislation, and told everyone that the meeting was still on.

By the date of the meeting most of the invitees had read *Furman*. They realized that if the referendum passed, the California legislature would no longer be totally prohibited from enacting new capital punishment laws, to the extent that *Furman* still permitted the states to pass such laws. The meeting began with the unstated assumption that the groups had to do everything possible to prevent passage of the amendment. Speaker after speaker stated the same theme: ironically, for several reasons, *Furman* would make defeat of the referendum difficult if not impossible. Persons who had been prepared to contribute money for a campaign against the measure had already concluded that with the battle almost won with *Furman,* they had better uses for their cash. Political leaders who had taken the abolitionist side in a matter of conscience when life was at stake would now withdraw to noncommittal postures, in the belief that life was no longer at stake. The *Furman* decision would itself account for a considerable know-nothing vote in favor of the amendment. So the arguments ran on. Finally, amused by the bombardment of pessimistic rhetoric directed to a nine-year-in-the-making landmark decision, Amsterdam threw up his hands in mock dismay: "This group has me seriously wondering whether winning *Furman* was a good thing after all."

In December 1972, with Governor Reubin Askew's approval, the Florida legislature met in special session and adopted new death penalty legislation which created three capital crimes: premeditated murder, felony murder, and rape of a child. Under the new legislation, the jury may recommend that the judge impose either life imprisonment (without possibility of parole for twenty-five years) or capital punishment. But the final sentencing decision is made by the judge alone, after he weighs aggravating and mitigating circumstances. In January 1973, a revision of the Ohio

Criminal Code went into effect, providing for a scheme similar to Florida's to be administered by a three-judge sentencing panel.

The National Association of Attorneys General voted 32 to 1 to ask Congress and the states to authorize capital punishment for ten offenses by enactment of legislation tailored to avoid the constitutional defects identified by the *Furman* decision. Before the top law enforcement officers convened, the Gallup Poll reported that 57 percent of the people it questioned—a twenty-year high—supported the death penalty.

As state legislators assembled for their 1973 legislative sessions, Douglas Lyons reported that bills to restore capital punishment would be introduced in three-fourths of the former capital punishment states, as well as in Michigan, which had abolished 127 years earlier.

In Massachusetts a teen-ager, convicted of the rape and murder of an elderly woman, was sentenced to death under an old Massachusetts statute carrying a mandatory death penalty for the crime. Because the penalty was mandatory, the trial judge ruled that *Furman* did not apply.

On March 2, Arab terrorists assassinated the American Ambassador and chargé d'affaires to The Sudan after President Nixon had refused to ransom the diplomats by arranging for the release of Sirhan Sirhan, Robert F. Kennedy's murderer. Secretary of State William P. Rogers told a Senate committee that the death penalty was the only appropriate punishment for the terrorists.

New York Governor Nelson Rockefeller, who in 1965 had signed legislation repealing capital punishment for most offenses, announced to five hundred cheering labor leaders that he was seriously considering proposing the death penalty for "major drug pushers."

After it had become apparent that death penalty legislation commanded considerable support, the Nixon Administration sponsored its own capital punishment bill. Nixon's approach involved a two-stage capital trial. At the first stage, guilt would be determined. Upon conviction, a second stage would be held to decide whether the death penalty should be imposed. The defendant would have the burden of proving mitigation to the satisfaction of a judge or jury; the prosecution, of proving aggravation. If the defendant proved at least one mitigating factor (age below eighteen, duress, only minor participation in the crime, lack of mental capacity to appreciate the wrongfulness of his conduct, or inability to foresee that the offense would cause or create a grave risk of death), capital punishment could not be imposed. In the absence of mitigation, establishment of one or more aggravating factors would make death "automatic," as Nixon put it. These included a killing done in a "heinous, cruel or depraved manner" or for hire, a homicide in the course of a kidnaping or aircraft hijacking, assassination of high federal officials or law enforcement officers, treason or espionage which created a grave threat to national security, and murder committed by a person who had been previously convicted of an offense for which a sentence of life imprisonment or death could have been imposed or of two or more felonies involving serious bodily injury. In a radio message explaining the proposal, Nixon took aim at the Supreme Court majority in *Furman*. He lambasted "soft-headed judges" who were responsible for misleading Americans that "the criminal was not responsible for his crimes against society, but that society was responsible."

Of course, it is to be hoped that study and debate ultimately will disenchant those whose initial reaction is to salvage what they can of the death penalty. Nevertheless, despite the political, intellectual, and practical problems with mandatory death sentencing laws, inevitably many will be enacted. They will face an uncertain future in the courts. It may take several years before such laws are actually employed by prosecutors and result in convictions. State appellate courts will have to construe the new laws. In some cases trial courts will apply them erroneously, and be reversed on appeal. No case demands more careful scrutiny than one in which a death penalty follows automatically upon conviction. Therefore it is likely that appellate courts will reverse convictions because of a variety of legal errors which do not directly relate to capital punishment. As a result, final resolution of the constitutionality of mandatory sentencing laws will be postponed.

What effect will several more years without a single execution have on the mind of the public, and on the attitude of the Supreme Court? Speculation is difficult. The compositon of the Court probably will have changed by the time the first cases are ripe for decision—thus introducing another political element into the future of capital punishment.

Even if one limits speculation to the views of the present Justices, predicting the Court's position in 1975 or 1977 on the constitutionality of mandatory capital sentencing laws is as risky as forecasting the weather for those years. Blackmun complained that the 1972 decision represented a too-sudden break with past decisions of the Court. But though he dissented, he may now respect the decision as precedent. It might influence him in the future to reject mandatory death statutes, given the "agony of the spirit" that he feels upon invoking the death penalty. Burger has decried the backwardness of mandatory sentencing and said that he prefers total abolition. Douglas, Stewart, and White, as well as Powell and Rehnquist, have not committed themselves— though Stewart, alone among the majority, has said that under certain circumstances retribution was a proper ingredient in the imposition of punishment.

Most important, the views and opinions of the Justices develop and grow as a result of their unique experience serving on the court of last resort for a nation of 200 million. Each of the Justices who voted to abolish had been exposed to at least five years of litigation challenging the constitutionality of the death penalty. During this period, the Court itself had vacated scores of death sentences on "narrow" procedural grounds and framed rules directing lower courts to do so in many more cases. By cutting back on the death penalty in *Witherspoon* and *Jackson,* the Court had created a situation where some death-row inmates would live solely because of the procedures that had been applied in their cases or because of accidents of timing. Suppose that the 1972 decision had resulted in a ruling that the death penalty was *not* cruel and unusual punishment as administered in twentieth-century America. Then the Justices themselves would have condemned some men, while in the recent past the Court's rulings had spared others whose culpability was not substantially different. Nothing would have been more "arbitrary" and "freakish." *Witherspoon,* for example, distinguished between cases where a juror had been wrongly excluded because of hesitant opposition to the death penalty and others where the prospective juror's response to voir dire questions was less uncertain. The difference might merely be a few words. A decision against the death-row inmates in *Furman* would have made life or death turn on such questions—notwithstanding the individual culpability of the offender. In the future, Justices considering whether to follow *Furman* will be faced with the same pressures that confronted the five who lived through years of gradual restriction of the death penalty: to authorize execution to begin again would be not only to decide that more men should die but to make that decision knowing that the men who would be killed were no more deserving of death than those whom *Furman* had spared.

No matter who sits on the Supreme Court when it confronts automatic death penalty statutes, the Justices will have to consider grave constitutional objections, and these are no less serious than those used successfully to challenge discretionary capital statutes. The Chief Justice has already declared that it was clear to him that Americans abhorred imposing a mandatory death sentence on all convicted murderers. Modern penology, he has pointed out, discredits sentencing practices which bar a judge or jury from considering the individual circumstances of the crime or the offender. Mandatory sentences in capital and non-capital cases were the rule at the time of the adoption of the Constitution; discretion had entered the criminal process in response to a clamor to reduce the scope of capital punishment. But if enough states reintroduce mandatory death statutes, states might claim that lawmakers seek to reflect the changing public temper by approving reintroduction of the earlier practice.

Little else can be said in favor of these statutes. The form in which they are likely to be introduced must contain inconsistencies so glaring as to mock the ideals of equal justice. Any lawyer familiar with homicide cases knows that one man may kill a police officer in a far less culpable manner than another man who kills his wife or business associate. A trained professional killer of a civilian might receive a life sentence, while a robber whose cohort's gun went off in a scuffle with a policeman would face death. There is no way to ensure that mentally disturbed but not legally insane killers like William Henry Furman will not commit an "aggravated" offense carrying a death penalty. In contrast, a killing by a man emotionally capable of conforming his conduct to the law might not qualify for the death penalty because, for example, the homicide did not take place in connection with another felony. Legislators will draft mandatory death statutes to net the Charles Mansons and Richard Specks of the future, but no set of rules will avoid catching men whose deeds are far less reprehensible, or whose character arouses sympathy.

Such laws face other formidable hurdles. Prosecutors and grand jurors usually have the power to charge a defendant with a lesser offense even though he could have been forced to defend against capital charges; judges and trial jurors also have the power to convict a defendant of a non-capital offense even if he is charged with a capital crime. Unless these options are eliminated, administration of the mandatory statutes may prove in practice to be as discretionary as administration of the statutes involved in *Furman.* The Nixon death penalty proposal, for example, purports to make capital punishment "automatic," but it actually does so only after a judge or jury has made a number of discretionary determinations about an offender's mental state, his culpability, or the impact of his crime—whether, for example, he could "appreciate the wrongfulness of his conduct," whether he committed the offense in an especially "depraved" manner, or whether the offense posed a "grave risk of substantial danger to the national security." Additionally, so long as state governors or pardon boards retain the power to commute mandatory death sentences, an element of discretion will remain which could make those actually executed "a capriciously selected random handful." But to abolish the power to extend mercy by executive clemency would be repugnant to centuries of Anglo-American legal practice.

The more numerous and complex the elements which constitute a mandatory capital offense, the more difficult it will be to show that the new laws actually change conduct. Lawyers will argue that the small number of executions resulting from an automatic sentencing law will not serve any significant deterrent or even retributive purpose. It is pure fiction, they will say, to pretend that potential killers are able to appreciate the numerous acts or omissions that separate capital from non-capital murder.

On the other hand, if the states broadly define the category of offenders subject to automatic execution upon conviction, jurors might acquit numerous guilty murderers or rapists rather than vote their execution. Failing this, the number of potential executions will skyrocket. As Professor H. Richard Uviller of Columbia Law School points out, the Court will have put itself in the "grotesque" position of having produced an increase in the use of capital punishment. (If so, the Justices will feel an enormous temptation to finish what *Furman v. Georgia* began.)

These defects and others derived from the language and form of each mandatory death statute will lead defense attorneys to argue that due process of law prohibits a system of sentencing which gives no weight to individual circumstances, background, and mental capacity. They will assert constitutional principles of equal protection of the laws to bar imposition of the death penalty on the ground that the legislatively defined class of capital murderers are actually no different in culpability from some of those who commit non-capital homicides or rapes. The Justices will be told that the prospect of even more killing than took place in the 1960's would be so odious to the public that they must follow the Brennan-Marshall route and completely forbid the death penalty.

Much litigation will be necessary before the Court accepts or rejects these arguments. Depending on the offense and the offender, a staggering number of potential challenges may be imagined. Plainly, the validity of legislative moves to retain the death penalty will remain for some time in "uncertain limbo," to use the Chief Justice's phrase. Just as plainly, the 1972 decision does not lay out a constitutional red carpet for mandatory death statutes, though a government claim that it has the right to execute in particularly outrageous, narrowly defined instances—such as killings in the course of aircraft piracy or kidnaping—will be hard to defeat. But in the dim light of these hazardous researches into the future, Jack Greenberg's prediction that no more executions will be held in the United States seems plausible.

The effect of the Supreme Court's decision in the four death penalty cases is not, of course, limited to forcing legislators to reappraise capital punishment laws. Policies governing parole of persons convicted of previously capital offenses, or violent crimes in general, are due for a tightening so that, as one governor puts it, "life imprisonment means life imprisonment." For some crimes, judges will be ordered to impose mandatory-minimum prison sentences, excluding the possibility of parole until the minimum term is served. The ancient right to bail—which never fully applied to capital offenses—may be modified to require the detention of some defendants prior to trial. "Maximum-maximum" security prisons might be introduced to contain criminals who correctional officials think particularly dangerous. If so, the combination of caged, violent men and apprehensive prison guards may spell increased conflict between the two groups.

Penologists hope that elimination of the death penalty will spur research into the causes of violent crime so that offenders may be more successfully deterred than in the past. Many prison reformers believe the decision to abolish the death penalty a necessary first step toward more civilized treatment of convicts. One scholar—Professor Harold S. H. Edgar of Columbia Law School—takes a gloomier view. He speculates that the decision may provoke interest in developing medical methods, including surgical techniques, to control violent behavior. Police officials fear a more primitive response: that some men on the beat will take the end of capital punishment as a signal for increased use of lethal force in apprehending criminals caught in the act.

The June 29 decision is also bound to have significant consequences for the American public transcending its effect on the criminal law and the court system. Of course the power of a great act of humanity is no less real for being difficult to trace, but to look hard for a connection between abolition and future events is to miss its most important aspect. The decision does not seem to have been impelled by an impulse to create a better world for Americans, or sustained by dreams of changing institutions or individual behavior. Rather the Supreme Court treated saving human life as an end in itself. The true character of the decision was moral, not utilitarian.

The Court, of course, spoke in legal, not moral terms, but the Justices asserted the preciousness of life despite claims advanced by forces far more powerful than the condemned that violence is necessary and wise. They acted to limit the human capacity for destructiveness against the strong tide of the urge to punish. A cloudy historical and empirical record was read to contain more respect than disregard for human beings. Although the majority opinions limited the scope of the result and left potential avenues open for the political process to explore, reverence for life—even life stunted, twisted, violent, or vexed—illuminated them all.

For centuries, attempts were made to justify the death penalty on the basis that the sanctity of life required that he who trespassed upon it had to forfeit his own. Four hundred years ago, Montaigne scoffed at such apologies. "The horror of one man killing another," he wrote, "makes me fear the horror of killing him; the hideousness of his cruelty makes me abhor any imitation of it."[11] If we have put behind us the notion that the second wrong makes a right, there is cause for rejoicing. But the sources of violence—including boredom as well as anger—are obscure, complex, and resistant to change. Philosophers and psychologists tell us that the will to create, to shape, to master, is hopelessly entangled with the urge to destroy. If it is wisdom to accept that we are both attracted and repelled by violence, that all of us harbor murderous wishes, then there will come a point where we dispense with the illusion that the violence within can be excised like a cancer. That state will govern best which gives us alternatives to violent physical expression, which helps us to confront with reason our capacity for chaos, and which teaches us to deal with the storms of our souls as we do with the storms of the rest of the natural world. In this, the politics of the future, *Furman v. Georgia* will have an honored place.

ACKNOWLEDGMENTS

As must appear from virtually every page, this book would not have been possible without the cooperation of the men and women whose story it tells. Rather than acknowledging individual generosity in sharing recollections, documents, and manuscript comments, I have hoped to honor their assistance by doing justice to their deeds. But I must single out Douglas Lyons, whose editorial guidance and dedicated efforts—assembling chapter notes and checking facts—greatly contributed to the finished work, and Anthony G. Amsterdam and Jack Himmelstein—the two men most responsible for *Furman v. Georgia*—both of whom were kind enough to read the manuscript.

I am also indebted to the research assistance of Diana Budzanoski, Theodore Ruthizer, Robert Kandel, and Stephen Zoukis, to the cooperation of Cordelia Jason, and to the comments of my friends, Victor Navasky and Harry Subin. Sir Leon Radzinowicz, and his associate Roger Hood, generously offered me use of the facilities of the Institute of Criminology at Cambridge, England, during the summer of 1971.

Preparation of the manuscript through many tedious drafts was largely the work of Kay Alicyn Ferrell. I owe much to her skill and judgment, as well as to the assistance of Maureen Carroll, Marcella Franklin, Shirley Grenoble, and Catherine Vickers.

I could not have completed this book while carrying on with my duties at the Columbia Law School without the cooperation of several colleagues and former colleagues: Dean Michael Sovern, George Cooper, William Fry, Harriet Rabb, Harold Rothwax, Philip G. Schrag, and H. Richard Uviller.

Over the years I have drawn heavily on the wisdom of Marcel Heiman.

My daughter Jessica contributed many helpful suggestions. From initial research to final revision, my wife Heli gave me the benefit of her keen eye for sense and nonsense, her good humor, and her demanding criticism.

1 THE FUND

[1] The early years of the Legal Defense Fund are described in Greenberg, *Race Relations and American Law* 34–39 (Columbia U. Press, New York; 1959).
[2] 163 U.S. 537 (1896).
[3] 347 U.S. 83 (1954).
[4] De Tocqueville, *Democracy in America*, Vol. I 283 (Vintage Books, New York; 1945).
[5] *Hamilton v. Alabama*, 368 U.S. 52 (1961).
[6] *Coleman v. Alabama*, 377 U.S. 129 (1964).
[7] *Coleman v. Alabama*, 389 U.S. 22 (1967).

2 THE COURT

[1] Alaska and Hawaii abolished in 1957. Delaware abolished the death penalty in 1958, and restored it in 1961. The story of the state's brief experience without the death penalty is told in Bedau, *The Death Penalty in America* 359 (Revised Ed.) (Anchor, New York; 1967).
[2] Royal Commission on Capital Punishment 1949–1953, Report 214 (1953).
[3] Model Penal Code § 201.6, Comment (Tent. Draft No. 9, 1959).
[4] *Id.* at 63–64.
[5] Gottlieb, *Testing the Death Penalty*, 34 So. Cal. L. Rev. 268, 281 (1961).
[6] Oberer, *Does Disqualification of Jurors for Scruples Against Capital Punishment Constitute Denial of Fair Trial on Issue of Guilt?*, 39 Tex. L. Rev. 545 (1961).
[7] Bickel, *The Least Dangerous Branch* 242 (Bobbs-Merrill, Indianapolis; 1962).
[8] Graham, *Will Earl Caldwell Go to Jail?* (More) A Journalism Review, 14 (June 1972).
[9] 372 U.S. 335 (1963).
[10] *Argersinger v. Hamlin*, 407 U.S. 25 (1972).
[11] *United States v. Frady and Gordon*, 348 F. 2d 84, 121 U.S. App. D.C. 78 (D.C. Cir. 1965).
[12] 375 U.S. 889 (1963).
[13] Packer, *Making the Punishment Fit the Crime*, 77 Harv. L. Rev. 1071 (1964).

[14] *Sims v. Balkcom,* 220 Ga. 7, 10, 136 S. E. 2d 766, 769 (1964).

[15] De Tocqueville, *op. cit, supra,* ch. 1, note 4 at 283.

[16] As quoted in Frankel, *Lawlessness In Sentencing,* 41 U. Cinc. L. Rev. 1 (1972).

[17] Weihofen, *The Urge to Punish* 138 (Farrar, Straus, & Cudahy, New York; 1956).

[18] Frankel, *supra,* note 16, *passim.*

[19] Wolfgang and Cohen, *Crime and Race, Conceptions and Misconceptions* 104–105 (Inst. of Human Relations Press, New York; 1970).

[20] *Mapp v. Ohio,* 367 U.S. 643 (1961).

[21] *Griffin v. Illinois,* 351 U.S. 12 (1956).

[22] *Miranda v. Arizona,* 384 U.S. 436 (1966).

[23] *Williams v. Florida,* 399 U.S. 446 (1970).

[24] *Terry v. Ohio,* 392 U.S. 1 (1968).

[25] Amsterdam, *The Supreme Court and the Rights of Suspects in Criminal Cases,* 45 N.Y.U.L. Rev. 785, 786 (1970).

[26] Taylor, *Nuremburg and Vietnam: An American Tragedy* 12 (Triangle Books, Chicago; 1970).

3 THE FACTS OF DEATH

[1] Bickel, *op. cit. supra,* ch. 2, note 7 at 242.

[2] Exodus 21:24.

[3] Cohn, *The Penology of the Talmud,* 5 Israeli L. Rev. 53, 66 (1970).

[4] Bedau, *op. cit. supra,* ch. 2, note 1 at 6. One colony (South Jersey) operated for almost fifty years under a Royal Charter which did not authorize capital punishment; for a time William Penn reduced the number of capital offenses in Pennsylvania to two—murder and treason.

[5] Beccaria, *On Crimes and Punishments* 47 (Bobbs-Merrill, Indianapolis; 1963) (tr. by H. Paolucci).

[6] Rush, *An Enquiry into the Effects of Public Punishments upon Criminals and upon Society* (Joseph James, Philadelphia; 1787).

[7] Rush, *Considerations on the Injustice and Impolicy of Punishing Murder by Death* (Mathew Carey, Philadelphia; 1792).

[8] Bradford, *Enquiry How Far the Punishment of Death Is Necessary in Pennsylvania,* 12 Amer. J. of Legal History 122, 131 (1968).

⁹ Such developments occurred at a time when in England "Sir Samuel Romilly was desperately trying to persuade Lord Ellenborough that the British character would not be hopelessly corrupted if Parliament repealed the death penalty for thefts from bleaching grounds and for stealing five shillings from a shop."— Davis, *The Movement to Abolish Capital Punishment in America 1787–1861,* 63 Amer. Hist. Rev. 23, 28 (1957).

¹⁰ Mackey, *Anti Gallows Activity in New York State, 1776–1861* (Univ. of Penn., 1969; Dissertation Order No. 70–7826).

¹¹ See, e.g., Select Committee on Capital Punishment of the Ohio Senate, Report, 5 Western L. J. 421 (1848).

¹² Brief of United States as *Amicus Curiae* 128–29, *McGautha v. California,* 402 U.S. 183 (1971).

¹³ Bedau, *op. cit. supra,* ch. 2, note 1 at 12, 407.

¹⁴ *Ibid.*

¹⁵ United States Dept. of Justice, Bureau of Prisons, National Prisoner Statistics, Bulletin No. 46, *Capital Punishment 1930–1970* at 11 (August 1971) [hereafter NPS].

¹⁶ *Ibid.*

¹⁷ Rose, *The Negro in America* 185 (Beacon, Boston; 1956).

¹⁸ Bedau, *op. cit. supra,* ch. 2, note 1 at 12–13.

¹⁹ Bedau, *The Death Penalty in America,* 35 Fed. Prob. 32, 38 (June 1971).

²⁰ *Id.* at 34, 35.

²¹ Capote, *In Cold Blood* 310–11 (Random House, New York; 1965).

²² Bedau, *op. cit. supra,* ch. 2, note 1 at 334.

²³ Hughes, *Sydney Silverman, Rebel in Parliament* (Skilton, London; 1969).

²⁴ Bedau, *op. cit. supra,* ch. 2, note 1 at 131.

²⁵ President's Commission on Law Enforcement and Administration of Justice, Report: The Challenge of Crime in a Free Society 143 (1967).

²⁶ State of New York Temporary Commission on Revision of the Penal Code, Special Report on Capital Punishment 2 (1965).

4 THE STRATEGY UNFOLDS

¹ Pearl, *Victorian Patchwork* 47 (Heinemann, London; 1972). The British have an incomparable flair for description of bawdy execution scenes, but there is ample evidence of similar occur-

rences in the United States. See Bedau, *op. cit. supra*, ch. 2, note
1 at 21.
2 Kubler-Ross, *On Death and Dying* 8 (Macmillan, New York;
1970).
3 Camus, *Resistance, Rebellion and Death* 187 (Knopf, New York;
1961).
4 Rubin, et al., *The Law of Criminal Correction* 324, note 47
(West, St. Paul; 1963).
5 Testimony of Clinton T. Duffy, *Hearings Before the Subcomm.
on Criminal Laws and Procedures of the Senate Comm. on the
Judiciary on S. 1760, To Abolish the Death Penalty*, 90th Cong.,
2d Sess. (1968) [hereafter *Hearings*].
6 Lawes, *Life and Death in Sing Sing* 170 (Doubleday, New York;
1928).
7 Murton, *Treatment of Condemned Prisoners*, 15 Crime and Delinquency 94, 98 (1969).
8 Kubler-Ross, *supra*, note 2 at 12.
9 Feifel, ed., *The Meaning of Death* xii (McGraw-Hill, New York;
1965).
10 *Missouri ex rel. Gaines v. Canada*, 305 U.S. 337 (1938).
11 Model Penal Code, *op. cit. supra*, ch. 2, note 3 at 74.
12 Brief of Berl I. Bernhard, et al., as *Amicus Curiae* in *Maxwell v.
Bishop*, O. T. 1969, No. 13.
13 *Hearings, supra*, note 5 at 93.
14 Cahn, *Confronting Injustice* 307 (Little Brown, Boston; 1966).

5 THE RACE FACTOR

1 Congressional Globe, 39th Cong., 1st Session, 2765 (1866).
2 A brief history of the punishment for rape in Georgia illustrates
how this system worked. In 1811, Georgia enacted a penal code
for whites that provided rape was punishable by imprisonment at
hard labor for not less than seven nor more than sixteen years,
and another code for slaves that authorized a death sentence for
any crime at the discretion of a special tribunal. Prior to the Civil
War, Georgia amended its rape laws to make a white man who
raped a white woman subject to imprisonment for a term of from
two to twenty years. Rape by a white man of a slave or a "free
person of colour" was made punishable "by fine and imprisonment at the discretion of the court." But rape of a white woman
by a slave or emancipated black remained punishable by death.

The Georgia Constitution of 1865 abolished slavery, and the following year a new rape statute was enacted which made all rapes punishable by death *or* by imprisonment for no less than one nor more than twenty years at the discretion of the jury. Ninety-five years later, in 1960, the Georgia legislature amended state law to provide a third option to the jury—life imprisonment. Despite the absence of racial reference in these post–Civil War statutes, Georgians well understood that there was a white penalty for rape and a black penalty—the latter being death, reserved primarily for blacks who raped white women. Since 1930, Georgia has executed 58 blacks and 3 whites for rape. See Brief for Petitioner 1b, *Jackson v. Georgia,* 408 U.S. 238 (1972).

[3] NPS, *op. cit. supra,* ch. 3, note 15 at 13.

[4] Wolf, *Analysis of Jury Sentencing in Capital Cases: New Jersey: 1937–1961,* 19 Rutgers L. Rev. 56 (1964).

[5] As quoted in Wolfgang and Cohen, *op. cit. supra,* ch. 2, note 19 at 89.

[6] U.N. Dept. of Economic and Social Affairs, Capital Punishment (ST/SOA/SD/9–10) (1968).

[7] *Hamilton v. Alabama, op. cit. supra,* ch. 1, note 5.

[8] Amsterdam, *The Void for Vagueness Doctrine in the Supreme Court,* 109 U. of Pa. L. Rev. 67 (1960).

[9] *Seale v. United States,* 461 F.2d 345 (7th Cir. 1972).

[10] *United States v. Caldwell,* 408 U.S. 665 (1972).

[11] *Crisis at Columbia: Report of the Fact-Finding Commission Appointed to Investigate the Disturbances at Columbia University in April and May, 1968* (Vintage Books, New York; 1968).

[12] *Moorer v. South Carolina,* 368 F. 2d 458 (4th Cir. 1966).

[13] *Maxwell v. State,* 236 Ark. 694, 370 S.W. 2d 113 (1963).

[14] *Fay v. Noia,* 372 U.S. 391 (1963); *Townsend v. Sain,* 372 U.S. 293 (1963); *Sanders v. United States,* 373 U.S. 1 (1963).

[15] *Maxwell v. Stephens,* 229 F. Supp. 205 (E. D. Ark. 1964).

[16] *Maxwell v. Stephens,* 348 F. 2d 325 (8th Cir. 1965).

[17] *Maxwell v. Stephens, cert. denied,* 382 U.S. 944 (1965) (Douglas, J., dissenting).

[18] 378 U.S. 368 (1964).

[19] 382 U.S. 399 (1966).

[20] 384 U.S. 998 (1966).

[21] 383 U.S. 375 (1966).

[22] *Maxwell v. Bishop,* 257 F. Supp. 710 (E.D. Ark. 1966).

[23] *Maxwell v. Bishop,* 385 U.S. 650 (1967).

[24] *Maxwell v. Bishop,* 398 F. 2d 138 (8th Cir. 1968).

6 MORATORIUM

1 *United States v. Jackson,* 262 F. Supp. 716 (D. Conn. 1967).
2 *United States v. Jackson,* 390 U.S. 570 (1968).
3 Ill. Rev. Stat. c. 38, § 743 (1959).
4 *Witherspoon v. Illinois,* 391 U.S. 510, 514 (1968).
5 Edison, *The Empirical Assault on Capital Punishment,* 23 J. of Legal Education 2, 13 (1971).
6 391 U.S. 543 (1968).
7 *Bell v. Patterson,* 402 F. 2d 394 (10th Cir. 1968).
8 *State v. Mathis,* 42 N.J. 238, 245 A.2d 20 (1968).
9 Ill. Rev. Stat., c. 38, § 1–7 (0) (1971).

7 SIMON'S FROLIC

1 See *State v. Pitts and Lee,* 249 So. 2d 47 (Dist. Ct. App., 1971).
2 See *Adderly v. Wainwright,* 272 F. Supp. 530 (M. D. Fla. 1967).
3 Eshelman, "San Quentin's Last Execution," San Francisco *Sunday Examiner and Chronicle* 40 (May 7, 1972).
4 *Hill v. Nelson,* 271 F. Supp. 439 (N.D. Calif. 1967).
5 *Hill v. Nelson,* 272 F. Supp. 790 (N.D. Calif. 1967).
6 *In re Anderson,* 69 Cal. 2d 613, 73 Cal. Rptr. 21, 447 P. 2d 117 (1968).
7 *People v. Massie,* 66 Cal. 2d 899, 59 Cal. Rptr. 733, 428 P. 2d 869 (1967).
8 West, *A Psychiatrist Looks at the Death Penalty,* reprinted in *Hearings, op. cit. supra,* ch. 4, note 5 at 123, 126.
9 Report of the Joint Conference on Professional Responsibility, 44 A. B. A. Journal 1159, 1162 (1958).
10 Massie, "Death by Degrees," 75 *Esquire* 179 (April 1971).
11 *Maxwell v. Bishop, cert. granted,* 393 U.S. 997 (1968).

8 MAXWELL

1 See 86 Harv. L. Rev. 303 (1972).
2 As quoted in Stern & Gressman, *Supreme Court Practice* 484 (4th ed.) (Bureau of National Affairs, Washington, D.C., 1969).

[3] *Witherspoon v. Illinois, supra* 391 U.S. at 532.
[4] 214 F. 2d 862, 94 U.S. App. D.C. 228 (D.C. Cir., 1954).
[5] 387 U.S. 1 (1967).
[6] *Duncan v. Louisiana,* 391 U.S. 145 (1968).
[7] *Witherspoon v. Illinois, supra,* 391 U.S. at 542.

9 BOYKIN

[1] Appendix p. 32, *Boykin v. Alabama,* 395 U.S. 238 (1969).
[2] *Boykin v. State,* 281 Ala. 659, 207 So. 2d 512 (1968).
[3] Elliot's *Debates* 447 (2d ed. 1876).
[4] 1 Annals of Congress 754 (1789).
[5] Granucci, *"Nor Cruel and Unusual Punishment Inflicted"—The Original Meaning,* 57 Calif. L. Rev. 839 (1969).
[6] *Wilkerson v. Utah,* 99 U.S. 130 (1878); *In re Kemmler,* 136 U.S. 436 (1890).
[7] 217 U. S. 349 (1910).
[8] Packer, *op. cit. supra,* ch. 2, note 13 at 1075.
[9] Brief *Amici Curiae* for the NAACP Legal Defense and Educational Fund, Inc., and the National Office for the Rights of the Indigent 70 in *Boykin v. Alabama,* 395 U.S. 238 (1969).
[10] *United States ex rel. Francis v. Resweber,* 329 U.S. 459 (1947).
[11] Prettyman, Jr., *Death and the Supreme Court* 83 (Avon Books, New York; 1961).
[12] 356 U.S. 44 (1958).
[13] 370 U.S. 660 (1962).
[14] *Powell v. Texas,* 392 U.S. 514 (1968).
[15] 395 U.S. 238 (1969).

10 HAYNSWORTH, CARSWELL, AND BLACKMUN

[1] See *Neil v. Biggers,* 409 U.S. 188 (1972).
[2] Quoted in Lewis, "The Same Justice Can Be Both a 'Strict' and a 'Loose' Constructionist," *The New York Times,* May 24, 1970 (magazine) p. 30.
[3] *Ibid.*
[4] *The New York Times,* August 19, 1969, p. 27, col. 5. See also *Crawford v. Bounds,* 395 F. 2d 297, 317 (4th Cir. 1968).
[5] *Darlington Manufacturing Co. v. NRLB,* 325 F. 2d 682 (4th Cir. 1963).

[6] *Textile Workers Union of America v. Darlington Manufacturing Co.* 380 U.S. 263 (1965).
[7] Douglas, *Points of Rebellion* (Vintage Books, New York; 1970).
[8] 115 Cong. Rec. 34039 (daily ed., Nov. 13, 1969).
[9] Harris, *Decision* 79 (Ballantine Books, New York; 1972).
[10] *Id.* at 54–55.
[11] *The New York Times*, March 25, 1970, p. 20, col. 4.
[12] *The New York Times*, Feb. 21, 1970, p. 50, col. 7.
[13] *The New York Times*, March 12, 1970, p. 40, col. 5.
[14] *The New York Times*, April 8, 1970, p. 42, col. 5.
[15] *The New York Times*, April 8, 1970, p. 42, col. 5.
[16] Hartz, "A Comparative Study of Fragment Cultures" in Graham and Gurr (eds.), *The History of Violence in America* 114 (Bantam, New York; 1969).
[17] *The New York Times*, April 10, 1970, p. 14, cols. 6–8.
[18] *Smith v. Morrilton*, 365 F. 2d 770 (8th Cir. 1966).
[19] *Maxwell v. Bishop*, 398 F. 2d 138, 153–54 (8th Cir. 1968).
[20] *Hearings Before the Comm. on the Judiciary, United States Senate, Nomination of Harry A. Blackmun*, 59–61, 91st Cong., 2d Sess. (1970).

11 MAXWELL *(Continued)*

[1] 396 U.S. 711 (1969).
[2] *Alderman v. United States*, 394 U.S. 165 (1969).
[3] 18 U.S.C. § 844(d).

12 TAKING STOCK

[1] NPS, *op. cit. supra*, ch. 3, note 15 at 2.
[2] *Sinclair v. Henderson*, 441 F. Supp. 1123 (E.D. La. 1971).
[3] *Brent v. White*, 398 F. 2d 503 (5th Cir. 1968).
[4] *Morford v. Hocker*, unreported, No. R-2174 (D. Nev., March 2, 1969).
[5] *Bean v. State*, 86 Nev. 80, 465 P. 2d 133 (1970).
[6] *In re Raggio*, 87 Nev. 100, 487 P. 2d 499 (1971).
[7] Bedau, *op. cit. supra*, ch. 3, note 19 at 34.
[8] *Spencer v. Beto*, 398 F. 2d 500 (5th Cir. 1968).
[9] Bedau, *op. cit. supra*, ch. 3, note 19 at 36.

[10] *Shuler and Chatman v. Wainwright,* 341 F. Supp. 1061 (M.D. Fla. 1972).

[11] *Washington v. State,* 269 Ala. 146, 112 So. 2d 179 (1959).

[12] *Washington v. Holman,* 245 F. Supp. 116 (M.D. Ala. 1965).

[13] *Washington v. State,* 46 Ala. App. 539, 245 So. 2d 824 (Crim. App. 1971).

[14] Murton, *op. cit. supra,* ch. 4, note 7.

[15] *United States ex rel. Smith v. Yeager,* 336 F. Supp. 1287 (D. N.J. 1971).

[16] 405 F. 2d 340 (4th Cir. 1969).

[17] *State v. Kilpatrick,* 201 Kan. 6, 439 P. 2d 99 (1968).

[18] *Thomas v. Arizona,* 356 U.S. 90 (1958).

[19] 384 U.S. 436 (1966).

[20] *Maxwell v. Bishop,* 398 U.S. 262 (1970).

[21] *People v. McGautha,* 70 Cal. 2d 550, 76 Cal. Rptr. 434, 452 P.2d 650 (1969).

[22] *People v. Crampton,* 18 Ohio 2d 182, 248 N.E. 2d 614 (1969).

13 "IF THE DEATH PENALTY IS TO BE RETAINED AT ALL"

[1] *Ralph v. Warden,* 438 F. 2d 786 (4th Cir. 1970).

[2] *Rehearing denied, Id.* at 794, 797.

[3] See *The New York Times,* Dec. 30, 1970, § A, at p. 26, col. 1; Rockefeller, *Executive Clemency and the Death Penalty,* 21 Cath. U. L. Rev. 94 (1971).

[4] National Commission On Reform of Federal Criminal Laws, Final Report, A Proposed New Federal Criminal Code, § § 3601–02 (1971).

[5] Goldberg and Dershowitz, *Declaring the Death Penalty Unconstitutional,* 83 Harv. L. Rev. 1773 (1970).

[6] Letter from Fred Speaker to Joseph Mazurkiewicz, Superintendent, Rockview State Correctional Institution, dated January 19, 1971.

[7] *Brown v. State,* 264 So. 2d 529, *rev'd,* 264 So. 2d 549 (1971).

[8] Lewis, "A Legal Nightmare," *The New York Times,* March 22, 1971, p. 33, col. 1.

[9] 402 U.S. 183 (1971).

[10] S. 1969, H.R. 8414, 92nd Cong., 1st Sess. (1971).

[11] 403 U.S. 952 (1971). For earlier proceedings, see *People v. Aikens,* 70 Cal. 2d 369, 450 P. 2d 258, 71 Cal. Rptr. 882 (1969);

Furman v. State, 225 Ga. 253, 167 S. E. 2d 628 (1969); *Jackson v. State,* 225 Ga. 790, 171 S. E. 2d 501 (1969); *Branch v. State,* 447 S. W. 2d 932 (Tex. Crim. App., 1969).
12 403 U.S. 946–68 (1971).
13 403 U.S. 953 (1971).

14 POWELL AND REHNQUIST

1 Sherrill, "The Embodiment of Poor, White Power," *The New York Times,* Feb. 28, 1971 (magazine), p. 48, col. 5.
2 402 U.S. 1 (1971).
3 50 A.B.A. Journal 891 (1964).
4 See ch. 3, note 25 at 305.
5 *Hearings before the Comm. on the Judiciary, Nominations of William H. Rehnquist and Lewis F. Powell, Jr.,* 309, 92nd Cong., 1st Sess. (1971).
6 *Id.* at 185–86.
7 118 Cong. Rec. E. 12, 378 (daily ed. Nov. 18, 1971).
8 *The New York Times,* Nov. 30, 1971, p. 38, col. 4.
9 *Senate Report from the Comm. on the Judiciary, Independent Views of Messrs. Bayh, Hart, Kennedy & Tunney, Nomination of William H. Rehnquist* 24–5, 92nd Cong., 1st Sess. (1971).
10 See note 5, *supra,* at 11.
11 *Senate Report No.* 92–16, 4–5, 92d Cong., 1st Sess. (1971).

15 CLOSING IN

1 *State v. Forcella,* 52 N.J. 263, 245 A. 2d 55 (1972).
2 *Funicello v. New Jersey,* 403 U.S. 948 (1971).
3 *State v. Funicello,* 60 N.J. 60, 286 A. 2d 55 (1972).
4 397 U.S. 742 (1970).
5 397 U.S. 790 (1970).
6 400 U.S. 25 (1970).
7 Black, *The Crisis in Capital Punishment,* 31 Maryland L. Rev. 289, 296 (1971).
8 *People v. Anderson,* 6 Cal. 3d 628, 493 P. 2d 880, 100 Cal. Rptr. 152 (1972).
9 Barrett, Jr., *Anderson and the Judicial Function,* 45 So. Cal. L. Rev. 739, 748 (1972).

[10] San Francisco *Chronicle,* Feb. 19, 1972, § 1 at p. 1, col. 3.
[11] Lublin, "Trailblazing Bench," *Wall Street Journal,* July 20, 1972, p. 1, col. 1.

16 CRUEL AND UNUSUAL

[1] *Johnson v. Louisiana,* 406 U.S. 356 (1972); *Apodaca v. Oregon,* 406 U.S. 404 (1972).
[2] *Kirby v. Illinois,* 406 U.S. 682 (1972).
[3] *United States v. Wade,* 388 U.S. 218 (1967); *Gilbert v. California,* 388 U.S. 263 (1967).
[4] *Laird v. Tatum,* 408 U.S. 1 (1972).
[5] *Aikens v. California, dismissed as moot,* 406 U.S. 813 (1972).
[6] Bronson, *On The Conviction Proneness and Representativeness of the Death Qualified Jury: A Study of Colorado Veniremen,* 42 U. of Colo. L. Rev. 1 (1970).
[7] Jurow, *New Data on the Effect of a "Death Qualified" Jury on the Guilt Determination Process,* 84 Harv. L. Rev. 567 (1971).
[8] *Furman v. Georgia; Jackson v. Georgia; Branch v. Texas,* 408 U.S. 238 (1972).
[9] Black, *op. cit. supra,* ch. 15, note 7 at 294.
[10] Barrett, Jr., *op. cit. supra,* ch. 15, note 9 at 747–78.
[11] *The Autobiography of Michel de Montaigne* 197 (Lowenthal Ed.) (Vintage Books, New York; 1935).

INDEX

About the Author

MICHAEL MELTSNER was born in New York City and educated at Oberlin College and Yale Law School. In 1961 he joined the staff of the NAACP Legal Defense and Educational Fund, and from 1963 until 1972 he and his colleagues represented over three hundred death-row inmates.

Mr. Meltsner has argued a number of constitutional cases before the Supreme Court. Now a professor at Columbia Law School, he lives in New York City with his wife and two daughters.